Praise for the Author and the Book

'His commentaries are in precise classical English'

The late Trevor Bailey, *England all-rounder and BBC expert commentator*

'I have known Ashis Ray for many years and have found him outstanding in his work in the media'

The late Richie Benaud, *former Australian captain, TV presenter and commentator*

'Authoritative reading'

The Hindu

CRICKET WORLD CUP

CRICKET WORLD CUP
THE INDIAN CHALLENGE

(UPDATED EDITION 2023)

ASHIS RAY

B L O O M S B U R Y
NEW DELHI • LONDON • OXFORD • NEW YORK • SYDNEY

BLOOMSBURY INDIA
Bloomsbury Publishing India Pvt. Ltd
Second Floor, LSC Building No. 4, DDA Complex, Pocket C – 6 & 7,
Vasant Kunj New Delhi 110070

BLOOMSBURY, BLOOMSBURY INDIA and the Diana logo are
trademarks of Bloomsbury Publishing Plc

First published in India 2015
Updated edition published 2019
This updated edition published 2023

ISBN: 978-93-56406-35-3; eBook: 978-93-56406-37-7

2 4 6 8 10 9 7 5 3 1

Typeset by Manipal Digital
Printed and bound in India by Replika Press Pvt. Ltd.

To the countless who have over the years tolerated with such kindness my commentaries and writings

Contents

Preface

This book is a chronicle of the Cricket World Cup from an Indian perspective and not a glorification of Indian cricket. It is an attempt at a dispassionate appraisal of the rise, fall and revival of Indian cricket in the one-day realm. It is a saga one cannot ignore, for to it has inextricably been linked the financial fortunes of world cricket since 1983.

It is a volume not merely for Indians, but for anyone interested in cricket. The book reviews all tournaments from 1975 to 2019. Each of India's matches, since the inaugural World Cup 49 years ago, is recorded as well as every semifinal and final regardless of whether India featured in them or not. It would have been absurd to even contemplate writing an account like this after India's ridiculous performance in the first two editions of the competition. But 1983 dramatically transformed everything. That summer in England, India, led by Kapil Dev Nikhanj, not just convulsed the world of cricket by thrillingly capturing the coveted crown—against the then seemingly unassailable West Indies. But Indians thereafter got so inebriated by limited overs cricket, that a comparatively Cinderella sport—restricted to a handful of Commonwealth countries—was catapulted into a big money extravaganza. Corporates and television networks based in India bankrolled the shorter version of the game and the 2011 World Cup culminated with India, much to the delight of their delirious supporters, lifting the trophy a second time.

The Cricket World Cup is a phenomenon well within the compass of my lifetime. I have, in fact, witnessed every single championship except the inaugural tournament, which I experienced by virtue of extended highlights. This book is, therefore, written considerably from a first-hand encounter and memory, upgraded and refreshed by reference work.

My presence at so many World Cups would not have been possible without assignments from various media houses. So, I should record my debt to *BBC, United News of India, Ananda Bazar Group, ABC* (Australia), *The Times* (UK), *The Statesman* (Kolkata), *The Tribune* (Chandigarh), *Daily News & Analysis* (*DNA*, Mumbai), *Indo-Asian News Service* (IANS) and *Sony Entertainment Television* for utilising my services.

Quotes from players who participated in the competitions have enhanced the evaluation. This is especially true of the chapter on the 1983 World Cup. The reactions are sourced from a television documentary on the competition—*1983: India's World Cup*—which I co-produced with Century TV in 2008 to mark the 25th anniversary of India's historic win.

Sachin Tendulkar's release of his autobiography *Playing It My Way* in the last quarter of 2014 was timely. This placed his impressions of India's successful campaign in the 2011 World Cup in the public domain. A few of these, as well as a couple of other comments have been incorporated in the text.

The first chapter deals with the World Cups of 1975 and 1979—both agonising and embarrassing from an Indian standpoint.

The next is devoted wholly to the remarkable turnaround in 1983, beginning with success against the indomitable West Indies in their backyard—Berbice in the interior of Guyana—and ending with the slaying of the same side on a heady, sun-drenched evening at Lord's, which snatched the silver away from the Caribbean.

The third chapter is a deliberate departure to drive home the point that the 1983 victory was not a flash in the pan. India's victory in the one-off 'World Championship of Cricket' in Australia in 1985 was, in fact, more emphatic than in either the 1983 or the 2011 World Cup. Indeed, it underlines that their bowling strength was the mainspring behind their breakthrough in the 1980s.

This is followed by four World Cups—1987, 1992, 1996 and 1999—compressed into an omnibus chapter. For Indians, this was obviously a disappointing phase when exuberance was deflated by repeated failure.

Not that interest in cricket in India ever really declined, but it was reignited as it were by India finishing runners-up in 2003 under the captaincy of Sourav Ganguly, a fighter and a skilful one-day batsman. It was India's best display since 1983 and a trigger for higher expectations. So, this encouraging exhibition is the subject of Chapter Five.

Given that India had, by this stage, reached a certain level of competence and seasoning in one-day cricket, being jettisoned in the 2007 World Cup at the preliminary stage—primarily because of a defeat to unfancied Bangladesh—was a rude shock for Indian fans. This justified a chapter by itself because of the controversies preceding and succeeding India's exit. The treatment here is different in that, I have simply reproduced relevant extracts from my reports for *The Tribune*, *DNA* and *IANS*. I thank them for permitting me to do so. Former premier batsman and Australian skipper Greg Chappell as India's coach was mostly the cause of the furore. His efforts to shake-up Indian cricket were clearly resisted by senior Indian players. Even the otherwise taciturn Tendulkar has in his book deemed it fit to scathingly criticise Chappell. Such censure has not been overlooked.

1983 and 2011—the two Everests for India—have been accorded pride of place and most wordage. Therefore, the seventh chapter is devoted accordingly to the latter. This is not merely a narration of a dream victory at home—dashed in 1987—but of a new lease of life for 50-over cricket.

The ascending popularity of Twenty20 after the introduction of a world tournament dedicated to it in 2007 had cast doubts about the future of one-day internationals. This ceased to be a topic of discussion after a buoyant 2011 World Cup, with the International Cricket Council (ICC) reassured about continuing with their three-format policy.

Indeed, the 2015 tourney was no less a success. Admittedly, India did not retain the title, but gave a decent account of themselves, maintaining a clean slate in the league phase, before critically losing in the knockout stage. Chapters Eight and Nine cover the last two editions of the tournament—the 2019 tournament also resulting in India being eliminated in the semifinals.

Full scorecards are presented for matches of the 1983 and 2011 World Cups and scores in brief are provided for all other games.

Finally, a review of the 2019 competition held in England completes the contents. Rohit Sharma's prolific run-getting here, if repeated in India in 2023, should go some way towards enhancing India's prospects.

A mere three months before the event, the composition of the Indian squad was in a state of flux. The hosts were sweating on an extended list of injuries—the recovery of fast bowler Jasprit Bumrah, opening batsman KL Rahul, batsman-wicket-keeper Rishabh Pant and middle-order batsman Shreyas Iyer, among others, in a limbo; while Surya Kumar Yadav was taking time to echo in ODIs his explosive performances in T20s.

If Indian cricketers have carved a niche for themselves and carried their country to distinction, even if intermittently, they have accomplished this in spite of the Board of Control for Cricket in India (BCCI), the Indian affiliate of the ICC and the administrative authority for the game in the country. Deriving revenue when people have gone berserk about the shorter formats of the sport is, arguably, a no-brainer. This has happened notwithstanding the incompetence of the BCCI. They have been, until a few years ago, unimaginative about harnessing the income for the development of acumen and ensuring steady success for India, particularly in test matches outside the subcontinent.

How could the bowling have been so unpenetrative—except on slow turners—for the greater part of India's involvement in cricket? Why does the batting in test matches so often disappoint in Australia, England and South Africa, when the BCCI in the past 20 years have possessed more money to plough into cricket than the rest of the world put together? The president of BCCI has been looked upon as being more powerful than an Indian cabinet minister. Thus, vested interests have occupied this space to control the running of a key element of life in India.

Where sporting bodies in most parts of the world have modernised, with professionals entrusted with day-to-day management, the BCCI has moved from mismanagement to a state of limbo, with *ad hoc* honorary officials hanging on to a historically obsolete culture, notwithstanding a clear Indian Supreme Court judgement to the body to reform. After the maharajas, office-bearers have predominantly been businessmen, politicians or bureaucrats. Very few have been caring or competent enough to capitalise on the extraordinary riches at the BCCI's disposal to India's benefit. Indeed, it has been a decade since India won an ICC event.

To make matters worse, sections of the BCCI were suspected of being mired in corruption. This made it imperative for the Supreme Court to intervene. A committee appointed by it and headed by a former judge, Justice Mukul Mudgal, found *prima facie* evidence of betting by officials of franchises in the Twenty20 Indian Premier League (IPL). Rules framed to govern the conduct of the IPL strictly forbade an insider from participating in any type of gambling—which is illegal in India in any case, other than in horse racing—with disenfranchisement laid out as the consequent punishment.

Gurunath Meiyappan, son-in-law of the once all-powerful president of the BCCI Narayanaswami Srinivasan was indicted by the Mudgal Committee. The franchise concerned, Chennai Super Kings (CSK), was owned by Indian Cements Limited. Srinivasan was the vice chairman, managing director and a significant shareholder of the company.

Originally, IPL rules debarred BCCI office-bearers from having any stake in any of the franchises, as this was tantamount to a clear conflict of interests. These though were amended to accommodate Srinivasan, who was then treasurer of the BCCI. Srinivasan was—before he was banished by a court order—simultaneously a member of the BCCI board, the IPL's governing council as well as the owner of an IPL franchise. After a two-year suspension, CSK is back in business in the IPL. Srinivasan even became chairman of the ICC. In other words, in a climate where the BCCI exerted disproportionate influence on the ICC, his grip on world cricket was complete and unprecedented. He was subsequently relieved of this post.

Suppression of independent television coverage of matches held under the auspices of the BCCI also demands closer inspection. A commentator hired for the purpose is unlikely to be critical if his pay packet is disbursed by the BCCI. Thus, not a word is uttered about the mistakes of the BCCI on the medium the Indian public overwhelmingly tunes into to follow cricket, namely television. India ignominiously lost eight test matches in a row in England and Australia in 2011-12. Nobody was taken to task for this abject showing.

My association with the ICC Cricket World Cup is personally memorable. It includes being the only Asian ball-by-ball commentator in BBC's coverage of the 1979 and 1983 World Cups. My three esteemed colleagues in the final of the latter were Brian Johnston, Christopher Martin-Jenkins and Tony Cozier—all of whom have now sadly passed away.

One of the objections to limited overs cricket is that it is loaded in favour of batsmen. Besides, today's willow is of a quality unimaginable in yesteryears. The game's founders conceived an even battle between bat and ball. So partiality to please the lowest common denominator infringes on the purity of the sport.

The batting powerplay, with its fielding restrictions, is a welcome innovation; but even greater elasticity to reduce predictability needs to be considered. The greater the uncertainty, the more thrilling it is for the spectator. Furthermore, either an amendment of Law 1.2 (which effectively stipulates no player can be nominated after the toss) or a relook at the earlier 'super sub' experiment could be explored. Advantage obtained from the weather and gained from pure luck with the coin should ideally be minimised.

It has been a rollercoaster ride for India in the World Cup. At the end of it though, Tendulkar is the highest run-getter in its history, Ganguly is credited with the second highest individual score (183) and Zaheer Khan's strike rate of 1.91 wickets per match in taking 44 wickets from 23 matches is, in fact, superior to Glenn McGrath's 1.82 wickets per match from his 71 scalps in 39 games. To cap it all, Mahendra Singh Dhoni wears the triple crown of having captained India to triumphs in the World Cup, the Champions Trophy and the World Twenty20. Besides, since the 2015 World Cup, Virat Kohli and Rohit Sharma have been batting-wise in a league of the own. Last but not least, Indians comprise more avid adherents to the sport than all other nationalities put together.

I sympathise with cricket connoisseurs, the test match brigade, who suffer in silence as an excess of limited overs cricket is heaped on them. But the shorter formats contribute invaluably to revenues, which are much needed for the prosperity of the game, including sustenance of tests. In fact, the World Test Championship is a most welcome addition to the ICC calendar.

I would like to thank Bloomsbury for publishing the updated edition of the book.

I am indebted to my family, who suffer from my inattention when I get engrossed in a literary project. My wife Pritha, daughter Debika and son Agnish, though, worry the most about typos not being corrected! I am also conscious of the moral support I have received over decades from my mother Roma and sister Pia.

Rechecking facts, first names of lesser-known players and scores were essential. In this respect, editions of the *Wisden Cricket Almanack*, *cricinfo.com* and *icc-cricket.com* were invaluable. At the outset, I consulted the Association of Cricket Statisticians and Historians in England, especially Andrew Hignell, for the same purpose.

London, August 2023

CHAPTER ONE

Before 1983

Agony

THE 1975 WORLD CUP

IN 1964, THE IMPERIAL CRICKET CONFERENCE, THE GOVERNING body of the game, renamed themselves the International Cricket Conference (ICC). As the previous nomenclature suggested, it was an entity born in an age when the sun never set on the British Empire and, therefore, of an imperious mindset. Cricket was treated by the English, especially the Marylebone Cricket Club (MCC), as a private fiefdom, with the president of this club automatically the ICC's ex-officio chairman (a convention that continued until suspended in 1989). No one questioned this practice or, if anyone did, such challenges were promptly shot down. The fact that a great pastime—which the MCC, admittedly, created and must be accorded full credit for—was stagnating commercially as well as in terms of its popularity, without any imagination on the part of its administrators to enhance its appeal and expand it beyond the shores of a handful of participants, appeared to be of no consequence to people preoccupied with clinging to the past. These Little Englanders with myopic vision had clearly outlived their utility, and were seen by progressive forces to be acting merely to protect Anglo–Saxon interests.

In Australia and New Zealand, England enjoyed active and dependable allies. They were, after all, nothing but an extension of the Anglo–Saxon conglomerate, owing allegiance to the British Queen and echoing London's worldview. The façade of the Ashes rivalry between England and Australia rapidly melted in the boardrooms of Lord's, as the duo closed ranks in a spirit of mutual back scratching. In fact, until 2000, both England and Australia had to agree on an ICC decision before this could be executed, which effectively gave them veto powers over other members. Then, there was a sure bet in the support of the West Indies, who were, financially, heavily reliant on England, apart from some of their constituents still being actual colonies of the United Kingdom.

In other words, the poor sods from the subcontinent, India and Pakistan, were voiceless. In any case, if one of them raised an issue, the chances were the other—because of the hostility between the two for political reasons—would automatically side with the majority foursome. It was in such an environment that the concept of a World Cup played on over-limit lines was mooted in 1971 at an ICC meeting and approved in 1973. 1975 was chosen as the year of the inaugural tournament, with England as the venue.

So, when the first one-day summit was staged, only those who were representing first-class county teams in England were really accustomed to limited-overs cricket. There was a sneaking suspicion that the intelligent English cricket administrator saw an opportunity to obtain an advantage over sides comparatively uninitiated to the abbreviated format by springing a 'World Cup'—such branding almost certain to capture the imagination of cricket lovers internationally - on them.

For instance, as compared to England, who had chalked up 15 one-day international (ODI) appearances (and their players, countless limited-overs outings domestically since 1963), Australia, West Indies, New Zealand, Pakistan and India had only seven, two, seven, three and two such experiences, respectively. West Indies and Pakistan were relatively less affected, as most of their players were engaged in English county cricket over the summer, while Australia had had their own one-day domestic tournament for six years and New Zealand theirs for four years. India were, therefore, the ones who were really left high and dry, and this plight could, of course, be equally attributed to a lack of alertness and inclination on the part of the Board of Control for Cricket in India (BCCI).

40 years have elapsed since the opening tournament; yet, the apparently carefully laid plan has failed to bear fruit for England. Even Sri Lanka, only an associate member of the ICC in the first two World Cups, have lifted the trophy, but not the founder-member who probably foresaw easy success!

However, the event has grown in stature quadrennially as well as in terms of mass appreciation. It has also, from its humble beginnings, become comparatively, a huge financial success. This upsurge has occurred largely because of the accident of India winning the World Cup in 1983, and the BCCI riding piggyback on the frenzy for the one-day game that overtook Indians. Limited-overs cricket in general, the World Cup and now the World Twenty20 are today monetary marvels because of the unforeseen but fortuitous shift in the balance of fiscal power in world cricket consequent to this outcome. Right of entry into the competition would probably have remained restricted; and the derivation and distribution of greater revenues, unambitious. Before 1983, the commercial success of the Olympics, football, golf and tennis had eluded cricket because of the stubbornness of the game's controllers. No sooner Kapil Dev held aloft the World Cup on the pavilion balcony at Lord's Cricket Ground, Narendra Salve, then president of BCCI, Sheshrao Wankhede, his immediate predecessor, and fellow officer bearers were informally assembled in a suite at the Westmoreland (as this hotel opposite the venue was then called) drawing up plans to host the next World Cup.

In the 1975 World Cup, sponsored by Prudential Assurance, the eight invited sides were split into two equal bunches, with each team pitted against the other three on a league basis. In Group A were England, New Zealand, India and East Africa; the stronger Group B was comprised of the West Indies, Australia, Pakistan and Sri Lanka. The top two on points in each cluster would qualify for the semifinals, with the champions of one clashing with the runners-up of the other. It envisaged 15 matches with each side restricted to 60 overs.

Srinivasaraghavan Venkataraghavan (generally abridged to 'Venkat') was appointed captain of India. The elevation of this Tamil Brahmin (or an upper caste Hindu) was prompted by a vacuum created by the premature retirement of Ajit Wadekar, and by Tiger Pataudi declaring himself to be over the hill. The former received a rather rumbustious reception in Mumbai upon India being whitewashed in a three-test series in England in 1974, which provoked his hasty departure. As for Pataudi, then 34, he had virtually ruled himself out by struggling as a batsman against the pace of Andy Roberts in the 1974–75 home season. Venkat, the off-spinner from the southern Indian state of Tamil Nadu, who made his test debut in 1965, was among the senior players still available and suitable for selection. He was credited with a fairly sharp cricketing brain—being his state's skipper—but also reputed to have an impatient streak.

Bishan Singh Bedi, a Sikh, who migrated from the northern state of Punjab to Delhi and who became captain of his country in 1976, could have been in the reckoning. Indeed, this left-arm spin bowler was a more regular member of the test eleven than Venkat. The latter, despite being a high-quality performer, was often sidelined because of his competition for a place in the side with another off-spinner, Erapalli Prasanna, from Mysore (later Karnataka) state, who fairly spun the ball like a top, with masterly control over flight and variation. But Bedi, reportedly, behaved rebelliously during the 1974 tour to England, which probably postponed his promotion. Venkat, on the other hand, was uncontroversial, a better batsman than either Bedi or Prasanna, an excellent fieldsman and had some experience of limited-overs cricket as a result of playing for Derbyshire. Besides, he had an influential southern Indian lobby, led by an industrialist and BCCI heavyweight, Muttaiya Chidambaram, to endorse his candidature.

7 June: Lord's, London

India's unpreparedness was soon confirmed. On the opening day of the competition at the Mecca of world cricket, they collided against England, as if bumping into a brick wall in a dark corridor.

With Dennis Amiss, a technically correct opening batsman but not noted for flair in strokeplay, in exceptional form and Keith Fletcher, too, in excellent touch, England amassed a record total for a 60-over ODI. The pipe-smoking Warwickshire opener, later this county's chief executive, powered to 137, with 18 fours and put on 176 for the second wicket with the Essex man. To rub salt into the wound, Yorkshire fast bowler, Chris Old, also enjoyed a salad day, helping himself to 51 off just 30 balls. England's score was—for that era—a staggering 334 for four.

India—or more precisely, Sunil Gavaskar—made no effort to respond in the spirit of one-day cricket, let alone pick up the gauntlet. Indeed the Bombay batsman batted out the entire 60 overs as if entrusted to save a test match, remaining not out on 36. Irate Indian supporters ran on to the pitch to protest against Gavaskar's skeptical display. India, in course of their innings, procured a pathetic 132 for three. As the *Wisden Cricketers' Almanack* succinctly put it, Gavaskar 'sat on the splice' throughout the innings.

Both the Indian manager, Gulabai Ramchand, and Venkat (the only Indian bowler, incidentally, to concede less than 50 runs in the allotted 12 overs per bowler) criticized Gavaskar for his cynicism. But no action was ever taken by the BCCI against him. Many years later—after Gavaskar had retired—Raj Singh, a stakeholder in the Indian princely state of Dungarpur, in Rajasthan, former chairman of Indian selectors, president of the BCCI and, most honourably, a distinguished president of the Cricket Club of India (India's MCC)—which he rendered more magnificent during his leadership—raised this issue in the middle of a public spat with the Mumbai legend. The truth is he and his colleagues in the BCCI had remained silent at the time of the outrageous performance.

Gavaskar, in his defence, argued, since there was no possibility of India surpassing England's compilation, he used the opportunity to obtain some batting practice! In hindsight, I am sure he regrets his attitude that day. But then, his upbringing was to secure matches first, before trying to win them—which he did with the historical valour and heroism of the Marathas (of whom he was one) on numerous occasions in tests. The win-or-lose circumstance of the one-day scenario was alien to his nature.

India, incidentally, excluded Bedi from their eleven. This omission raised a few eyebrows, since the spinner had indulged in a fair amount of over-limit operations for Northamptonshire, where he was contracted for six years from 1972. Instead, the Indians plumped for five medium pacers, all of whom could bat in varying degrees—Madan Lal Sharma, Mohinder Amarnath, Syed Abid Ali, Karsen Ghavri and Eknath Solkar. Venkat, too, pushed his off-breaks through faster than usual. Tilting towards seam in the first half of an English summer was correct thinking. But none of the quicker bowlers possessed much quality and were, predictably, treated with disdain by the English batsmen.

Toss: England
Man of the Match: DL Amiss
England 334/4 in 60 overs (Dennis Amiss 137, Keith Fletcher 68, Syed Abid Ali 2/58). **India** 132/3 in 60 overs (Sunil Gavaskar 36*, Gundappa Viswanath 37, Peter Lever 1/16, Geoff Arnold 1/20).

11 June: Headingley, Leeds

After being slaughtered by England, India breathed a sigh of relief at being squared off against part-time cricketers representing East Africa, whose players were mostly of subcontinental origin. There was, however, an Englishman in Donald Pringle, father of Derek Pringle, who later played for England principally as a medium pacer but was also a decent lower order batsman and is presently a cricket writer.

Not unexpectedly, India flourished against such modest opposition. The East Africans won the toss and batted first. There was no venom in the pitch, but they lacked the wherewithal to combat consistent line and length. India, on their part, fielded well. East Africa scored just 36 runs in their first 22 overs and could eventually muster a total of only 120. Indeed, it was a scramble for the ball between the bowlers, as Bedi, returning to the fold with a vengeance, posted figures of 12-8-6-1. Jawahir Shah, though, stood valiantly on the burning deck with an attacking 37, resplendent with cover drives, before he was bowled by Amarnath.

Farokh Engineer, too, was back in the side after missing the first outing due to injury. A batsman-wicketkeeper for Lancashire and, therefore, quite seasoned in the shorter version of the game, he seamlessly slipped into this role for his country. He (with seven fours) and Gavaskar (with nine) duly reached the team's target in the 30th over without any mishap. Frasat Ali, who opened the batting and bowling for East Africa, exhibited an accurate opening spell for his team; but Pringle, who shared the new ball with him, proved to be expensive and was taken off after only three overs. Tragically, Pringle died in a car accident when only 43.

Toss: East Africa
Man of the Match: FM Engineer
East Africa 120 all out in 55.3 overs (Jawahir Shah 37, Sharma Madan Lal 3/15, Syed Abid Ali 2/22, Bishan Bedi 1/6). **India** 121/0 in 29.5 overs (Sunil Gavaskar 65*, Farokh 54*).

Meanwhile...

England built on their overwhelming win over India by eclipsing East Africa by 181 runs and then New Zealand by 80 runs. They, therefore, comfortably occupied the foremost position in their group.

14 June: Old Trafford, Manchester

So India versus New Zealand became the make-or-break match for the second qualifiers from the group for the semifinals. India won the toss on a palatable pitch. However, Gavaskar, who notched a notable test hundred on the same ground a year earlier, failed to ignite, caught as he was by Richard Hadlee off elder brother Dayle Hadlee, who proved to be the pick of the New Zealand bowlers. Engineer set off with characteristic briskness, but was trapped leg before wicket by Richard, later to emerge as one of the greatest fast bowlers of all time.

Although Anshuman Gaekwad produced a useful 37, India fragmented to 101 for six, before Abid Ali, an all-purpose man from the southern Indian city of Hyderabad, with a doughty innings of 70 at number seven, restored respectability. This effort included a six and five fours. Madan Lal provided some support to Abid, as did Venkat, who remained not out on 26 as India finished with a reasonably defendable total.

Man to man, India were not inferior to the Kiwis even on the unfamiliar stage of one-day cricket. But the person who made the difference was Glen Turner. A batsman in the Gavaskar mould, he was by no means a natural in the one-day realm. Yet, his long stint with Worcestershire had honed his skills for limited-overs requirements. His undefeated 114 off 177 balls, with 13 boundaries, essentially settled the issue for the New Zealanders.

India chipped away at the other end. Abid Ali, a Muslim educated in a Christian school, whose nephew, Mohammed Azharuddin, was to subsequently captain India, capped his batting display with an impressive bowling stint. And Bedi was again economical. New Zealand were at one point 70 for three. But with Turner unruffled and collecting runs crisply, they cruised home by four wickets with seven balls to spare. India, thus, made an early exit from the first World Cup.

Toss: India
Man of the Match: GM Turner
India 230 all out in 60 overs (Syed Abid Ali 70, Anshuman Gaekwad 37, Brian McKechnie 3/49, Dayle Hadlee 2/32). **New Zealand** 233/6 in 58.5 overs (Glen Turner 114*, Brian Hastings 34, Syed Abid Ali 2/35, Bishan Bedi 1/28).

Elsewhere...

It was a resurgent West Indies after their travails in the late 1960s and early 1970s. This revival was first felt in India, with the flowering of Andy Roberts, Gordon Greenidge and Vivian Richards, in addition to the endurance of Clive Lloyd and Alvin Kalicharran. Now, they stamped their authority by defeating Sri Lanka by nine wickets and Australia by seven wickets, but were lucky to get the better of Pakistan, the winning run being scored off the fourth ball of the last over—in what's looked upon as one of the great ODIs. This riveting encounter hung in the balance until the very end; and the West Indies could not have been confident when their eighth wicket fell on 166 and their ninth at 203. But amazingly, the last pair of Deryck Murray and Andy Roberts, who came together in the 46th over, scored the necessary 64 runs for victory. The Pakistani batsmen followed Majid Khan's example, punishing anything not on a length and going boldly for their strokes. But Mushtaq Mohammad and Wasim Raja, who prematurely passed away in August 2006, were unfortunate to play-on when both threatened to dominate the bowling. The West Indies batsmen showed almost indecent haste and, with the exception of Lloyd and Murray, lacked the patience to build a major innings. Murray's brand of discipline and the courage of Roberts eventually carried them through.

On the basis of this win, the West Indies headed their group, with the Aussies securing second place after beating Pakistan and Sri Lanka by 73 runs and 52 runs, respectively.

Semifinal, 18 June: Headingley, Leeds

If it was sunny at the headquarters of Yorkshire County Cricket Club, it was generally heavenly for batting. But once an overcast sky enveloped the industrial pollution that hung in the air, conditions became beastly for batsmen. Apart from aiding movement in the air, such an environment assisted a greening of the pitch, converting it into a quicker bowler's paradise. Sometimes an uneven bounce made life more miserable for batsmen.

The wicket was the same as the one used for the Australia-Pakistan game, in which 483 runs were scored. But 10 days later, it looked grassy and the players complained it was also damp.

Australia won the toss and unhesitatingly inserted England.

Indeed, the Aussies ran rather than walked to change ends (much in the style of today's 20:20 cricket) to get through as many overs as possible before the wicket dried out. England were soon 37 for seven and then 93 all out in 36.2 overs. Gary Gilmour, left-arm fast medium, tore through the English line-up. Bowling a good length, he swung and cut the ball disconcertingly in the heavy atmosphere. Four of his victims were trapped leg before wicket to incoming deliveries, including Amiss and Fletcher, while Tony Greig was caught behind. Bowling unchanged for his 12 overs, he finished with quite sensational figures of six for 14. Captain Mike Denness and the tail staged a slight rally from 52 for eight; otherwise, it would have been worse.

But there was excitement yet in the encounter. At first, there was relative calm as the Australian openers resisted inroads by the England new ball operators for the first seven overs. But Geoff Arnold, John Snow and Chris Old—all adept at swinging and seaming the ball—performed predictably. The conditions were less challenging for batsmen than in the morning. Yet the trio had the Australians tottering on 39 for six. At this stage, though, Gilmour joined Doug Walters and this pair ensured England made no further headway. They added 55 and the Aussies won quite comfortably by four wickets, with 31 overs to spare.

Recrimination followed, as both sides castigated the strip, particularly England. Such reactions even raised questions about Headlingley's suitability as an international venue.

Toss: Australia
Man of the Match: GJ Gilmour
England 93 all out in 36.2 overs (Mike Denness 27, Gary Gilmour 6/14, Max Walker 3/22). **Australia** 94/6 in 28.4 overs (Doug Walters 20*, Chris Old 3/29, John Snow 2/30).

Semifinal, 18 June: The Oval, London

Two hundred miles south of Leeds, the West Indies took on New Zealand in the last four. Possessing an all-pace attack, it was no surprise the former's captain Clive Lloyd invited the opposition to bat. Thus, New Zealand took first strike and initially fared quite well against some sustained hostility. Their run rate of around three an over was sluggish, but they adequately advanced to 98 for one. Geoff Howarth pushed the score along as best he could, playing some delightful shots *en route* to a well-deserved 50. But Turner, on whom New Zealand banked heavily after his two centuries in the championship, failed to cut loose, his technical competence notwithstanding. With his departure and then Howarth's in the following over—both dismissed by Andy Roberts—the Kiwis were disembodied like a pack of cards.

Left-arm fast-medium exponent, Bernard Julien, swung the ball both ways to return four for 27 in his 12 overs; Roberts dug it in awkwardly and Vanburn Holder and Keith Boyce provided equally disobliging support. The Kiwis folded up for 158.

When the Windies began the chase, Roy Fredricks left early to a lackadaisical stroke; but Greenidge and Kalicharran realized 125 runs for the second wicket to largely put the issue beyond doubt. Richard Collinge created a stir by capturing three quick wickets. But the evergreen Rohan

Kanhai, recalled for the World Cup, was in attendance to steer the West Indians past the finishing line by five wickets.

Toss: West Indies
Man of the Match: Al Kallicharran
New Zealand 158 all out in 52.2 overs (Geoff Howarth 51. Glen Turner 36, Bernard Julien 4/27, Vanburn Holder 3/30). **West Indies** 159/5 in 40.1 overs (Alvin Kallicharan 72, Gordon Greenidge 55, Richard Collinge 3/28).

Final, 21 June: Lord's, London

With no spinner in his ranks, Ian Chappell asked the West Indies to bat and the decision seemed to be justified. The left-handed Fredricks hooked a bouncer for six only to loose his balance and swivel on to his stumps. Greenidge just could not get going and Kalicharran essayed an indiscreet cut. Both were caught behind. West Indies were, thus, 50 for three.

But Lloyd filled the breach and with Kanhai, his Guyanese compatriot, put on 149 runs for the fourth wicket to radically reverse the Australian advantage. While the tall, bespectacled left-hander bludgeoned the ball, Kanhai anchored his way to a half-century. However, the day really belonged to the former as he sculpted a sizzling hundred off 85 balls, punctuated by a brace of sixes and a dozen fours. Boyce and Julien, then, took over from where the skipper left off to set their opponents a stiff target.

The Aussies, through with their never-say-die approach, were undeterred. Chappell led the way with a skilful 62, but he was one of five to be run out, which, arguably, cost Australia the match. Vivian Richards, unsuccessful with the willow, twice hit the stumps from square leg and was also involved in a third dismissal. Yet, Jeff Thomson and Dennis Lillee, generally feared for their bowling, batted like a trigger-happy twosome emerging from an under-siege saloon in a Hollywood western. Australia perished, but they went down guns blazing, as the pace partners rattled up 41 for the last wicket. The West Indies were generally dominant and edged home by 17 runs, but the Australians had made a match of it.

As finals go, this unquestionably lived up to its billing. It was the longest day of the year and possibly the most extended day in cricket history. The match started at 11 a.m. and concluded at 8.43 p.m., when the light was just about enough on a luminous evening. The cavaliers from the Caribbean had jousted with the dashers from Down Under. It had proved to be a classic and secured the future of the World Cup!

Millions watched the tournament on television. A full house witnessed the final, which produced gate receipts of £66,950, a record for a one-day match in England at the time. The 15-day extravaganza, governed by good weather, was underwritten by Prudential to the tune of £100,000. The sale of tickets fetched over £200,000, as 158,000 spectators waded through the turnstiles. The winners received £4000 and the runners-ups £2000. England and New Zealand went home with £1000 each.

Ten per cent of the profits was retained by the UK. The other seven participating sides were each allocated 7.5 per cent of the surplus. The rest went to the ICC.

Toss: Australia
Man of the Match: CH Lloyd
West Indies 291/8 in 60 overs (Clive Lloyd 102, Rohan Kanhai 55, Gary Gilmour 5/48, Jeff Thomson 2/44). **Australia** 274 all out in 58.4 overs (Ian Chappell 62, Alan Turner 40, Keith Boyce 4/50).

About a week after the finals, the ICC assembled for their annual meeting to discuss, among other business, proposals for the next World Cup. The BCCI submitted that they were enthusiastic about hosting the event. Not surprisingly, there were no takers for this bid, as most members concurred 'it was hard to beat England as the venue'.

It was, of course, true that India's shorter daylight hours would have made it impossible to stage 120 overs of cricket in a day.

THE 1979 WORLD CUP

The summer of 1979 was a significant one for Indian cricketers. This was the first time they were returning to play test matches in England after the dreadful tour of 1974—when, among other indignities, the visitors were shot out for 42 in an innings at Lord's. But before the test series, there was the business of the second World Cup, again sponsored by Prudential Assurance.

Indeed, it was *déjà vu.* Venkataraghavan was again, unexpectedly, retained as captain; and India appeared to be as unripe for the task as four years earlier. In the autumn of 1978, the Indians had resumed cricket relations with Pakistan after 17 years. Playing away, they lost a three-test series 2–0. Following this defeat, Bishan Bedi was forthwith relieved of the captaincy and his second in command, Sunil Gavaskar, assumed charge. By this stage, Kerry Packer, an Australian tycoon, piqued by the Australian Cricket Board's refusal to award television rights to his Channel Nine network, had retaliated by lucratively luring three dozen top players from Australia, England, West Indies, New Zealand and Pakistan to participate in his 'World Series Cricket' Down Under, in defiance of cricket approved by and under the auspices of the ICC or its member boards. For the first time, it was cricket in coloured clothing, under floodlights and with a white, rather than a red, ball.

In the winter of 1978–79, a second-string West Indies squad under Alvin Kalicharran—for the bulk of their leading lights had gone over to Packer—visited India. The depth of talent in the Caribbean in that period was such that even a side without stars consisted of exponents who were strongly competing for places in the first XI, among them the effervescent Barbadian fast bowler, Malcolm Marshall. But the Indians duly recorded their maiden series victory over the West Indians at home; and Gavaskar, unaffected by the burden of leadership, aggregated 732 runs in the six tests at an average of 91.50.

Yet he was relieved of the captaincy for the trip to England. None of the Indian cricketers had been tempted to join Packer. But it was widely rumoured that Gavaskar had been approached and the BCCI feared he would cross over. While this has never been officially confirmed, it was surmised that Indian officials, not wanting to be embarrassed if he announced his departure after being retained as skipper, pre-emptively stripped him of his job. As it transpired, their apprehensions were misplaced, as Gavaskar never signed up with Packer. Indeed, he was probably never seriously approached, as a criterion for consideration was ability to play limited-overs cricket;

and in this respect, the Indian run-glutton had not shown himself to be particularly enthusiastic.

As in 1975, eight sides took part in the 1979 World Cup, the six test-playing ones, namely, England, Australia, West Indies, New Zealand, India and Pakistan, and two associate members of the ICC, Sri Lanka (who had also partaken four years earlier) and Canada, both of whom emerged from the ICC Trophy qualifying tournament. As per the draw, England, Australia, Pakistan and Canada featured in Group A; West Indies, New Zealand, India and Sri Lanka figured in Group B.

The English establishment's heart bled that South Africa had been spurned for a second time. It was astonishing that such elements could be so insensitive to the heinous crimes being systematically committed against human beings under institutionalized brutality—that, too, on a majority by a minority, racist government. For such behaviour, South Africa had become the pariah of the world. Yet, a majority of MCC members, the TCCB and the right wing of British media were advocating contravention of the 1977 Gleneagles Agreement, reached between Commonwealth Heads of Government, which imposed a ban on all sporting links with Pretoria and was binding on all Commonwealth countries. Indeed, it took the reluctant ICC 12 years to ratify the Gleaneagles resolution, when, in 1989, it finally debarred cricketers with South African ties from playing tests and ODIs.

Before the curtain ascended on the 1979 World Cup, India had featured in 10 ODIs, as compared to England's 36, Australia's 22, West Indies' 14 and Pakistan and New Zealand's 16 apiece. The Pakistani and West Indian cricket boards had forgotten and forgiven their Packer rebels; so, they were at full strength. England too had recovered from the likes of Tony Greig deserting them. But Australia continued to be without, among others, Greg Chappell and Dennis Lillee. Most were, however, more attuned to the needs of one-day cricket, especially those with the additional experience of the quite competitive limited-overs matches in Packer's World Series Cricket. The Indians had neither much practice in domestic competition nor the privilege of figuring in over-limit cricket in England. Only Bedi and Venkat in the Indian squad had experience of playing for English counties.

9 June: Edgbaston, Birmingham

To India's misfortune, their very first outing was a stern challenge—against the defending champions, no less, now approaching the height of their powers. Clive Lloyd won a significant toss and was able to unlatch his fearsome foursome—Andy Roberts, Michael Holding, Joel Garner and Colin Croft—on a wicket with residual moisture. With an umbrella field plucking catches as India slipped to 77 for five, the action paralleled more a test match than a one-day game. Only Gundappa Viswanath tackled with any conviction such sustained hostility, which was characterized by an overdose of bouncers, ignored by umpires David Evans and John Langridge—those were the days of all-English officials supervising World Cup fixtures!

It was, obviously, not a case of bias, but a lack of vigilance. The umpires appeared to solely interpret the situation on the basis of whether it was intimidation or not, forgetting that deliveries sailing well over a batsman's head—and 'Vishy', as the Bangalore batsman 'without an enemy in the world' was popularly addressed, was barely five foot five even with his spikes—were impossible to score of and should, therefore, have been penalized. Thus, the West Indies—not that they needed any help—not only benefited from the life in the pitch, but also from the benevolence of the umpires. As conditions eased, the Indian tail mustered a slight resistance, but overall the effort was insufficient.

At the customary cocktails after the match, Venkat expressed his displeasure with the umpiring in no uncertain terms. I immediately sensed a 'scoop'. Reporting for United News of India (UNI)—an Indian wire service—I carried his comments verbatim, which were published by newspapers in various parts of India, including his home city of Chennai. Before the next match, though, I observed Venkat had turned grumpy and sneerful. The manager of the team, Coimbatarao Gopinath, a former test player also from Chennai, explained the captain's remarks were not meant to be quoted. I remonstrated he never qualified his remarks by saying so. I also offered to despatch a denial, if this is what either he or Venkat desired. He didn't accept this offer. He elucidated it was not that Venkat did not make the statement, but he was upset about this being sourced to him.

As a stickler for journalistic ethics and diligent about not attributing remarks which are meant to be off-the-record, I was fairly clear in my mind Venkat's observations were not provided as background information. His subsequent stance, I felt, stemmed from his corporate and cricketing bosses in Chennai, with strong business links with Britain, censuring him for his criticism of umpires, that, too, English officials. I understood his circumstances, but could not sympathise with these. He was, after all, captain of India. But it took him four years—until half way through India's 1983 tour of the West Indies, for which he had been recalled—to snap out of his sulk. As far as I am concerned, I have never had any ill-feeling towards him before, during or since the incident; and I watched in admiration as he became the first Indian test player to don an umpire's coat (which many of his predecessors and peers deemed beneath their dignity) and established himself, for a spell, as the best in this trade. Not that it matters, but I hope that if 'Venky' ever writes his memoirs, he will reiterate what he told me that evening at Edgbaston—to put the record straight!

In reply, the West Indies batted exactly the same number of lawful deliveries as India. Despite some disciplined bowling by Kapil Dev and Karsen Ghavri, Gordon Greenidge took charge, completing a century, and realizing 138 runs for the opening partnership with his fellow Barbadian Desmond Haynes, before Viv Richards helped to finish the job. The West Indians cruised home by nine wickets.

Toss: West Indies
Man of the Match: CG Greenidge
India 190 all out in 53.1 overs (Gundappa Viswanath 75, Michael Holding 4/33, Andy Roberts 2/32). **West Indies** 194/1 in 51.3 overs (Gordon Greenidge 106*, Desmond Haynes 99, Kapil Dev Nikhanj 1/46).

13 June: Headingley, Leeds

Under sullen skies and given a slightly moist pitch, it was small wonder New Zealand's captain Mark Burgess invited India to bat. Sunil Gavaskar offered a difficult return catch to Richard Hadlee, but otherwise batted meticulously. However, Anshuman Gaekwad, Dilip Vengsarkar and Viswanath failed to forge any significant partnerships with him and India were soon 53 for three. Furthermore, their run rate was an indolent 2.5 an over. At this point though, Brijesh Patel filled the breach more inventively. This also instigated Gavaskar to take the cue. Kapil Dev and Ghavri, then, delivered a few lusty blows. But the Kiwis made the best of the conditions, which were not dissimilar to what one often encountered at Wellington or in their South Island in general. Richard Hadlee conceded only 20 runs in 10 overs, capturing two wickets, including the prized scalp of Gavaskar.

John Wright, later India's coach, and Bruce Edgar posted three figures for the opening wicket for the New Zealanders, which laid a launch pad for victory. At one stage they fell behind in their run rate, only to be resuscitated by Glen Turner, who, with an undefeated 43, featured in an unbroken partnership of 80 with Edgar. New Zealand won by eight wickets.

Toss: New Zealand
Man of the Match: BA Edgar
India 182 all out in 55.5 overs (Sunil Gavaskar 55, Brijesh Patel 38, Lance Cairns 3/36, Richard Hadlee 2/20). **New Zealand** 183/2 in 57 overs (Bruce Edgar 84, John Wright 48, Mohinder Amarnath 1/39).

16 and 18 June: Old Trafford, Manchester

In 1979, Sri Lanka were only an associate member of the ICC or, in other words, had not yet been granted test status. Indeed, at this juncture, they still figured in an annual clash alternately at home and away across the Palk Straits—22 miles of sea that separates the Indian Ocean island from mainland India—with the southern Indian state of Tamil Nadu for what was called the Gopalan Trophy (named after M. J. Gopalan, who played his only test for India at Kolkata against England in 1933–34). Tamil Nadu was a first-class side, though not among the topmost Ranji Trophy teams. And Sri

Lanka did not always win, either. Moreover, on this occasion at the World Cup, they were without the services of their skipper, Anura Tenekoon, who had pulled a hamstring at practice the day before the match. To top it all, they lost the toss and were asked to bat.

It was a Saturday and overcast as only Lancashire's commercial and cultural hub—notorious for its inclement weather—could be. Indeed, commencement of play had been delayed by drizzles. But the pitch was unharmed and against a blunt Indian attack, which, additionally, underperformed, the Sri Lankans batted with a nothing-to-lose spirit. Sidath Wettimuny and Roy Dias, both to subsequently acquit themselves with credit in official tests, erected a foundation with a 96-run second-wicket association at around four runs an over, before Duleep Mendis, another batsman to catch the eye in tests in the 1980s, drove home the advantage.

Wettimuny played correctly as befits an opener, driving with precision; Dias worked the ball away wristily, while the thickset Mendis carted the Indian seamers to distant corners on the leg side. Kapil, Ghavri and Amarnath were each despatched for six. All three Sri Lankan batsmen registered half-centuries. Even Sudath Pasqual, a left-handed schoolboy and the youngest participant in the 1979 World Cup, partook of the jollity, adding 52 runs in seven overs for the fifth wicket with Mendis, before the latter, not the swiftest over 22 yards, was run out.

Although secular in practice, Britain is on paper a Christian state; and, in the 1970s, Sundays were still strictly a day of rest, when test and county championship matches would come to a standstill only to resume on Mondays. Whether cricketers attended church or not—some did—they were, by tradition, not meant to be seen frolicking on a cricket field, or anywhere else for that matter. But confronted by realities, English authorities were compelled to relax such rigidity by permitting a 40-overs-a-side competition (the John Player League) between first-class counties on Sunday afternoons following religious services in the morning. Indeed, the gravelly voice of John Arlott accompanied by the pleasant cockney of Jim Laker on BBC TV would lift the boredom of a sleepy Sabbath.

But full-day cricket had not yet been introduced on a Sunday; therefore, a 60-over match, which is what a World Cup game then amounted to and which would consume both morning and afternoon, was still not admissible. Consequently, the India–Sri Lanka match, which could not be finished on a Saturday because of the late start, was carried over into the Monday.

Gavaskar and Gaekwad put on 60 for the first wicket and India needed 4.88 runs an over off the last 25 with eight wickets in hand. But no worthwhile stand bloomed to tackle this task. Somachandra de Silva, a leg spinner, enticed the Indian middle order to their doom. Tony Opatha, a medium pacer, who had made no impact with the new ball, then extinguished the tail. India crashed to ignoble surrender by 47 runs. It was Sri Lanka's first victory in two World Cups.

It was the only upset by a non-test-playing side in the tourney. As for India, far from progressing from their display in the previous World Cup, they had actually regressed. Indeed, if 1975 had been an embarrassment, 1979 now turned out to be an unalloyed *contretemps*.

Toss: India
Man of the Match: LRD Mendis
Sri Lanka 238/5 in 60 overs (Sidath Wettimuny 67, Duleep Mendis 64, Roy Dias 50, Mohinder Amarnath 3/40). **India** 191 all out in 54.1 overs (Dilip Vengsarkar 36, Anshuman Gaekwad 33, Somachandra de Silva 3/29, Tony Opatha 3/31).

Earlier...

The points from India were not the only ones acquired by the Sri Lankans. They obtained two more from their match against the West Indies, which even after three days of efforts—13, 14 and 15 June—was abandoned without a ball being bowled. Unrelentingly heavy downpours at The Oval left the outfield waterlogged and unsuitable for play even when there were a few dry spells.

The misfortune, though, did not prevent the West Indians from topping their group, with New Zealand finishing as runners-up. In the other cluster,

England won all three of their games, while Pakistan edged out Australia. The two, thus, qualified for the semifinals.

Semifinal, 20 June: Old Trafford, Manchester

Burgess won the toss for New Zealand and sent England into bat; and Hadlee restrained as well as threatened immediately. He had Geoffrey Boycott caught at third slip in the fifth over. But both skipper Mike Brearley and Graham Gooch chiselled half-centuries, the latter more aggressively. Indeed, stepping out, he sent Brian McKechnie sailing over the sightscreen before being bowled by the same bowler. Brearley had departed by then, snicking Jeremy Coney to the wicketkeeper. So, as most of the middle order collapsed—David Gower was run out and Ian Botham was lbw to one that kept low—Derek Randall, at number seven, conjured a neat cameo, playing sensibly rather than flamboyantly, while Bob Taylor chipped in with a six to long on off Lance Cairns. The Englishmen, thus, scrambled 25 runs in the last three overs.

The left-handers, Wright and Edgar, launched New Zealand's chase. But none, other than the former, even crossed 50 and only Turner made a meaningful contribution before he became Bob Willis' only victim. They ought to have done better, as the Warwickshire paceman had an injured leg and Botham and Mike Hendrick (the most successful of the English bowlers), too, had niggles. The attack (which included Boycott with his gentle medium pacers and he had Geoff Howarth lbw with a full toss bowled round the wicket) lacked a single spinner, as left-armer, Phil Edmonds, had been left out amidst some criticism in the English media. Wright kept the Kiwis' hopes alive until Randall brilliantly ran him out from square leg. Warren Lees and Cairns struck a six each at the expense of Hendrick and Botham, respectively, and took the New Zealanders close, but these were only the last strokes of a drowning swimmer.

As Botham began the last over, New Zealand needed 14 runs to win. They ultimately got only four of them, thereby losing by nine runs. It was a well-contested game played at an unusually sunny Old Trafford. For the near-capacity crowd, it was quite pulsating as the pendulum swung from one end to the other before coming to rest in the home side's favour.

Toss: New Zealand
Man of the Match: GA Gooch
England 221/8 in 60 overs (Graham Gooch 71, Mike Brearley 53, Brian McKechnie 2/46, Richard Hadlee 1/32). **New Zealand** 212/9 in 60 overs (John Wright 69, Glen Turner 30, Mike Hendrick 3/55, Geoff Boycott 1/24).

Semifinal, 20 June: The Oval, London

The other clash amongst the last four—staged simultaneously—also lived up to the occasion. Pakistan, perhaps wanting as much to avoid the opposition's quartet of serious quicks as to exploit the morning conditions with Imran Khan, Sarfraz Nawaz and Sikander Bakht, inserted the West Indies; but came up against the roadblock of in-form Caribbeans.

Greenidge and Haynes posted an opening stand of 132, although the latter was lucky to be dropped by Imran at long leg off the amiable pace of Mudassar Nazar when he was 32. Eventually the slow but slippery medium pace of Asif Iqbal, vastly seasoned in the art of one-day cricket by virtue of his long stint at Kent, collected four of the six wickets that fell; but not before Richards and Lloyd had sprayed the field with an array of shots. Sarfraz was a particular spendthrift, donating 71 runs in his 12 overs before he had Collis King caught and bowled. The West Indians set their opponents a target of 294. Match over? Not yet.

Sadiq Mohammad, the left-handed brother of the more famous Hanif and Mushtaq, was snuffed out peremptorily by the hostility of Holding, as he attempted to ward off a bouncer. But his dismissal brought together Majid Khan and Zaheer Abbas in the most exhilarating partnership of the day. As the sun bathed this lustrous ground on a glorious south London afternoon, the two Pakistani stroke players, adept at the one-day game, having spent years at Glamorgan and Gloucestershire respectively, mirrored nature's splendour. Admittedly, Majid was given a life by Greenidge off Holding when only 10, but the duo added 166 runs for the second wicket in 36 overs to give their side an even chance of victory. My colleague Trevor MacDonald, Britain's Independent Television News' newscaster of Trinidadian origin and an occasional cricket writer, was on his feet in the Long Room of the pavilion, smiling nervously, tankard in hand. But where Roberts, Holding and Garner were seen off by the skill of a talented twosome, ultimately the West Indians' bowling depth had the last say.

Colin Croft, an awkward speedster as any, was brought back from the Vauxhall end—the side of the river Thames. He had Zaheer and Majid caught and trapped Javed Miandad, a potential match winner, leg before in 12 balls for four runs. Pakistan never recovered from this. More importantly, the West Indies reached the World Cup final for the second time running.

Toss: Pakistan
Man of the Match: CG Greenidge
West Indies 293/6 in 60 overs (Gordon Greenidge 73, Desmond Haynes 65, Vivian Richards 42, Asif Iqbal 4/56, Imran Khan 1/43). **Pakistan** 250 all out in 56.2 overs (Zaheer Abbas 93, Majid Khan 81, Colin Croft 3/29, Vivian Richards 3/52, Andy Roberts 2/41).

Final 23 June: Lord's, London

The home of cricket was filled to the rafters as a clear blue sky provided a magnificent canopy over proceedings. Many who had come to St John's Wood, the north London quarter that houses the ground, in expectation of picking up returned tickets left disappointed.

That no side relished facing the West Indian pacemen of the late 1970s vintage in the freshness of an English forenoon was once again testified to by Brearley, a shrewd judge of the game, who invited Lloyd to bat. England were handicapped by the absence of Willis. But Edmonds, Brearley's Middlesex teammate, replacing him, emerged as the most economical of the English bowlers. This performance was offset, though, by Boycott, Gooch and Will Larkins, combining to bowl 12 overs, haemorrhaging 86 runs without any purchase.

Earlier, England's bowlers had got off to a dream start, as Botham, Hendrick and Chris Old—and an under-arm run out from midwicket by Randall—reduced the favourites to 99 for four. Richards was in control, but by his sublime standards, not his contemptuous self. The man who joined him at this point, though, evidently was. In about an hour and a quarter, Collis King smashed three sixes and 10 fours in an awesome power play. He drove, hooked and pulled *en route* to 86 in a fifth-wicket association of 139 with Richards, and by the time he holed out at square leg off Edmonds, he had all but taken the game away from England.

Richards thereafter completed his hundred and famously flicked Old's last ball of the innings over square leg for six to remain unconquered on 138, with three hits over the fence and 11 fours.

A dry pitch under a salubrious afternoon glow was perfect for batting. But while Boycott and Brearley, opening for England, both crossed 50 and were unseparated for 130 minutes, they never managed to stamp their authority on the West Indian bowling. Indeed, Boycott spent 17 overs just to reach double figures. After Brearley left—caught off Holding—for 64, England required 158 runs in 22 overs, too tall an order by 1970s definition. Gooch made a valiant attempt to step up the scoring, but in vain. In hot pursuit of their target, the Englishmen crumbled. In a sensational spell, the 6-ft-8-inch Garner snapped up five wickets for four runs in 11 balls and was twice on a hat trick.

As the giant Barbadian tightened his team's grip on the match, the music and dancing among the West Indian supporters in the stands grew in magnitude. And when the West Indies completed their 97-run win to retain the Prudential World Cup, their compatriots fittingly converted the hallowed abode of cricket into an arena for a Caribbean carnival.

Toss: England
Man of the Match: IVA Richards
West Indies 286/9 in 60 overs (Vivian Richards 138*, Collis King 86, Phil Edmonds 2/40, Ian Botham 2/44). **England** 194 all out in 51 overs (Mike Brearley 64, Geoff Boycott 57, Graham Gooch 32, Joel Garner 5/38, Colin Croft 3/42).

Although the second World Cup did not enjoy the fairly uninterrupted sunshine of four year earlier, it was still an unqualified success. Prudential contributed £250,000 and revenues from ticket sales fetched £359,700—almost double the takings in the first competition. But because of the sketchy weather, spectator presence dropped from 160,000 in 1975 to 132,000 in 1979. Eventually, the profit of £350,000 was shared between the full and associate members of the ICC.

Out of the £25,900 reserved for prize money, the West Indies received £10,000 and England £4000. New Zealand and Pakistan, the losing semifinalists, went home with £2000 each, while winners of group matches got £500. Richards won £300 for his Man of the Match award in the final; £200 were paid out in each of the semifinals and £100 in the league matches to such nominated players.

With this championship, the ICC formally resolved to make the World Cup a four-yearly event, with the 1983 tournament once again allocated to England.

CHAPTER TWO

1983

Ecstasy

GUYANA, SITUATED IN THE NORTHEAST OF SOUTH AMERICA, with Venezuela to its west, Suriname to its east and Brazil to the south, is a country of around one million people. The Dutch, who founded colonies in the seventeenth and eighteenth centuries, imported African slaves for plantations producing sugar, coffee and cotton. The territories were, then, ceded to Britain in 1814.

With the abolition of slavery in 1834, labourers were imported from India, mainly from the northern provinces of Bihar and Uttar Pradesh, many of whom settled in the country after their indentures. As a result, people of Indian decent are in a slight majority in the country, with Afro-Caribbeans largely constituting the rest of the population.

This only non-island state in the cricketing consortium that comprises the West Indies has sprouted significant talent. Among the Afro-Caribbeans, there have been Basil Butcher, Lance Gibbs, Roy Fredericks, Clive Lloyd, Colin Croft and Carl Hooper, while the Indo-Caribbeans have included Rohan Babulal Kanhai, Alvin Kallicharran, Shivnarine Chanderpaul and Ramnaresh Sarwan. Typically, the blacks came from the country's coastal areas, including the capital Georgetown, which are generally inhabited by people of their background, whereas the Indians hailed from the 'interior', a term commonly used for inland areas.

The third leg of the visit by Kapil Dev's team in 1983—the first two having been Jamaica and Trinidad in that order—was Guyana, which was, then, in a rather impoverished and lawless condition. The Dutch colonial architecture of the country was in a state of disrepair. Food was in short supply, of dodgy quality and quite unvaried even in the towering Pegasus Hotel at Georgetown—the best in the country-overlooking the Atlantic Ocean where the two sides stayed. A practice known as 'choke and rob' made it hazardous to venture onto the streets. But the hospitality of the local Indians enlivened the evenings.

On the morning of 29 March, the Indian and West Indians players as well as mediapersons were transported on military aircraft from Georgetown, which was also on the mouth of the Demerara (of sugar fame) river to Albion town in the rice-bowl region of Berbice (otherwise a five-hour drive), for a one-day international. The West Indians were, at the time, not only by far the most dominant force in tests, but also the best at limited-overs cricket, for which they had a natural propensity. They had, in fact, won both the Prudential World Cups held up to this juncture—in 1975 and 1979—and were odds-on favourites to complete a hat trick in the one scheduled for June of that year.

In contrast, the Indians, who had performed abysmally in the two events and also been soundly beaten in the first one-dayer of this tour at Port of Spain, Trinidad, gave the impression of being unenthusiastic about the shorter format. They were, thus, only expected to serve as cannon fodder in the Guyanese countryside.

For the greater part of the 1970s, compilation of runs by India depended heavily on Kapil's predecessor Sunil Gavaskar and his brother-in-law, Gundappa Viswanath. There was limited luxury or leeway to play shots. Gavaskar's mentality was, therefore, to save a match first and to go on the offensive only if a genuine opportunity arose. He could apply this philosophy in tests with a degree of success, but not in one-dayers, where India were ill-equipped for the compulsions of an attacking game. They were accoutred with neither the batting talent nor the bowling prowess to flourish in a one-day situation. The Mumbai maestro tried to invigorate himself in the Benson & Hedges Series with Australia and New Zealand Down Under in 1980–81, where there was an incentive of prize money. But his pre-determined mindset prevailed over him.

However, in the Caribbean, in 1983, Gavaskar was replaced by Kapil, an athletic, sports-loving member of a Chandigarh-based business family. This all-rounder from the northern agricultural state of Haryana, bordering the capital, New Delhi, was of a different mould. He was a belligerent swing bowler and naturally strokeful in his batting. He played the game with a carefree candour, instinctively and without worrying too much about the consequences. Safety first or unentertaining cricket was foreign to his thinking. He once innocently asked me after one of his pleasing performances whether I had enjoyed it. The uncomplicated character that he was, it probably never occurred to him that I hadn't been at the ground as a paying spectator, but as an unsentimental journalist. Quite simply, his doctrine was to dish out delight to anyone caring to watch.

India had just been thrashed 3–0 in a test series in Pakistan, yet the composition of the squad despatched to the West Indies under Kapil was suddenly more promising. The resurfacing of Mohinder Amarnath in a brilliant, new incarnation, the advance of Dilip Vengsarkar (later to become the world's highest ranked batsman) and the performance of the stoic utilitarian, Ravi Shastri, had lessened the burden on Gavaskar, while Balwinder Singh Sandhu, a Sikh swing bowler from the cosmopolitan metropolis of Mumbai, provided a decent foil to Kapil. (India were, of course, beaten 2–0 in the five-test series on the 1983 tour by the irrepressible West Indian bulldozer navigated by Lloyd; but went down without discredit!)

The batting of Amarnath, the second son of Lala Amarnath, who scored India's first test century against England in Mumbai in 1933, was particularly riveting. Continuing from where he left off in Pakistan, he met fire with fire, driving and hooking the West Indian fast bowlers in a manner they had rarely been treated before. With centuries at Port of Spain and St John's, Antigua, and four other half-centuries, including two rip-roaring innings of 91 and 80 on a characteristically bouncy track at Bridgetown, Barbados—batting with stitches after being struck on his lips—he was at that stage incomparable against pace. Vivian Richards, a premier batsman in that era, but who had, admittedly, never had the unenviable task of facing the fearsome foursomes of West Indian cricket, graciously conceded as much at Kapil's birthday bash at Port of Spain on the same tour. He, however, mischievously added to Amarnath: 'I take my hats off to you maan for the runs you got in Pakistan!' Inherent in the remark was Richards' belief—which he went on to elaborate—that the Pakistanis tampered with the ball, thus obtaining movement by unfair means. Amarnath, nicknamed 'Jimmy', smiled appreciatively. He had registered three hundreds on India's neighbouring soil a few months earlier to the Antiguan's solitary three-figure knock in Pakistan in his entire career. Indeed, while batting in a test and after being beaten several times by bending deliveries, Richards demanded to see the ball in order to check if it had been scuffed up.

Albion, located on the alluvial, foliaged plains of the Berbice region, sometimes depicted as the 'ancient county', through which the Berbice river meandered, had once been a major sugar plantation hub. Masses of East Indian faces—not the ruddy skins of indigenous Indians of the American continent—glistened in the hazy, humid sunshine. They had mushroomed as if to greet and inspect messengers from the mother country. Among others, Kanhai, who originated from here, was concurrently visiting his mother, who still lived nearby. Some Afro-Caribbeans, too, bestrewed the welcome party. Basil Butcher, after all, came from the same area. What caught the eye were banana groves and coconut trees half-concealing Biswasian cottages of Naipaulian description (though this was Guyana, not Trinidad). Small, red, triangular flags—with a clearly Hindu connotation—fluttered in the breeze. A boisterous crowd of 15,000, with distinctly divided loyalties, were assembled at the town's Sports Complex.

Lloyd, the West Indian skipper, had settled in England, where he had long worn Lancashire's colours in the county scene. Now back on native soil, he won the toss. With the battery of fast bowlers at his disposal, he generally fancied unleashing them while the pitch was still fresh in the morning, regardless of the opposition. This time, too, he made no exception. He inserted India; and let loose his speed merchants, who indicated a change, with an injured Garner being rested for Winston Davis, who was making his ODI debut. But contrary to all expectations, India did not surrender a wicket until Shastri, opening the innings with Gavaskar, was caught behind off Marshall with the total on 93.

Gavaskar, a middle-class Maharashtrian groomed in the batting mill of Mumbai's Dadar Union club, had been the bane of West Indian bowlers with record-breaking aggregates in test series in 1971 and 1976. But he had, thus far on this visit, not been his normal, prolific self. Not only had he disappointed in the previous one-dayer, but also had a top score of just 32 in four test innings, which included a first ball duck at Sabina Park, Kingston, where his stumps were spectacularly sent cantering by the local limousine, Michael Holding.

Nephew of a former test wicketkeeper, Madhav Mantri, Gavaskar was, of course, the primary target of the West Indian quicks, with Lloyd not averse to employing them around the wicket to pretty much aim every ball at his head or ribs. With no fixed ceiling on bouncers in those days, nothing, I daresay, in cricket history could have been as threatening as this four-pronged offensive against Gavaskar, not even the Douglas Jardine-inspired bodyline bowling of Harold Larwood in Australia in 1932–33 to contain Donald Bradman. Gavaskar's absence of form, though, might also have been caused by the fact that he was yet to come to terms with being deposed as captain. To return to the ranks from a lofty pedestal is never easy. In his case, to play under someone considerably his junior could also have been a factor. Besides, relations between him and his successor, Kapil had become a little tense. This, because of a West Zone–North Zone rivalry that still existed in Indian cricket at the time and also because of the misleading influence of their cronies.

At Albion, though, he carved one of the most significant limited-overs knocks of his career. Indeed, by the time he was run out for 90 and India had progressed to 152 for two—he had the Windies really worried. More pertinently, Gavaskar was delighted with his Albion essay. It was as if he had crossed the Rubicon and proved to himself and the world that he was now ready for the one-day requirements.

Kapil replaced Gavaskar. He connected with the ball like a Muhammad Ali punch. Aware that his opponents had been softened up, he was determined not to allow them to return to their feet. With languid ease, he floated down the wicket like a butterfly but stung the bowlers, especially Gomes and Holding, like a bee! With seven fours and three sixes, he raced to a stunning 72 in 38 balls. Like the Hindu God, Hanuman torching pre-historic Lanka in the mythological epic, Ramayana, he set Albion ablaze. The match had been reduced to 47 overs for each side; yet the West Indies, faced an uncommonly stiff target of 283.

Greenidge and Haynes strode out, but were soon separated as Sandhu trapped the latter leg before wicket. The other followed not long afterwards—caught and bowled by Kapil—and Lloyd, too, perished cheaply, falling victim to Madan Lal. His exit reduced the home side to 62 for three, to which the imperious Vivian Richards had contributed the most. As far as the Indians were concerned, his was the key wicket. He majestically moved to 64, but at this point, Madan Lal shattered his stumps.

Eight years previously, I had seen the same, underrated bowler send back this burgeoning batsman with a ball that swung away to start with and then moved back at the Eden Gardens in Kolkata. It was in the final session of play—when a breeze used to emanate from the nearby Hooghly river and assist deviation in the air at this ground—on the fourth day of the third test in a best-of-five series. Tiger Pataudi, leading India, reintroduced the medium-pacer against the wind. Madan Lal disfigured Richards' sticks after the batsman had ominously progressed to 47. It was the only wicket he took in that innings, but the menacing Richards' was, arguably, the most valuable scalp.

Now, a maturer and more determined West Indies did not cave in that easily. Faoud Bacchus and Jeff Dujon, with half-centuries, resisted spiritedly. But Shastri, with his left-arm orthodox stuff, chipped in with three wickets. And so, the undisputed champions of both forms of cricket crashed to unprecedented defeat by 27 runs. It was the first time that a full-strength West Indian side had lost a one-day international at home. The only other instance was in 1978, when they went down to Australia by two wickets—in a match restricted to 36 overs by rain—when both teams were weakened by the exodus of a majority of their leading cricketers to Kerry Packer's rebel 'World Series'.

For India, this was their first-ever win over the West Indies in an ODI anywhere. Balwinder Sandhi said: "That win gave us the belief that we can beat them; and that was the turning point in our confidence."

Tension intensified at the ground as the possibility of an Indian win increased. Having applauded Gavaskar and Kapil in the morning, the Indo-Caribbeans in attendance could not help appreciate the combined effort of the visiting bowlers. This annoyed the Afro-Caribbeans. At one stage, scuffles spilling over from the temporary stands, not to mention the worsening light, raised fears of an abandonment, which the West Indians wouldn't have objected to.

Bacchus' presence in the side notwithstanding, Guyanese Indians were generally dissatisfied with the West Indian team selection. They felt Kalicharran, among others, had received a raw deal under the Lloyd regime—a point rubbed in to me in no uncertain manner by the former.

The West Indies, not unexpectedly, proceeded to win the third and final ODI at Queen's Park, St George's, in Grenada.

The significance of the Indian triumph at Albion, though, is immeasurable. It helped the Indians to realize they were not so useless in one-day cricket; that what was hitherto deemed to be unimaginable beating the West Indies in the abbreviated form—had, actually, been achieved, that, too, in the West Indians' backyard. The victory converted an erstwhile apathy towards the shorter version of the game into a calculated keenness for it.

While the attainment could well have been labelled a flash in the pan, it soon became obvious that the psychological gain from it was enormous. It signified that India entered the Prudential World Cup less than three months later in a completely different frame of mind as compared to the two previous such competitions. They were more self-assured against all teams, including the formidable West Indies. This aspect was, in fact, to manifest itself in their very first outing against the defending champions at Old Trafford, Manchester.

In more ways than one, therefore, the ascent at Albion was the turning point in India's odyssey in limited-overs cricket, which was soon to lead to a glittering display in the 1983 Prudential World Cup.

Toss: West Indies

Man of the Match: N Kapil Dev

India innings (47 overs maximum)			R	B
SM Gavaskar	run out		90	117
RJ Shastri	c Dujon	b Marshall	30	56
M Amarnath		b Richards	30	34
*N Kapil Dev		b Roberts	72	38
Yashpal Sharma	c Greenidge	b Davis	23	26
DB Vengsarkar	not out		18	19
AO Malhotra	not out		1	3

Extras: (b 1, lb 9, w 4, nb 4) 18

Total: (5 wickets, 47 overs) 282

DNB: S Madan Lal, +SMH Kirmani, BS Sandhu, S Venkataraghavan.

FoW: 1-93 (Shastri), 2-152 (Gavaskar), 3-224 (Amarnath), 4-246 (Kapil Dev), 5-277 (Yashpal Sharma).

Bowling	O	M	R	W
Holding	7	0	49	0
Roberts	9	0	44	1
Davis	8	0	40	1
Marshall	7	0	23	1
Gomes	10	0	64	0
Richards	6	0	44	1

West Indies innings (target: 283 runs from 47 overs)			R	B
CG Greenidge	c & b Kapil Dev		16	28
DL Haynes	lbw	b Sandhu	2	7
IVA Richards		b Madan Lal	64	51
*CH Lloyd	c Amarnath	b Madan Lal	8	4
SFAF Bacchus	c Yashpal Sharma	b Shastri	52	65
HA Gomes	c Kapil Dev	b Shastri	26	28
+PJL Dujon	not out		53	64
1MD Marshall	c Sandhu	b Shastri	5	6
AME Roberts		b Kapil Dev	12	10
MA Holding	c Malhotra	b Sandhu	2	8
WW Davis	not out		7	12

Extras: (lb 6, w 1, nb 1) 8

Total: (9 wickets, 47 overs) 255

FoW: 1-6 (Haynes), 2-22 (Greenidge), 3-62 (Lloyd), 4-98 (Richards), 5-154 (Gomes), 6-181 (Bacchus), 7-192 (Marshall), 8-228 (Roberts), 9-232 (Holding).

Bowling	O	M	R	W
Kapil Dev	10	0	33	2
Sandhu	10	0	38	2
Madan Lal	9	0	65	2
Venkataraghavan	10	0	63	0
Shastri	8	0	48	3

'THE SUN NEVER SHINES AT OLD TRAFFORD,' HAS BEEN AN endless refrain about the opprobrious weather at Manchester's iconic cricket ground. This is where the Lancashire and England fast bowler, Brian Statham, flourished in the 1950s and early 1960s as the pitch acquired a greenish hue under cloud cover exacerbated by industrial pollution, but where batsmen would make hay when the sky cleared.

I had always felt attracted to Old Trafford, with its pavilion a chaplet of red brick, Victorian masonry; and unlike most other international cricket grounds the wicket positoned square to it—though no longer the case. This affection was triggered in my teens, when reading the *doyen* of English cricket writers, Sir Neville Cardus, himself a Mancunian. Among many gems, I came across his description of Kumar Sri Ranjitsinhji's batting, especially his leg glance—a shot he invented and even executed from off-stump—as 'esoteric *legerdemain*'. 'Ranji', the first Indian to play test cricket and later the Jam Saheb or ruler of the princely state of Nawanagar, in the western Indian state of Gujarat, made his debut at Old Trafford in 1896.

Not only that; he became the second batsman after W. G. Grace, the Gloucestershire doctor recognized as the father of batsmanship, to score a hundred on his maiden appearance for England—from all accounts a magical display. In so doing, he also became the first player to complete a hundred runs before lunch in a test match. On the third morning, he took his overnight contribution of 41 to 154, thus adding 113 runs in a session and setting a record that remains unsurpassed in Ashes series.

The fact that Farokh Engineer, the Indian wicketkeeper-batsman of the 1960s and 1970s from Mumbai, joined Lancashire County Cricket Club—whose home is Old Trafford—in 1968, further enhanced my interest. 'Rooky', as he came to be called in England, was a swashbuckling cricketer who caught the imagination of many in my generation, especially after he almost reached three figures before the luncheon interval at Chennai in 1967 against the West Indies led by Garry (later Sir Garfield) Sobers. His 94 not out at the interval on the first day was no mean effort, for it was at the expense of Wesley Hall, Charlie Griffith, Sobers himself and Lance Gibbs. He went on to post 109.

Last but not the least, on a grey afternoon, within weeks of my arrival in England for the first time as an adult, I saw Greg Chappell, then Australia's captain and some three decades later India's coach, etch an innings of 112 out of a total of 218. Remembering Cardus, I was inspired to characterize his footwork against England's left-arm spinner Derek Underwood on a difficult pitch (Australia lost the test by nine wickets) to the felicity of the Russian ballet dancer Rudolf Nureyev, whom I had just seen on the London stage.

Cardus was also the music critic of *The Manchester Guardian*, later *The Guardian*, the respected British daily, in addition to being its cricket correspondent. John Arlott, who succeeded Cardus as cricket correspondent, fulfilled a dual responsibility, as well. He was the wine appraiser of the paper. In the summer of 1979, he was seated immediately behind me at the old press box at Lord's, when he narrated a friendly banter between him and Cardus about who had enjoyed the better position overall. They agreed, in terms of cricket, they were at par. But what about the additional role? Arlott insisted his was the cushier circumstance since he got to savour the finest wines in the market. Cardus thought about this for a while, then retorted: 'But who would you rather spend an evening with? A drunk or a soprano?' Arlott of a bass voice was stumped!

India, though, had mixed memories of Manchester. In 1936, Vijay Merchant, a textile tycoon and a prolific run-getter from Mumbai, and Mushtaq Ali, the light-footed Virender Sehwag of his era, put on 203 for the first wicket, but in 1952, India were bowled out for 58 and 82 to lose by an innings. India also went down in 1959, despite the elegant Hyderabadi Abbas Ali Baig posting a hundred on debut, and succumbed once more in 1974, in spite of a Sunil Gavaskar century. However, the Indians drew in 1982, when Sandip Patil, a Bombay belter, pummelled Bob Willis for six fours—a world test record—in a seven-ball over (one of which was a no-ball). His 24 runs also equalled the test record for the highest number of runs scored in an over, held by Andy Roberts. Indeed, Patil fairly motored from 73 to 104 off a mere nine balls. (I was also a witness to this feat being replicated by Ramnaresh Sarwan of the West Indies at St Kitts in June 2006 at the expense of paceman Munaf Patel.)

Patil, chairman of the Indian selection committee that chose the 2015 squad, was a natural and powerful stroke player. But hard work was not his forte. Gavaskar, his captain both at state and national levels, used to virtually beseech his parents to ensure that he attended nets and training regimens. In fact, Patil had looked rather out of sorts in county games on the 1982 tour and, consequently, wasn't selected in the side for the first test at Lord's. But after India lost this match, the tour selectors decided to gamble with him. That they were not exactly confident about him was reflected by he being held back to number seven in the batting order. Indeed, he walked in at 136 for five, with his side still requiring 90 runs to save the follow-on. But what an exhibition he, then, proffered! Willis, a redoubtable fast bowler, probably still wakes up with a sweat from the mauling meted out to him.

This was the second of two heroic performances from Patil I had had the pleasure of observing. The previous one was at the Adelaide Oval, a year and a half earlier.

In the first test of that series at the Sydney Cricket Ground, he had been fearfully hit on the head by a Lenny Pascoe bouncer on a lively first-day wicket. As he saw this, Tiger Pataudi, sitting next to me in the press box, unconsciously grabbed my arm in a grip that left me a bit bruised. As Patil—batting on 65 (which transpired to be the top score in an innings of

201)—crumpled before our eyes, Pataudi had visions of Nari Contractor being near-fatally struck on the head by a short-pitched delivery from Charlie Griffith that failed to rise in the Barbados game in 1962. Contractor, leading the side on that ill-fated trip (India lost all five tests), gave way to Pataudi, then only 21, for the rest of the tour.

As Bapu Nadkarni, the slender erstwhile test player, who was India's assistant manager on that tour, struggled to lift—let alone carry—a concussed Patil back to the pavilion, an otherwise phlegmatic Pataudi, couldn't help exclaiming loudly: 'Get help, Bapu!' When Patil came out to bat with a helmet (not yet a universal feature) in the second innings, he shakily spooned a catch close to the wicket off Dennis Lillee to be dismissed for four.

The consensus based on such evidence was: he would be hard put to make a comeback to international cricket; the matter of his participation in the rest of the prevailing series was completely ruled out. Experts averred: the psychological trauma of the injury was difficult to overcome. India were defeated in the match by an innings.

Less than three weeks later was the second test at Adelaide. To most people's surprise, Patil was included in the eleven. Australia piled up 528 and India in reply were starkly looking down a barrel at 130 for four, when he entered the fray. Not unexpectedly, he was greeted by a barrage of bumpers. At first, he ducked and let them sail over his shoulders. Thereafter, he embarked on hooking Lillee, Pascoe and Rodney Hogg through midwicket in a fierce riposte. Indeed, he stormed to 174 off 240 balls, with 22 fours and a six. It was a remarkable rejuvenation after such a frightful jolt. India drew the match and proceeded to win the next at the Melbourne Cricket Ground to avoid defeat in a test series in Australia for the first time.

In 1983, the third and final World Cup to be sponsored by the Prudential Assurance Company was still a 60-overs-a-side competition. A bowler was allowed a maximum of 12 overs per innings, and the umpires became perceptibly stricter in applying the rules in respect of wides and bouncers.

There were once more eight participants, who were divided into two groups. But the build-up was different from that of the preceding World Cups in that, in the preliminary phase, the sides played each other not once but twice. This was partly to enhance revenue but also to reduce the chances of a team being eliminated because of worse luck with the weather than their rivals. In actual fact, after one of the wettest Mays on record, the clouds all but disappeared in June; and of the 27 matches played, only three were not concluded in a day. The first two from each group in the league stage qualified for the semifinals and the knockout portion, with the winners of a cluster taking on the runners-up of the other. India's section had the West Indies, Australia and Zimbabwe, while the other assembly was made up of England, Pakistan, New Zealand and Sri Lanka. India, 66:1 outsiders before the tournament began, commenced their campaign in Old Trafford's fluctuating conditions. It could not have been a more foreboding challenge, for the opposition were again the Windies!

The contrast between 1979 and 1983 was that the Indians had in the interim undergone a grinding in Australia in 1980–81 when they took part in the triangular Benson & Hedges World Series Cup, which exposed them to 10 ODIs on the trot. Ultimately, they prevailed in only three of these outings, but perforce gained useful experience in the ways and means of dealing with the shorter version of the game. Indeed, they made a surprisingly good start, winning three of their first four matches, but subsequently fell away to seldom look like winning another game. The batsmen seemed untuned to the urgency demanded in instant cricket. Much of the bowling was uncontrolled and the fielding, overall, was not up to scratch.

I checked in at a hotel in Manchester's city centre, where the Indian team were also staying. It was a bit of a reunion, for we had parted company only a month earlier. There were few barriers between the Indian players and the press in those days. In a way it was socializing between the scanned and the scanner, yet in those days such interaction was an integral part of an overseas tour. The meeting point was generally the watering hole of the team hotel. It was no different on this occasion. But such bonding was forgotten the next next morning as the participants resumed their respective roles of cricketer and commentator or chronicler.

9–10 June: Old Trafford, Manchester

It was a tricolour attendance—whites, Afro-Caribbeans and Asians. The indigenous folks had come to catch a glimpse of the then most respected cricketing outfit in the planet, and the West Indians and Indians had turned up to support their respective sides—the former more unabashedly, as they were sanguine about the outcome. The latter were more subdued, indeed nervous that their compatriots might end up as lambs for slaughter.

Greater Manchester and cities and town around it, from Liverpool in the west, Birmingham to the south and West Yorkshire to the east across the Pennine mountain range, have absorbed multitudes of immigrants from both the Caribbean and the Indian subcontinent. From upwardly mobile Afro-Caribbeans in felt hats to men in boiler suits, from Indian medical practitioners to factory workers, the stands reflected a variety of pastels and people. The West Indians were soon into their rum and music. The Indians watched in admiration and amusement, tucking into benign sandwiches.

The West Indies won the toss and—as you would expect—put India in after a delayed start caused by inclement weather. Indeed, India struggled on a damp pitch and indifferent light to lose three wickets for 79. But a splendid innings of 89 by Yashpal Sharma, Kapil Dev's Haryana teammate, in 120 balls, before he was bowled by Michael Holding, boosted them to their highest total in three World Cups. Sharma's became at that point the best-ever score by an Indian batsman in the World Cup. His 73-run partnership for the sixth wicket with Roger Binny, who got 27, principally contributed to the total. Patil chipped in with a sprightly 36. As the sun filtered through the clouds, the Indian innings brightened with it. Of the first eight batsmen, only Kapil Dev did not record double figures.

In reply, Gordon Greenidge and Desmond Haynes began confidently, scoring 49 before the latter was run out. From that moment, India began to tighten their grip on the match. With play spilling over to the reserve day, the West Indies recommenced on 67 for two in the 23rd over. To India's relief, Richards departed early caught behind off Binny and skipper Clive Lloyd was bowled by the same bowler. The champions rapidly collapsed to 157 for nine. Binny recalled: "Initially, I found it difficult to control the ball; but when I got my line, I found it easy and had them in trouble, straightway." Andy Roberts and Joel Garner demonstrated fortitude by realizing 71 runs before wicketkeeper Syed Kirmani smartly stumped the latter off Ravi Shastri to seal the West Indies' fate.

This was their first-ever loss in the World Cup. The West Indies caved in by 34 runs; their venture lasting merely 54.1 overs. It was only India's second win in the World Cup—the previous one being against an unpretentious East African side in 1975. Shastri and Binny, an Anglo-Indian all-rounder from Bangalore, were slightly expensive, but both captured three wickets apiece, while medium pacers Madan Lal and Balwinder Singh Sandhu were the most economical. Where Yashpal Sharma had found the fence nine times, the West Indians, albeit on a slow outfield, failed to hit a single four. Garner, though, struck a six.

The cricketing world was stunned. But to some of us who had witnessed the Indian win at Albion, the result, while, admittedly, unexpected, was not an absolute surprise. It suggested that Albion was probably not a fluke, and that 'Kapil's devils' could now be treated as dark horses for the tournament. The advantage India possessed, as compared to the other sides, was that they were fresh from encountering the West Indian quicks—their most potent weapon—less than a couple of months earlier and had almost come to terms with them by compiling 457 runs in an innings in the final test at Antigua. It had also dawned on the Indians that after Albion the West Indians were no longer impregnable. Amarnath remarked: "We had won against the world champions... so there is a possibility we can do a miracle in the World Cup."

Toss: West Indies
Man of the Match: Yashpal Sharma
Close of Play: **Day 1:** India 262/8,
West Indies 67/2 (Richards 12*, Bacchus 3*, 22 ov)

India innings (60 overs maximum)			R	B
SM Gavaskar	c Dujon	b Marshall	19	44
K Srikkanth	c Dujon	b Holding	14	17
M Amarnath	c Dujon	b Garner	21	60
SM Patil		b Gomes	36	52
Yashpal Sharma		b Holding	89	120

*N Kapil Dev	c Richards	b Gomes	6	13
RMH Binny	Lbw	b Marshall	27	38
S Madan Lal	not out		21	22
+SMH Kirmani	run out		1	2
RJ Shastri	not out		5	3

Extras: (b 4, lb 10, w 1, nb 8) 23

Total: (8 wickets, 60 overs) 262 DNB: BS Sandhu.

FoW: 1-21 (Srikkanth), 2-46 (Gavaskar), 3-76 (Amarnath), 4-125 (Patil), 5-141 (Kapil Dev), 6-214 (Binny), 7-243 (Yashpal Sharma), 8-246 (Kirmani).

Bowling	O	M	R	W
Holding	12	3	32	2
Roberts	12	1	51	0
Marshall	12	1	48	2
Garner	12	1	49	1
Richards	2	0	13	0
Gomes	10	0	46	2

West Indies innings (target: 263 runs from 60 overs)			R	B
CG Greenidge		b Sandhu	24	55
DL Haynes	run out		24	29
IVA Richards	c Kirmani	b Binny	17	36
SFAF Bacchus		b Madan Lal	14	24
*CH Lloyd		b Binny	25	38
+PJL Dujon	c Sandhu	b Binny	7	12
HA Gomes	run out		8	16
MD Marshall	st Kirmani	b Shastri	2	5
AME Roberts	not out		37	58
MA Holding	b Shastri		8	11
J Garner	st Kirmani	b Shastri	37	29

Extras: (b 4, lb 17, w 4) 25

Total: (all out, 54.1 overs) 228

FoW: 1-49 (Haynes), 2-56 (Greenidge), 3-76 (Richards), 4-96 (Bacchus), 5-107 (Dujon), 6-124 (Gomes), 7-126 (Marshall), 8-130 (Lloyd), 9-157 (Holding), 10-228 (Garner).

Bowling	O	M	R	W
Kapil Dev	10	0	34	0
Sandhu	12	1	36	1

Madan Lal	12	1	34	1
Binny	12	1	48	3
Shastri	5.1	0	26	3
Patil	3	0	25	0

The outcome at Old Trafford was not the only upset in the opening round of matches. More sensationally, Australia lost to Zimbabwe by 13 runs (starring in this win was skipper Duncan Fletcher, later England and India's coach, who with an unbeaten 69 and four wickets for 42, almost single-handedly overcame the Aussies and was, duly, adjudged the Man of the Match).

11 June: Leicester

India's next engagement was at Leicester, a central England city, which is home to Leicestershire County Cricket Club, whose colours the languorously graceful left-handed batsman, David Gower, once wore. It had also become a sanctuary for people of Indian origin fleeing persecution in East Africa, notably at the hands of the Ugandan dictator, Idi Amin. India, thus, anticipated exuberant support from the crowd; and this was commensurately extended.

The opposition were Zimbabwe, who were taking part in a World Cup for the first time, having qualified by virtue of winning the ICC Trophy in 1982. Though still not a test-playing nation, they were fresh from toppling Australia. Their side included several players with first-class experience, acquired from representing Rhodesia (as Zimbabwe was previously known) in the quite competitive Currie Cup of South Africa. As a matter of fact, in the 1960s, Colin Bland, a Rhodesian, was a conspicuous member of the South African test team, he being the Jonty Rhodes of his generation or a fielder *par excellence.*

Indeed, in 1965, before the start of South Africa's match with Sussex, a contest had been arranged between him and Pataudi, then on this county's staff, to determine the world's best fieldsman. Reportedly, a delayed arrival on the part of the nawab, forced a cancellation. The moral of the story: Zimbabwe could not to be taken lightly.

A drizzle postponed start of play until after lunch. Then, having to bat first, the Zimbabweans were shaken by the extent of swing and bounce extracted by the Indian medium pacers, notably Madan Lal. This Delhi all-rounder boasted an analysis of three for 27, as Zimbabwe were bundled out cheaply. The Indian fielding was frail, but Kirmani, a Bangalorean Muslim with a Telly Savalas-style shaven head—'Kiri' to his mates and the best Indian wicketkeeper I have ever seen—took five catches to establish a new World Cup record, improving on the West Indian Deryck Murray's four victims against Sri Lanka in the inaugural event.

In persistently murky conditions, India slumped to 32 for two, as the fast-medium, Peter Rawson, too, exploited the heaviness in the air; and the 36-year-old off-spinner John Traicos, who played for South Africa in tests in 1970—more than 22 years before he did so for Zimbabwe—bowled a tight spell. At this point in the Indian innings, one of my colleagues on the host broadcaster BBC's panel, a Zimbabwean commentator, jumped the gun in visualizing a second upset. But a 69-run association between Mohinder Amarnath and Patil, who was dropped at 12, cleared the mist. India ultimately cruised home by five wickets with 22.3 overs to spare.

Toss: India
Man of the Match: S Madan Lal

Zimbabwe innings (60 overs maximum)			R	B
AH Omarshah	c Kirmani	b Sandhu	8	32
GA Paterson	lbw	b Madan Lal	22	51
JG Heron	c Kirmani	b Madan Lal	18	30
AJ Pycroft	c Shastri	b Binny	14	21
+DL Houghton	c Kirmani	b Madan Lal	21	47
*DAG Fletcher	b Kapil Dev		13	32
KM Curran	run out		8	16
IP Butchart	not out		22	35
RD Brown	c Kirmani	b Shastri	6	27
PWE Rawson	c Kirmani	b Binny	3	6
AJ Traicos	run out		2	13

Extras: (lb 9, w 9) 18
Total: (all out, 51.4 overs) 155
FoW: 1-13 (Omarshah), 2-55 (Heron), 3-56 (Paterson), 4-71 (Pycroft), 5-106 (Fletcher), 6-114 (Houghton), 7-115 (Curran), 8-139 (Brown), 9-148 (Rawson), 10-155 (Traicos).

Bowling	O	M	R	W
Kapil Dev	9	3	18	1
Sandhu	9	1	29	1
Madan Lal	10.4	0	27	3
Binny	11	2	25	2
Shastri	12	1	38	1

India innings (target: 156 runs from 60 overs)			R	B
K Srikkanth	c Butchart	b Rawson	20	27
SM Gavaskar	c Heron	b Rawson	4	11
M Amarnath	c sub	b Traicos	44	79
SM Patil		b Fletcher	50	54
RJ Shastri	c Brown	b Omarshah	17	27
Yashpal Sharma	not out		18	19
*N Kapil Dev	not out		2	8

Extras: (w 2) 2

Total: (5 wickets, 37.3 overs) 157

DNB: RMH Binny, S Madan Lal, +SMH Kirmani, BS Sandhu.

FoW: 1-13 (Gavaskar), 2-32 (Srikkanth), 3-101 (Amarnath),4-128 (Patil), 5-148 (Shastri).

Bowling	O	M	R	W
Rawson	5.1	1	11	2
Curran	6.5	1	33	0
Butchart	5	1	21	0
Traicos	11	1	41	1
Fletcher	6	1	32	1
Omarshah	3.3	0	17	1

June 13: Trent Bridge, Nottingham

I have fond memories of Trent Bridge, Nottinghamshire County Cricket Club's seat of power, where Harold Larwood—a collier from the county's mineral belt—first caught the attention of England's selectors before going on to shatter the serenity of cricket with superfast deliveries at batsmen's bodies at the behest of his captain, Douglas Jardine, in the 1932–33 tests Down Under.

It was here that I was for the first time invited to join BBC's Test Match Special (TMS) team at lunch in the 1977 Ashes test to answer questions from listeners. The other two on the panel were the well-known English commentators, John Arlott and Christopher Martin-Jenkins. I cite this episode only because it was, then, uncommon, possibly unheard-of, for a broadcaster from a third country to figure on TMS during an Anglo–Australian contest. The English, in particular, were rather protective of what they perceived as a kind of private battle.

But India's remembrance of Trent Bridge wasn't exactly inspiring. In 1959, they had been thrashed by an innings and 59 runs. Now, though, they took the field maintaining a clean slate in the tourney. Australia, however, won the toss and capitalized on a gloriously sunny East Midland morning and a beautiful batting wicket. Trevor Chappell was dropped by Binny off his own bowling when 27 and this youngest of three brothers—the others being the more eminent Ian and Greg—to wear the baggy green cap made the Indians pay with a stroke-filled 110. With his captain, Kim Hughes, he put on 144 runs for the second wicket in 29 overs, which laid the foundation of a demanding total. Graham Yallop, then, proceeded to post an unbeaten 66. Only Kapil made any impression on the Aussies, finishing with five for 45, which included four in his last three overs.

A sidelight remains engraved in memory. When towards the closing stages of the Aussie innings, a batsman holed out to Kapil near the boundary, far from celebrating—as quick bowlers do in such circumstances these days—he hardly smiled. It wasn't the grimness of India's situation that precluded happiness. It was in that era an insult for a fast bowler to be lofted that far afield. Kapil, with an instinctive grasp of the finer points of the game, was conscious of this and conveyed it in unmistakable terms.

India were without Gavaskar—officially injured, although some suspected he had been dropped—and when they batted, the sky turned surly, and stoppages caused by indifferent light, intermittent drizzle or both, made their challenging task even more difficult. With the wicket freshening, the young fast-medium bowler, Ken MacLeay, reaped a harvest of six for 39. Kapil, rounding off a singular resistance, reached a quickfire 40 until he was bowled by the left-arm slow bowler, Tom Hogan, who had replaced the out-of-form Dennis Lillee in the Australian eleven. India were cut to size by 162 runs.

Toss: Australia

Man of the Match: TM Chappell

Australia innings (60 overs maximum)			R	B
KC Wessels		b Kapil Dev	5	11
TM Chappell	c Srikkanth	b Amarnath	110	131
*KJ Hughes	b Madan Lal		52	86
DW Hookes	c Kapil Dev	b Madan Lal	1	4
GN Yallop	not out		66	73
AR Border	c Yashpal Sharma	b Binny	26	23
+RW Marsh	c Sandhu	b Kapil Dev	12	15
KH MacLeay	c & b Kapil Dev		4	5
TG Hogan		b Kapil Dev	11	9
GF Lawson	c Srikkanth	b Kapil Dev	6	3
RM Hogg	not out		2	2

Extras: (b 1, lb 14, w 8, nb 2) 25

Total: (9 wickets, 60 overs) 320

FoW: 1-11 (Wessels), 2-155 (Hughes), 3-159 (Hookes), 4-206 (Chappell), 5-254 (Border), 6-277 (Marsh), 7-289 (MacLeay), 8-301 (Hogan), 9-307 (Lawson).

Bowling	O	M	R	W
Kapil Dev	12	2	43	5
Sandhu	12	1	52	0
Binny	12	0	52	1
Shastri	2	0	16	0
Madan Lal	12	0	69	2
Patil	6	0	36	0
Amarnath	4	0	27	1

India innings (target: 321 runs from 60 overs)			R	B
RJ Shastri	Lbw	b Lawson	11	18
K Srikkanth	c Border	b Hogan	39	63
M Amarnath	run out		2	17
DB Vengsarkar	Lbw	b MacLeay	5	14
SM Patil		b MacLeay	0	7
Yashpal Sharma	c & b MacLeay		3	11
*N Kapil Dev		b Hogan	40	27
S Madan Lal	c Hogan	b MacLeay	27	39
RMH Binny	lbw	b MacLeay	0	6

+SMH Kirmani		b MacLeay	12	23
BS Sandhu	not out		9	12

Extras: (b 1, lb 4, w 3, nb 2) 10
Total: (all out, 37.5 overs) 158
FoW: 1-38 (Shastri), 2-43 (Amarnath), 3-57 (Vengsarkar), 4-57 (Patil), 5-64 (Yashpal Sharma), 6-66 (Srikkanth), 7-124 (Madan Lal), 8-126 (Binny), 9-136 (Kapil Dev), 10-158 (Kirmani).

Bowling	**O**	**M**	**R**	**W**
Lawson	5	1	25	1
Hogg	7	2	23	0
Hogan	12	1	48	2
MacLeay	11.5	3	39	6
Border	2	0	13	0

Elsewhere...

In Group A, England won all their three games in the opening round in convincing fashion and New Zealand beat Pakistan; the latter's sole victory being against Sri Lanka. In India's group, the West Indies, after the embarrassment of the first outing, brushed aside Australia and Zimbabwe.

15 June: The Oval, London

The world's first two cricket tests were played in March and April of 1877 and the third in January 1879—all at the Melbourne Cricket Ground. The maiden test in England was held at The Oval, south of London's River Thames, in September 1880.

India's saga at this venerable venue had been one of agony and ecstasy. In 1936, India lost a test to England by nine wickets, were thumped by an innings and 27 runs in 1959, won by four wickets in 1971 and almost pulled off an amazing run chase in 1979. Set 438 to win in 498 minutes, India failed to reach their target by nine runs with two wickets to spare. The man instrumental in making the impossible nearly possible was Gavaskar, whose 221 was hailed by Sir Leonard Hutton, the former England captain and superlative opening batsman, in Britain's *Observer* newspaper, as the greatest innings he had ever seen.

I had commentated ball-by-ball on this match and to me Gavaskar's innings was certainly something special. Later, I asked Hutton if he was sure of what he had said. He put his hand on my shoulder and said he had fielded in the covers for most of Stan McCabe's 232 in 235 minutes at Trent Bridge in 1938—considered by many cricket historians to be the greatest test innings. Therefore, he was in an enviable position to judge which was the better effort. Bradman, captaining Australia, reportedly, ordered his players on to the dressing room to see McCabe in action, telling them: 'You'll never see the like of it again!' Hutton himself responded with 364 in the final test of that series at The Oval to establish a new record for the highest individual score in tests before this was surpassed by Garry Sobers' 365 not out against Pakistan in 1958.

The Oval is in the vicinity of the Afro-Caribbean district of Brixton. Buoyed by calypsos, improvised steel bands, salutations and taunts, Richards uncoiled an uncharacteristic sheet-anchor knock of 119. He had registered a paltry 40 runs in three visits to the crease in the competition and was determined not to miss out again. The Indian bowlers, Binny and Amarnath, cooperated fully by bowling an untidy line and length. With Haynes keeping the Antiguan company to stitch a 101-run second-wicket partnership and Lloyd with a sledge-hammer 41 adding 80 with him for the third wicket in 14 overs, the West Indians were virtually supreme.

However, it was interesting that Lloyd, unlike his normal practice, had refrained from giving use of the morning wicket to his fast bowlers. Twice bitten—at Albion and Old Trafford—he was third time shy. India had, thus, already made inroads into the psychological ascendancy of the West Indies.

In reply, India lost openers Srikkanth and Shastri for 21, but Amarnath and Vengsarkar were showing symptoms of a recovery—which raised excitement among the relatively smaller contingent of Indian supporters—when the latter was struck on the mouth by a viciously lifting delivery from Malcolm Marshall. He retired hurt with the score on 89 for two.

A degree of animosity had existed between the Mumbai batsman, also from the cradle of Dadar Union club, and the West Indians for some time.

They reckoned Vengsarkar had once or twice not respected the spirit of the game, and it was rumoured, they were out to teach him a lesson. The Barbadian, then the speediest of his team's bowlers, possibly sent down his fastest and nastiest spell of the tournament. Indeed, when he persisted with his short-pitched stuff to Patil, who replaced Vengsarkar, umpire David Shepherd had no alternative to cautioning him. Though he was denied the Man of the Match award, Amarnath's knock of 80 was really the pick of the day. Once he and a vigorous Kapil departed—both to Holding—wickets fell in a heap, with India folding up after being 193 for four. In effect, the West Indies reasserted their authority by a margin of 66 runs.

Toss: West Indies
Man of the Match: IVA Richards

West Indies innings (60 overs maximum)			R	B
CG Greenidge	c Vengsarkar	b Kapil Dev	9	13
DL Haynes	c Kapil Dev	b Amarnath	38	93
IVA Richards	c Kirmani	b Sandhu	119	146
*CH Lloyd	run out		41	42
SFAF Bacchus		b Binny	8	8
+PJL Dujon	c Shastri	b Binny	9	13
HA Gomes	not out		27	22
AME Roberts	c Patil	b Binny	7	9
MD Marshall	run out		4	7
MA Holding	c sub	b Madan Lal	2	5
WW Davis	not out		0	2

Extras: (lb 13, w 5) 18
Total: (9 wickets, 60 overs) 282
FoW: 1-17 (Greenidge), 2-118 (Haynes), 3-198 (Lloyd), 4-213 (Bacchus), 5-239 (Dujon), 6-240 (Richards), 7-257 (Roberts), 8-270 (Marshall), 9-280 (Holding).

Bowling	O	M	R	W
Kapil Dev	12	0	46	1
Sandhu	12	2	42	1
Binny	12	0	71	3
Amarnath	12	0	58	1
Madan Lal	12	0	47	1

India innings (target: 283 runs from 60 overs)			R	B
K Srikkanth	c Dujon	b Roberts	2	9
RJ Shastri	c Dujon	b Roberts	6	15
M Amarnath	c Lloyd	b Holding	80	139
DB Vengsarkar	retired hurt		32	59
SM Patil	c & b Gomes		21	31
Yashpal Sharma	run out		9	10
*N Kapil Dev	c Haynes	b Holding	36	46
RMH Binny	lbw	b Holding	1	4
S Madan Lal	not out		8	15
+SMH Kirmani		b Marshall	0	2
BS Sandhu	run out		0	2

Extras: (b 3, lb 13, nb 5) 21

Total: (all out, 53.1 overs) 216

FoW: 1-2 (Srikkanth), 2-21 (Shastri), 3-130 (Patil), 4-143 (Yashpal Sharma), 5-193 (Amarnath), 6-195 (Binny), 7-212 (Kapil Dev), 8-214 (Kirmani), 9-216 (Sandhu).

Bowling	O	M	R	W
Roberts	9	1	29	2
Holding	9.1	0	40	3
Marshall	11	3	20	1
Davis	12	2	51	0
Gomes	12	1	55	1

18 June: Tunbridge Wells

The Nevill county ground at Tunbridge Wells is a magical cricketing *mise en scène*. Surrounded by blooming rhododendron bushes, colourful marquees and neatly erected wooden stands, this became the setting of a great escape by India, prompted by a landmark personal performance.

The train from London's Charring Cross station to Tunbridge was late; and, so, by the time I surfaced at the park, India were six for two, with openers Gavaskar and Srikkanth already back in the pavilion without bothering the scorers. Fortunately, mine was not the first stint on the commentary rota. By the time my turn came, India had crumbled to 17 for five, with Rawson and Kevin Curran ruling the roost.

"We just stayed back in the basement of the dressing room. We didn't feel like coming up... And then when we got the news the runs were coming, Kapil is batting beautifully, scoring runs at will, we started coming up and watching the game," Amarnath recounted.

India had misread the pitch, for the ball moved both in the air and off the wicket, but, as Binny now joined Kapil, it was the captain who stood Horatio-like as the last brown hope in the Kent countryside. Zimbabwe, though, were devoid of that extra bit of experience as well as bowling depth to deliver a *coup de grâce;* and the wicket was also drying rapidly under a hot sun. Besides, Binny, who had opened for both his state, Karnataka, and country, was not incapable of negotiating the lateral movement.

So, with his partner an ideal foil, not failing to get behind the line of the ball, Kapil unfurled one of the most astonishing innings in limited-overs history. It was a scientific assault, not a slog. He pierced the off-side field with perfect technique. With Binny and then Madan Lal, he boosted the score to 140. Thereafter, with Kirmani proving to be a sensible prop for an unbroken ninth wicket stand of 126 in 16 overs, he hoisted the total to 266 for eight. Once in full flow, he used his feet to unleash a barrage of sixes, hitting half a dozen altogether, in addition to 16 fours. His unconquered 175 extinguished the previous highest in World Cup competition—New Zealander, Glenn Turner's 170 against East Africa at Edgbaston in 1975.

Dave Houghton, Zimbabwe's wicket-keeper, remembered: "It was absolutely amazing. He never mishit the ball, we never dropped him, he never gave us a chance. Anything that went in the air, generally went out of the ground."

Kapil's own impression was: "I think in every cricketer's life—when you've played for 15-20 years—some of the days come out as your days, manufactured by God, given to you. Whatever you do, nothing can go wrong. Perhaps, that innings was like that."

But the match was far from decided. The undaunted Zimbabweans continued to defy the odds. Six of their batsmen perished for a modest 116, but for Curran it wasn't over yet. He kept India at bay with an adventurous essay of 73 before paying the penalty of skying the ball once too often.

Zimbabwe were eventually bowled out for 235 in 56.5 overs, leaving their opponents victors by 31 runs. The fact is, notwithstanding the rope trick the Indians pulled off in the first half of the day, they remained on tenterhooks until the ninth Zimbabwean wicket fell—that of Curran.

Toss: India
Man of the Match: N Kapil Dev

India innings (60 overs maximum)			R	B
SM Gavaskar	lbw	b Rawson	0	2
K Srikkanth	c Butchart	b Curran	0	13
M Amarnath	c Houghton	b Rawson	5	20
SM Patil	c Houghton	b Curran	1	10
Yashpal Sharma	c Houghton	b Rawson	9	28
*N Kapil Dev	not out		175	138
RMH Binny	lbw	b Traicos	22	48
RJ Shastri	c Pycroft	b Fletcher	1	6
S Madan Lal	c Houghton	b Curran	17	39
+SMH Kirmani	not out		24	56

Extras: (lb 9, w 3) 12
Total: (8 wickets, 60 overs) 266 DNB: BS Sandhu.
FoW: 1-0 (Gavaskar), 2-6 (Srikkanth), 3-6 (Amarnath), 4-9 (Patil), 5-17 (Yashpal Sharma), 6-77 (Binny), 7-78 (Shastri), 8-140 (Madan Lal).

Bowling	O	M	R	W
Rawson	12	4	47	3
Curran	12	1	65	3
Butchart	12	2	38	0
Fletcher	12	2	59	1
Traicos	12	0	45	1

Zimbabwe innings (target: 267 runs from 60 overs)			R	B
RD Brown	run out		35	66
GA Paterson	lbw	b Binny	23	35
JG Heron	run out		3	8
AJ Pycroft	c Kirmani	b Sandhu	6	15
+DL Houghton	lbw	b Madan Lal	17	35
*DAG Fletcher	c Kapil Dev	b Amarnath	13	23

KM Curran	c Shastri	b Madan Lal	73	93
IP Butchart	b Binny		18	43
GE Peckover	c Yashpal Sharma	b Madan Lal	14	18
PWE Rawson	not out		2	6
AJ Traicos	c & b Kapil Dev		3	7

Extras; (lb 17, w 7, nb 4) 28

Total: (all out, 57 overs) 235

FoW: 1-44 (Paterson), 2-48 (Heron), 3-61 (Pycroft), 4-86 (Brown), 5-103 (Houghton), 6-113 (Fletcher), 7-168 (Butchart), 8-189 (Peckover), 9-230 (Curran), 10-235 (Traicos).

Bowling	**O**	**M**	**R**	**W**
Kapil Dev	11	1	32	1
Sandhu	11	2	44	1
Binny	11	2	45	2
Madan Lal	11	2	42	3
Amarnath	12	1	37	1
Shastri	1	0	7	0

20 June: Chelmsford

Chelmsford, less than an hour to the east of London, is Essex county's cricketing headquarters. From here have sprung the likes of Trevor Bailey, Graham Gooch and Nasser Hussain. The first mentioned, though, whose company as an expert commentator on BBC I cherished, for he was not only an accurate judge of ability, but lucid in elaborating on it, actually came from Southend-on-Sea on the English coast.

The clash between India and Australia here would decide the qualifier with the West Indies from Group B in the semifinals. The Indians had three wins from five outings. Their opponents had two, but a faster overall run rate, which meant a win would clinch them a place in the last four.

Binny felt: "We were confident at that point of time; but we were also tense. In these situations, it's a give and take. You either stay in the tournament or you get out."

It was another day of bright sunshine; and the temperature, too, had begun to soar by this stage of the championship. India had no hesitation to bat, but after losing three wickets for 65, were rather forced into reconstruction mode. Indeed, it was a collaborative effort—for the highest individual score was Yashpal's 40—that saw them attain a respectable total. The Australian bowlers helped undistinguishedly with 15 no-balls and nine wides in extras of 37—the second highest score of the venture.

The wicket was a featherbed, but Australia were missing captain and leading batsman Hughes, absent because of a thigh strain. In his place, they selected an extra bowler. Binny, introduced in the 16th over, swung the ball just enough to consistently find the edge, and with Madan Lal an able ally, the Aussies nose-dived from 46 for one to 78 for seven, never to recover. It was nothing short of a crushing victory for India. Those in Anglo–Australian media who complained that the men from the Antipodes gave a 'poor performance' were pandering to a preconceived notion that Australia were a superior side *vis-à-vis* India. Admittedly, form on the day counts in over-limit cricket. But at the juncture of the 1983 World Cup, India's hardening experience in the West Indies just a few months earlier, endowed them with a capability to beat the Australians of that generation. Certainly, batting-wise, on that decisive day at Chelmsford, Australia were as good as they were allowed to be.

Toss: India
Man of the Match: RMH Binny

India innings (60 overs maximum)			R	B
SM Gavaskar	c Chappell	b Hogg	9	10
K Srikkanth	c Border	b Thomson	24	22
M Amarnath	c Marsh	b Thomson	13	20
Yashpal Sharma	c Hogg	b Hogan	40	40
SM Patil	c Hogan	b MacLeay	30	25
*N Kapil Dev	c Hookes	b Hogg	28	32
KBJ Azad	c Border	b Lawson	15	18
RMH Binny	run out		21	32
S Madan Lal	not out		12	15
+SMH Kirmani	lbw	b Hogg	10	20
BS Sandhu		b Thomson	8	18

Extras: (lb 13, w 9, nb 15) 37

Total: (all out, 55.5 overs) 247

FoW: 1-27 (Gavaskar), 2-54 (Srikkanth), 3-65 (Amarnath), 4-118 (Patil), 5-157 (Yashpal Sharma), 6-174 (Kapil Dev), 7-207 (Azad), 8-215 (Binny), 9-232 (Kirmani), 10-247 (Sandhu).

Bowling	O	M	R	W
Lawson	10	1	40	1
Hogg	12	2	40	3
Hogan	11	1	31	1
Thomson	10.5	0	51	3
MacLeay	12	2	48	1

Australia innings (target: 248 runs from 60 overs)			R	B
TM Chappell	c Madan Lal	b Sandhu	2	5
GM Wood	c Kirmani	b Binny	21	32
GN Yallop	c & b Binny		18	30
*DW Hookes		b Binny	1	2
AR Border		b Madan Lal	36	49
+RW Marsh	lbw	b Madan Lal	0	2
KH MacLeay	c Gavaskar	b Madan Lal	5	6
TG Hogan	c Srikkanth	b Binny	8	10
GF Lawson		b Sandhu	16	20
RM Hogg	not out		8	12
JR Thomson		b Madan Lal	0	5

Extras: (lb 5, w 5, nb 4) 14

Total: (all out, 38.2 overs) 129

FoW: 1-3 (Chappell), 2-46 (Wood), 3-48 (Hookes), 4-52 (Yallop), 5-52 (Marsh), 6-69 (MacLeay), 7-78 (Hogan), 8-115 (Lawson), 9-129 (Border), 10-129 (Thomson).

Bowling	O	M	R	W
Kapil Dev	8	2	16	0
Sandhu	10	1	26	2
Madan Lal	8.2	3	20	4
Binny	8	2	29	4
Amarnath	2	0	17	0
Azad	2	0	7	0

Meanwhile...

In the other group, England slipped against New Zealand, but repeated their first round successes over Pakistan and Sri Lanka. But the Kiwis lost to Pakistan and astoundingly also to the Lankans, then the minnows of test cricket—to facilitate a Pakistani entry into the semifinals behind the Englishmen.

The West Indians, on the other hand, rampaged through the return matches to race past India in the final group standings. Australia finished third after staving off another energetic challenge from Zimbabwe.

Semifinal, 22 June: Old Trafford, Manchester

So, from the south-east of England the Indians drove back on their coach to the north-west and to Old Trafford. It was virgin terrain for India in that they had never progressed beyond the preliminary, league stage of a World Cup, yet a beaten track, as they were back in the familiar surroundings of Old Trafford, where they had eclipsed the West Indies at the start of the tournament. Many estimated, this is where the dream sequence would end. After all, England were vastly seasoned in the art and craft of one-day cricket. They had been semifinalists in 1975 and finalists in 1979; and, not to be forgotten, enjoyed home advantage.

Unlike a fortnight before, the weather was luminous, even humid; and the wicket, while seaming a bit, was slow and low and not dissimilar to those in the subcontinent—as indeed were most tracks in the tournament, in general, especially after the mercury levels mirrored more an Indian summer.

It was a foregone conclusion that any side winning the toss would bat first; so it was no surprise England did just that. But after openers Graeme Fowler and Chris Tavare put on 69 at four runs an over—before both became victims of Binny—England struggled against the slower part-timers, Amarnath and Kirti Azad, whose 24 overs cost a mere 55 runs and captured the wickets of Gower, Mike Gatting and the dangerous Ian Botham, while Allan Lamb was run out. With the ball not quite coming on to the bat, boundaries were difficult to come by, while lofting the ball on a sluggish pitch was also hazardous. As wickets fell at regular intervals, the Englishmen fragmented in the face of a disciplined but by no means unplayable attack. Their total was, in fact, an injustice to the conditions.

David Gower analysed: "In essence what happened was, every time we tried to force the pace—and this happened to me personally—there was just a little bit of something there, didn't come on to the bat ... And that was pretty much the case throughout our top and middle order."

Amarnath revealed: "Roger Binny was I think the man of the series as a bowler ... I thought instead of bowling outswingers—I hadn't been very successful in earlier games—let me bowl inswingers ... The ball was keeping low and it was coming into the batsman and it was difficult to force."

For once in the tournament, Gavaskar showed glimpses of his pedigree before he was caught at the wicket. Then, a 92-run partnership for the third wicket between Amarnath and Yashpal Sharma laid the foundation for the latter and Patil to finish the job with 5.2 overs to spare. As the Indians raised the tempo, Amarnath stepped out to clobber Vic Marks for a straight six and Sharma flicked Willis off his toes for another over the ropes. Amarnath narrated: "I told Yash, 'Yash, one of us has to take some risks'. I suggested to him, 'You stay around and I will go for the bowling', So straighaway I started hitting the bowlers over the top. And what do I see in the next over? Yashpal doing the same thing, because he didn't want to stay behind." Thereafter, Patil again feasted on Willis by despatching him thrice to the fence in an over. India, thus, sailed into the final with a six-wicket win.

Toss: England
Man of the Match: M Amarnath

England innings (60 overs maximum)			R	B
G Fowler	b Binny		33	59
CJ Tavare	c Kirmani	b Binny	32	51
DI Gower	c Kirmani	b Amarnath	17	30
AJ Lamb	run out		29	58
MW Gatting		b Amarnath	18	46
IT Botham		b Azad	6	26
+IJ Gould	run out		13	36

VJ Marks		b Kapil Dev	8	18
GR Dilley	not out		20	26
PJW Allott	c Patil	b Kapil Dev	8	14
*RGD Willis		b Kapil Dev	0	2

Extras: (b 1, lb 17, w 7, nb 4) 29

Total: (all out, 60 overs) 213

FoW: 1-69 (Tavare), 2-84 (Fowler), 3-107 (Gower), 4-141 (Lamb), 5-150 (Gatting), 6-160 (Botham), 7-175 (Gould), 8-177 (Marks), 9-202 (Allott), 10-213 (Willis).

Bowling	**O**	**M**	**R**	**W**
Kapil Dev	11	1	35	3
Sandhu	8	1	36	0
Binny	12	1	43	2
Madan Lal	5	0	15	0
Azad	12	1	28	1
Amarnath	12	1	27	2

India innings (target: 214 runs from 60 overs)			**R**	**B**
SM Gavaskar	c Gould	b Allott	25	41
K Srikkanth	c Willis	b Botham	19	44
M Amarnath	run out		46	92
Yashpal Sharma	c Allott	b Willis	61	115
SM Patil	not out		51	32
*N Kapil Dev	not out		1	6

Extras: (b 5, lb 6, w 1, nb 2) 14

Total: (4 wickets, 54.4 overs) 217

DNB: KBJ Azad, RMH Binny, S Madan Lal, +SMH Kirmani, BS Sandhu.

FoW: 1-46 (Srikkanth), 2-50 (Gavaskar), 3-142 (Amarnath), 4-205 (Yashpal Sharma).

Bowling	**O**	**M**	**R**	**W**
Willis	10.4	2	42	1
Dilley	11	0	43	0
Allott	10	3	40	1
Botham	11	4	40	1
Marks	12	1	38	0

Simultaneously...

Semifinal: The Oval, London

Two hundred miles down south, the West Indies tackled Pakistan in the other semifinal. This match, too, turned out to be a one-sided affair. The venom of the Caribbean pacemen proving too much for the Pakistani batsmen to digest. Marshall once again bowled with utmost hostility and Holding, Roberts and Garner were almost as disconcerting. Pakistan only managed a humble total, with Mohsin Khan painstakingly collecting 70 with 43 singles and off 176 balls. The only other batsman to make an impression was Zaheer Abbas before the underrated off-spin of Gomes cut short his ambitions. Only three boundaries were logged in the innings, one of them a bye. With Imran Khan unfit to bowl, Richards swiftly took control, cutting, driving and hooking imperiously to peg an unbeaten 80. The West Indies galloped past the post by eight wickets, with 12 overs to spare.

Toss: West Indies
Man of the Match: IVA Richards

Pakistan innings (60 overs maximum)			R	B
Mohsin Khan		b Roberts	70	176
Mudassar Nazar	c & b Garner		11	39
Ijaz Faqih	c Dujon	b Holding	5	19
Zaheer Abbas		b Gomes	30	38
*Imran Khan	c Dujon	b Marshall	17	41
Wasim Raja	lbw	b Marshall	0	3
Shahid Mahboob	c Richards	b Marshall	6	10
Sarfraz Nawaz	c Holding	b Roberts	3	12
Abdul Qadir	not out		10	21
+Wasim Bari	not out		4	7

Extras: (b 6, lb 13, w 4, nb 5) 28

Total: (8 wickets, 60 overs)184 DNB: Rashid Khan.

FoW: 1-23 (Mudassar Nazar), 2-34 (Ijaz Faqih), 3-88 (Zaheer Abbas), 4-139 (Imran Khan), 5-139 (Wasim Raja), 6-159 (Shahid Mahboob), 7-164 (Sarfraz Nawaz), 8-171 (Mohsin Khan).

Bowling	O	M	R	W
Roberts	12	3	25	2
Garner	12	1	31	1
Marshall	12	2	28	3
Holding	12	1	25	1
Gomes	7	0	29	1
Richards	5	0	18	0

West Indies innings (target: 185 runs from 60 overs)			R	B
CG Greenidge	lbw	b Rashid Khan	17	38
DL Haynes		b Abdul Qadir	29	58
IVA Richards	not out		80	96
HA Gomes	not out		50	100

Extras: (b 2, lb 6, w 4) 12

Total: (2 wickets, 48.4 overs) 188

DNB: *CH Lloyd, SFAF Bacchus, +PJL Dujon, MD Marshall, AME Roberts, J Garner, MA Holding.

FoW: 1-34 (Greenidge), 2-56 (Haynes).

Bowling	O	M	R	W
Rashid Khan	12	2	32	1
Sarfraz Nawaz	8	0	23	0
Abdul Qadir	11	1	42	1
Shahid Mahboob	11	1	43	0
Wasim Raja	1	0	9	0
Zaheer Abbas	4.4	1	24	0
Mohsin Khan	1	0	3	0

Final, 25 June: Lord's, London

Lord's, adjoining Regent's Park and nestling in north-west London's leafy St John's Wood area, home of the Marylebone Cricket Club, founders and guardians of the game, is recognized by purists to be the Mecca of cricket.

It was here, in 1932, that India made their advent on the international arena and had played a test on all visits to England since, losing every time barring 1971 and 1979 (India later won in 1986 and 2014). A total of eight defeats rendered the venue a veritable crematorium of Indian cricket. The catalogue incorporated the ignominy of being bowled out for their lowest test score ever of 42 in an incredible 77 minutes in 1974, which provoked a sneering cartoon in a British paper of a man scolding his friend: 'I told you not to go to the toilet!' Even in the 1975 World Cup, England pulverized the Indians to post a record score of 334 for four as India lost by a shameful margin of 202 runs.

Only Dilip Vengsarkar's centuries in consecutive appearances in 1979 and 1982—which was inflated to a hat trick in 1986—had slightly lightened the load of embarrassment. In short, there was cause for trepidation in the Indian camp on the eve of the 1983 World Cup final.

But Lord's, hosting its third consecutive World Cup final, was dressed to kill. To complement this, it transpired to be a radiantly sunny midsummer day.

Tickets for the finale had been sold out months in advance—bought mostly by the English. They expected England to qualify for this culmination, like they had done four years earlier. So, their hopes were dashed by England's capitulation to India. As a result, a flood of 'returns', officially and unofficially, became available after the semifinals with Indians of all descriptions and from a variety of destinations—including India itself—mopping these up.

Ticket touts outside the ground—who in India are branded black marketeers—have been commonplace at English grounds, including Lord's. It was, until recently, not looked upon as an illegal activity. On this occasion, as one approached the Grace Gates (named after the illustrious W. G.), such peddlers accosted you every few yards, and only the flashing of a medallion—proof of media accreditation in that age, as opposed to laminated cards with photo identities of this security-conscious generation—deterred their doggedness. It was, obviously, good business, for tickets—genuine or counterfeit—were exchanging hands thick and fast and at a considerable premium.

Inside there was a festive atmosphere. West Indian supporters, with their improvised musical instruments, had arrived in strength, many, perhaps, from their south London base. Correspondingly, hirsute Sikhs, generally unfailing cheer leaders for India outside the country (noticeably at Olympic and World Cup hockey championships, where India used to dominate for decades until overshadowed by the Europeans and Australia), armed with bugles, stood out in the Indian section; many, presumably, descending from west London suburbs like Southall and Hounslow. Conch shells were in evidence in both segments.

While the galleries surrounding the immaculate turf were a kaleidoscope of sight and sound, a more subdued pavilion—a majestic, light brick mansion house, with three-tier seating and a spacious hall within known as the Long Room, where a tie and jacket are necessary to gain entry—presided over proceedings.

(Senior citizens, who used to serve as stewards at Lord's, were notorious for their inability to recognize non-white cricketers, including prominent figures like Gavaskar, who was once stopped at the main gate, following which he initially refused an honorary membership of the MCC. As for Tiger Pataudi, when he characteristically turned up at the pavilion entrance without a tie, it was pointed out to him that he was inadequately dressed. Tiger jestfully retorted: 'You can't stop royalty, can you?' and strode past the stupefied doorman, an old age pensioner, before he could recover from the remark.)

In the same spirit, Amarnath, who was vice-captain, emphasized: "There was no planning, no team discussion; no strategies were discussed... I think the motto was very simple in those days: that cricket we played very hard on the field and we used to party in the evenings."

Those who had left home early were tucking into their egg and toast, washed down with coffee. Others wasted no time in bracing themselves with beer or, as both Afro- and Indo-Caribbeans prefer, a dash of rum.

There was not much doubt about the outcome of the match among an overwhelming majority. India, they surmised, had had their moment in the sun, and even upset the titleholders at Old Trafford. Now it was time for the West Indians to monopolize the stage. Indeed, their form since the initial reverse suggested it was crunch time for the Indians. 'Thanks for coming,' a West Indian friend joked as I made my way through the aforementioned pavilion door. Only the blind, irrational India backer believed otherwise.

Ominously for India, Lloyd won the toss and, unsurprisingly, decided to give his commandos a crack at the Indians in lively morning conditions.

Kapil admitted: "I can't describe in words how unhappy we were (to see the wicket). It was totally green, and Garner, Michael Holding, Marshall and Andy Roberts, those type of bowlers they had. And they've (the organisers) have given us a green top."

Indeed, the ball seamed; and Joel Garner, with his extra height, consistently made the ball rise chest-high from three-quarter length. But it was the faster and flatter Andy Roberts who had Gavaskar caught behind in the third over, thus imprinting in this tournament the most barren phase of this otherwise hungry Indian batsman's career.

At the other end, though, Srikkanth, the buccaneer from Chennai, went about his task with a gay abandon. He hooked Roberts for four, pulled him for a six and then crashed him through the covers for another boundary.

"Once I got off the mark," Srikkanth reminisced, "I decided I am going to go for the bowling... So, if they are going to bounce, I am going to hook at it... The best shot I liked was actually when I hit Michael Holding over the (bowler's) stumps for four."

He was in full flow when he played across the line to Marshall to be trapped lbw for 38. "It was a ridiculous choice of a shot," Srikkanth conceded. I was on air then. Little did I realize I had just described the termination of the most substantive innings of the match.

Amarnath, as usual, steadied a capsizing ship before he was cleaned up by Holding; Patil portrayed a flurry of shots prior to becoming a victim of greed against the innocuous Gomes. India's total appeared woefully inadequate. Yet, they didn't lose heart. Having traversed a distance they had not dreamed of travelling before the tournament, they had nothing to lose. The ball was still seaming, and while it required another minor miracle to defend the modest score, nothing was impossible. In between my commentary spells from atop the pavilion, I would scurry to the Indian dressing room one floor down to check the atmosphere therein. As the

Indians took the field, Syed Abid Ali, a hero of India's maiden test series win in England in 1971 as well as a participant in the 1975 World Cup, was down on his knees in prayer.

In between innings, Kapil told his boys: "There's a lot of difference between there being already 183 runs on the board and they (the West Indies) having to make it."

The West Indians started inauspiciously. Greenidge shouldered arms to a ball from Sandhu he expected to move away but which instead came back to disfigure his stumps. "I knew Gordon was not able to pick my inswinger when I used to come close to the wicket (to bowl it). When I bowled that ball, it hit the seam and started coming in, I knew it was going to hit the wicket."

That, though, hardly unsettled Richards, who dismissively moved to 33 with seven fours to threaten to win the match by himself. Madan Lal bore the brunt of the onslaught.

Kapil and Madan's wives left the ground, unable to withstand the butchery. Kapil went to Madan and said: "Take a break for a while." Madan pleaded: "Give me one more over, I will get him out."

Soon, Madan Lal impelled the Antiguan to hook; he mistimed and the superb fielder that was Kapil ran back towards the midwicket boundary to take a marvellous catch over his shoulder. Richards, 25 years later still seemingly cross with himself, stated: "You get Viv Richards out, who was going so well at that particular time, you think you do stand a chance. It was a catch that was pretty inspirational to that (Indian) team."

Haynes and Gomes, too, departed, victims of Madan, as three wickets fell in 19 balls. With Lloyd handicapped by a torn hamstring, and Bacchus not lasting long either, the West Indies plummeted to 76 for six.

But it wasn't curtains yet. Wicketkeeper Dujon was joined by Marshall, who was no novice with the willow. Uncomfortably for India, they showed no signs of relenting as the score mounted to 119. Enter Amarnath with his deceptively slow seamers. The tinge of green made the ball hurry off the pitch. Marshall was caught, Dujon played on and Holding was plumb in front to reward Amarnath with three wickets for 12 runs in seven overs. India had worthily defeated the insurmountable West Indies by 43 runs.

Akin to the history of one-day cricket, the team that had acquitted themselves more capably on the day had triumphed. Yet, this was no accident, for it was the third time India had got the better of the Windies in their last five meetings over a period spanning three months.

In the BBC commentary box, some, evidently, expected me to start jumping with joy. I disappointed them. A list of 'dos' and 'don'ts', a creation of the BBC thrust before me the first time I commentated on a cricket match on All India Radio in 1972, had stressed the need for detachment. I have never consciously deviated from this. My job was to describe lucidly for listeners the drama unfolding before me, not to get drawn into it.

Aaj Kaal, a Bengali daily in my home city of Kolkata and a competitor of *Ananda Bazar Patrika*, which I then represented as its London correspondent, was generous enough to carry an editorial headlined 'ABHINANDAN ASHIS RAY' or 'Congratulations Ashis Ray'. It went on to say that while there were no Bengal players (Kolkata being the capital of the eastern Indian state of West Bengal) in the World Cup winning Indian squad, I had done Bengal proud with my radio commentaries on the event.

It had, obviously, been a rather low-scoring match, but this phenomenon reflected a seamer-friendly wicket. Indeed, the outcome was on a knife edge until Richards left the scene. Subsequently, the match tilted inexorably India's way. Thousands among the capacity crowd of over 24,000—mostly Indians—invaded the field to obtain a close-up of the presentation ceremony, which took place on the middle-level balcony of the three-tier pavilion. A thunderous roar rent the air as Kapil lifted the coveted trophy. It was India's day; their greatest moment till date in one-day cricket! The limited-overs game as far as India and Indians were concerned was never to be the same again!!

India's breakthrough owed much to their captain's positive frame of mind and the presence in their side of all-rounders like Kapil himself, Amarnath and Binny (the highest wicket-taker in the competition) and to the bowling of Madan Lal and Sandhu. None was express fast but of the right velocity to revel in the seaming conditions. The ball gripped even for the left-arm spin of Shastri, while, with the bat, Srikkanth, who was to become chief selector of India's successful 2011 World Cup squad, Patil and Sharma were there to be counted when the chips were down. It was an admirably collective feat.

It was also a dizzy moment for the Indian players and the countless aficionados, and the intoxication had only begun. As the magnitude of the attainment sunk in, hundreds of Indian fans waited outside the pavilion to not just catch a glimpse of their heroes, but also to usher them back to their hotel across the road, then known as the Westmoreland, to continue the celebrations. The bar and lobby of this establishment have probably never seen such crowds before or since. The inebriation and impromptu *bhangra* dancing lingered late into the night. The place was awash with champagne and the cricketers, having restrained themselves for weeks, finally let their hair down. A visibly tired Kapil, but still smiling, stayed up till the end, not disappointing the innumerable well-wishers. The camaraderie between the actors and their adherents mirrored an age of accessibility. It was a delight to witness the scene, indeed cherish it. Kapil doesn't know till date who provided or paid for the champagne that flowed like water!

Raj Singh, chairman of Indian selectors, president of the BCCI as well as of the Cricket Club of India and a cricket connoisseur, concluded: "Except for India's independence, I can't remember anything that brought so much of joy, so much of confidence in people and realization what the game of cricket meant to this country (India)."

Thus concluded the 1983 Prudential World Cup. It opened with two major shocks: when India beat West Indies and Zimbabwe defeated Australia in the opening round. And climaxed with the greatest surprise of all: when India once more trounced the West Indies. None of the eight sides that took part departed without a win.

"It's a billion dollar game," as David Gower put it. "I guess '83 was pretty much a starting point for it."

Prudential underwrote the event to the tune of half a million UK pounds and the gate receipts were UK £1.2 million. The aggregate attendance was 232,000.

In addition to the cup and silver medals for each player, India received £20,000, West Indies got £8000 and the losing semifinalists, England and Pakistan, took home £4000 each.

Toss: West Indies

Man of the Match: M Amarnath

India innings (60 overs maximum)			R	B
SM Gavaskar	c Dujon	b Roberts	2	12
K Srikkanth	lbw	b Marshall	38	57
M Amarnath		b Holding	26	80
Yashpal Sharma	c sub (AL Logie)	b Gomes	11	32
SM Patil	c Gomes	b Garner	27	29
*N Kapil Dev	c Holding	b Gomes	15	8
KBJ Azad	c Garner	b Roberts	0	3
RMH Binny	c Garner	b Roberts	2	8
S Madan Lal		b Marshall	17	27
+SMH Kirmani		b Holding	14	43
BS Sandhu	not out		11	30

Extras: (b 5, lb 5, w 9, nb 1) 20

Total: (all out, 54.4 overs) 183

FoW: 1-2 (Gavaskar), 2-59 (Srikkanth), 3-90 (Amarnath), 4-92 (Yashpal Sharma), 5-110 (Kapil Dev), 6-111 (Azad), 7-130 (Binny), 8-153 (Patil), 9-161 (Madan Lal), 10-183 (Kirmani).

Bowling	O	M	R	W
Roberts	10	3	32	3
Garner	12	4	24	1
Marshall	11	1	24	2
Holding	9.4	2	26	2
Gomes	11	1	49	2
Richards	1	0	8	0

West Indies innings (target: 184 runs from 60 overs)			R	B
CG Greenidge		b Sandhu	1	12
DL Haynes	c Binny	b Madan Lal	13	33
IVA Richards	c Kapil Dev	b Madan Lal	33	28
*CH Lloyd	c Kapil Dev	b Binny	8	17
HA Gomes	c Gavaskar	b Madan Lal	5	16
SFAF Bacchus	c Kirmani	b Sandhu	8	25
+PJL Dujon		b Amarnath	25	73
MD Marshall	c Gavaskar	b Amarnath	18	51
AME Roberts	lbw	b Kapil Dev	4	14

J Garner	not out		5	19
MA Holding	lbw	b Amarnath	6	24

Extras: (lb 4, w 10) 14

Total: (all out, 52 overs) 140

FoW: 1-5 (Greenidge), 2-50 (Haynes), 3-57 (Richards), 4-66 (Gomes), 5-66 (Lloyd), 6-76 (Bacchus), 7-119 (Dujon), 8-124 (Marshall), 9-126 (Roberts), 10-140 (Holding).

Bowling	**O**	**M**	**R**	**W**
Kapil Dev	11	4	21	1
Sandhu	9	1	32	2
Madan Lal	12	2	31	3
Binny	10	1	23	1
Amarnath	7	0	12	3
Azad	3	0	7	0

CHAPTER THREE

1985
Double Delight

IN 1985, TO COMMEMORATE 150 YEARS OF THE ESTABLISHMENT of the Australian state of Victoria, the Victorian Cricket Association organized what they dubbed a 'World Championship of Cricket', sponsored by Benson & Hedges. Floodlights were installed at the Melbourne Cricket Ground at a cost of over £3 million. They were switched on for the first time for the opening match between England and Australia, which attracted a crowd of 82,000. Of the 13 matches in the tournament, four were held at Sydney, which, of course, is in the state of New South Wales, and the rest in Melbourne. Only test-playing teams were invited; and they were divided into two groups. India, Pakistan, England and Australia featured in one; the West Indies, New Zealand and Sri Lanka in the other. The tourney confirmed 1983 hadn't been a fluke.

20 February: Melbourne Cricket Ground (MCG) (Day/Night)

Pakistan won the toss and chose to bat, but struggled with their run rate, as the Indian medium pacers moved the ball around capably. Then, when Sunil Gavaskar, back as skipper, introduced spin, Ravi Shastri was highly economical and Laxman Sivaramakrishnan (Siva for brevity among those acquainted with him) picked up two useful wickets. India also fielded assiduously. In contrast, Pakistan had a disappointing match. Briefly, though, playing his first match for Pakistan for over a year, Imran Khan threatened to turn the tables on India. In a fiery spell, he took three wickets in six overs for 13 runs as India slumped to 27 for three. But Mohammed Azharuddin and Gavaskar, coming together, added 132 in 31 overs to pave the way for an easy Indian win. Fresh from his remarkable test debut—in course of which he posted hundreds in his first three tests against England in India—Azharuddin created a brilliant impression on his first appearance in Australia. He survived one chance—to the wicketkeeper off Tahir Naqqash when he was on 37—but his 93 not out came off not more than 135 balls. India won by six wickets.

Toss: Pakistan
Man of the Match: M Azharuddin
Pakistan 183 all out in 49.2 overs (Qasim Umar 57, Roger Binny 4/35, Kapil Dev Nikhanj 2/31). **India** 184/4 in 45.5 overs (Mohammed Azharuddin 93*, Sunil Gavaskar 54, Imran Khan 3/27).

26 February: Sydney Cricket Ground (SCG) (Day/Night)

Put in to bat by David Gower, India were given a rousing start by Krishnamachari Srikkanth, who scored 42 of the first 52 runs in ten overs. Out of the 16 boundaries hit in the match, this Tamil Nadu opener struck 10. Indeed, England only found their feet after he was superbly run out from long leg by Ashley Cowans; they bowled and fielded much better thereafter. Subsequently, needing 236 to win, they seemed to be cruising until Gower hit a full toss down deep midwicket's throat. After that, the Englishmen's last eight wickets realized just 55 runs, as Siva and Shastri exploited a much-used pitch. India won by 86 runs.

Toss: England
Man of the Match: K Srikkanth
India 235/9 in 50 overs (Krishnamachari Srikkanth 57, Mohammed Azharuddin 45, Dilip Vengsarkar 43, Ashley Cowans 3/59, Neil Foster 2/33). **England** 149 all out in 41.4 overs (Martyn Moxon 48, Ravi Shastri 3/30, Laxman Sivaramakrishnan 3/39, Sharma Madan Lal 2/19).

3 March: MCG

The calculations were such that Australia had a dual opportunity of reaching the semifinal of the competition. These required them to win this match by either scoring at least 223 in 50 overs or, upon failing to do so, bowling India out for 160 or less. They came nowhere near achieving either. Inserted by Gavaskar (Rodney Hogg tossed the coin for Australia as Allan Border was temporarily indisposed), the Aussies were soon 37 for five—in a virtual re-run of Chelmsford 1983—owing to a succession of loose strokes. Wayne Phillips attempted something of a recovery; but when India batted, Srikkanth and Shastri made light work of maintaining their side's 100 per cent record in the group matches. India won by eight wickets and, by virtue of this victory, avoided meeting the West Indies in the last four.

Toss: India
Man of the Match: RJ Shastri
Australia 163 all out in 49.3 overs (Wayne Phillips 60, Roger Binny 3/27, Kapil Dev 2/25). **India** 165/2 in 36.1 overs (Krishnamachari Srikkanth 93*, Ravi Shastri 51, Terry Alderman 1/38).

Semifinal: 5 March, SCG

Gavaskar again fancied chasing instead of setting a target. On a pensive pitch, New Zealand lost John Wright in the first over and never really ameliorated their circumstances. There was a flicker of defiance when Lance Cairns and Ian Smith came together at 151 for seven in the 43rd over. But this was too little too late as the Kiwis became the fourth successive side to be bowled out by India in the competition. But needing 207 to win, India, initially, made heavy weather of their mission. After 20 overs they managed to reach only 46 for one. Mark Snedden was particularly impressive in giving away only seven runs in his first five overs. But when Geoff Howarth rested him, India slowly but surely asserted themselves, with Kapil Dev sharing a rip-roaring stand with Dilip Vengsarkar. The turning point was the 34th over, wherein the Haryana all-rounder cut loose against Richard Hadlee, hitting him for a quartet of streaking boundaries, besides of course surviving a difficult chance to mid-off. India won by seven wickets with 6.3 overs to spare.

Toss: India
Man of the Match: RJ Shastri
New Zealand 206 all out in 50 overs (John Reid 55, Lance Cairns 39, Sharma Madan Lal 4/37, Ravi Shastri 3/31). **India** 207/3 in 43.3 overs (Dilip Vengsarkar 63*, Kapil Dev Nikhanj 54*, Ravi Shastri 53, Lance Cairns 1/35).

Semifinal, 6 March: MCG (Day/Night)

Clive Lloyd, making what turned out to be his final appearance for the West Indies, won the toss against Pakistan and decided to take first strike. The West Indians had endured a rain-affected match against New Zealand and easily romped home against Sri Lanka. Consequently, they were a little short of match practice in the championship, though they were quite battle hardened and accustomed to Australian conditions at the end of a long tour Down Under. They were, however, without Larry Gomes, who was injured and whose off-spin may have proved useful. But the truth is, the Windies batted poorly and paid the penalty. Wasim Raja, with his leg-breaks, and Mudassar Nazar and Tahir Naqqash, with tidy medium pace, restricted them. Then Wasim's brother, Rameez, with an authoritative innings, Qasim Omar, with a sprightly, unbeaten effort and Mohsin Khan with an obdurate one pole-vaulted the Pakistanis over the fence. For the West Indies, Malcolm Marshall and Michael Holding frequently beat the bat, but to no avail. Pakistan, thus, swept to victory against the favourites by seven wickets.

Toss: West Indies
Man of the Match: Rameez Raja
West Indies 159 all out in 44.3 overs (Roger Harper 25*, Clive Lloyd 25, Mudassar 5/28, Tahir Naqqash 3/23). **Pakistan** 160/3 in 46 overs (Rameez Raja 60, Qasim Umar 42*, Joel Garner 1/19, Malcolm Marshall 1/25).

Final, 10 March: MCG (Day/Night)

In a matter of 12 overs, Kapil Dev and Chetan Sharma had Pakistan tottering at 33 for four. Only Javed Miandad and Imran's contribution for the 5th wicket and a last wicket stand of 31 averted an annihilation. But 177 was rather a small score to defend. To illustrate this, Srikkanth and Shastri, who constituted an outstanding opening combination in the

competition, made 103, the former, as usual, providing the fireworks, while his partner chugged along unnoticeably yet usefully. Following this partnership, Azharuddin contributed a-run-a-ball quarter century as India clinically finished the job. Pakistan were never really in the running. India won by eight wickets.

Indeed, India extended the infallibility they had indicated in previous matches. Mature batting coupled with penetrative bowling, smart out-cricket and adroit captaincy characterized their performance throughout. A 35,000 crowd provided them a lusty reception, as the Indians circled the ground in a lap of honour aboard an Audi car won by Shastri for being chosen 'champion of champions' or man of the tournament. India's 'take-home pay' for lifting the trophy was £22,500; Pakistan raked in £11,500 for finishing as runners-up.

India had played faultless cricket, winning all their five matches comfortably. This display was in pleasant contrast to their poor showing against England in the one-day series at home, which had preceded the visit to Australia. Gavaskar was a revelation. Seemingly eager to match Kapil's accomplishment of winning the World Cup, he redressed his previous allergy for one-day cricket to, first, lead India to victory in the inaugural Asia Cup tournament at Sharjah in the United Arab Emirates (UAE) in 1984 and follow this with an inspiring demonstration as captain in the 'World Championship of Cricket'.

At the age of 35, there was a new spring in his heels; he fielded smartly. Indeed he performed as if he wanted to prove a point—that he could be as good in limited-overs cricket as in test cricket, if he wanted to. That he had sufficient talent to adjust to the demands of the one-day game. When I spoke to him after the match, he was thrilled like I have rarely seen him in his career. He had disposed off the monkey on his back: that he lacked the talent to succeed in the over-limit theatre. As announced by him prior to it, he relinquished the captaincy at the end of the tournament.

For India, it was a notable double after triumphing in the World Cup. Australia's end of season, slower than normal wickets, which even turned a bit, suited them. Azhar and Siva caught the eye on their overseas debuts. To Australian spectators, the latter's leg-spin provided a refreshing change from

the invariableness of incessant fast bowling the West Indians had dished out earlier in the season.

Toss: Pakistan
Man of the Match: K Srikkanth
Man of the Series: RJ Shastri
Pakistan 176/9 in 50 overs (Javed Miandad 48, Imran Khan 38, Kapil Dev Nikhanj 3/23, Laxman Sivaramakrishnan 3/35). **India** 177/2 in 47.1 overs (Krishnamachari Srikkanth 67, Ravi Shastri 63*, Imran Khan 1/28, Tahir Naqqash 1/35).

CHAPTER FOUR

After 1985
Frustration

THE 1987 WORLD CUP

THE FOURTH WORLD CUP, HELD IN THE INDIAN subcontinent, attracted a much bigger audience, transpired to be more keenly contested and had an air of glamour about it as compared to its three predecessors held in England. Indeed, it got off to an a stimulating start, with thrilling opening matches taking place between Pakistan, the favourites, and Sri Lanka; India, the holders, and Australia; England and the West Indies; and New Zealand and non-test-playing Zimbabwe. Even if the rest of the Reliance Cup, as it was officially known, did not quite live up to such a beginning, the foray of the World Cup into warmer climes was still seen to be an unstinting success.

As before, there were eight participants, who were divided into two groups. Australia, New Zealand, India and Zimbabwe were concentrated in one; England, West Indies, Pakistan and Sri Lanka in the other.

Outside the subcontinent, the geographical enormity of the two host countries and the policy of the India–Pakistan Joint Management Committee to spread the games around in as many as 21 venues were seen as shortcomings. It was the equivalent of staging a tournament across the European Union without quite the same infrastructure of transport and telecommunications. Fewer centres would have meant less travelling; and a shorter and more compact competition. In some cases, teams travelled for days between matches, with hours spent in unexciting airport terminals.

Nonetheless, in arduous circumstances, the organizers fared capably. The weather was hot, but unoppressive. Only one match was affected by rain, when Australia and New Zealand were reduced to 30 overs each at Indore, in India's Madhya Pradesh state. (Mercifully, the rule that a match could not be carried over to a second day was never tested.) Otherwise, the matches were 50 overs per side; and, on placid pitches, totals similar to those in previous 60-over World Cups were raised. Viv Richards, individually, and West Indies, collectively, established new records against Sri Lanka for World Cup innings.

A subcontinental World Cup, refreshingly, encouraged spin, relieving, to some extent, the recurrence of seam in previous competitions in England. The 1975 final had been wholly pace or medium pace. Australia, however, stuck to their strength, in that they did not usually risk more than 10 overs of spin; a majority of other sides fielded two spinners. In the qualifying rounds, seven of the nine most economical bowlers were spinners. At the same time, the highest wicket-takers were Craig McDermott and Imran Khan, both fast bowlers. The former equalled the World Cup record of 18 wickets, while the latter took 17 in one match less.

Shorter daylight compelled an early start of play. But the concern over dew being a disadvantage to batsmen was misplaced. 19 of the 27 matches were won by sides batting first. The side taking first strike played normally; the side batting second seemed to panic.

As for the umpiring, even if this was not of the very highest standard, the redeeming factor was that its neutrality served to minimize grievances.

9 October: Chepauk, Chennai

The third test in the first ever test series in India—against Douglas Jardine's Marylebone Cricket Club or England side in February 1934—was staged at Chennai's Chepauk, thereby making it the country's third oldest test centre after the Bombay Gymkhana Ground and Kolkata's Eden Gardens.

Opening their campaign at the historic venue, India won the toss, but chose to field. On a docile pitch Geoff Marsh and David Boon put on 100 at almost five runs an over. Then, Dean Jones played quite beautifully, but the middle order lost the initiative. Marsh, in the 95-degree heat and high humidity, batted for more than three hours and hit a six and seven fours.

For India, Sunil Gavaskar (one six, six fours), Krishnamachari Srikkanth (seven fours) and Navjot Singh Sidhu (five sixes, four fours) sent India racing past 200 for the loss of only two wickets. The last-mentioned, known for fortitude rather than flinging his bat, demonstrated a new incarnation *en route* to becoming an effective batsman and the best Sikh wielder of the willow ever. Interestingly, he hailed from Patiala in Punjab, whose maharajas have been notable benefactors of cricket.

Craig McDermott's first four overs conceded 31 runs, but he came back strongly to whip out the middle order. Even so, India, with four wickets in hand, needed just 15 from the last four overs; when the last over began, the requirement was six, with the last man, Maninder Singh, taking strike. He managed two 2s, but along with his sang-froid collapsed his off stump. Australia's innings, like India's, had been built around the top-order batsmen. Also, Kapil Dev's sportsmanship proved to be a deciding factor in a close-run match. One of Jones's two sixes, in his 39 from 35 balls, had been signalled a four; but between innings Kapil relented to the Australians' insistence that the ball landed beyond the boundary. India's target was, thus, increased by two runs. Australia ultimately won by a solitary run.

Toss: India
Man of the Match: GR Marsh
Australia 270/6 in 50 overs (Geoff Marsh 110, David Boon 49, Manoj Prabhakar 2/47). **India** 269 all out in 49.5 overs (Navjot Siddhu 73, Krisnamachari Srikkanth 70, Sunil Gavaskar 37, Craig McDermott 4/56, Steve Waugh 2/52).

14 October: Chinnaswamy Stadium, Bangalore

With the progress of cricket in Mysore state, later Karnataka, its capital became a test centre in 1974 (with a stadium later dedicated to a former president of the Board of Control for Cricket in India, M. Chinnaswamy, from this state), hosting Clive Lloyd's West Indians.

New Zealand called correctly and asked India to bat on a pitch of mixed demeanour and a sluggish outfield. Besides, the Indians were not exactly helped by a suicidal Srikkanth, who contributed to the run-out of himself and Gavaskar. The quirky batsman was seemingly unconscious of the threat to himself when he was sent packing by Ken Rutherford. At 21 for three in the 10th over, it was certainly doom and gloom in the Indian dressing room. However, Sidhu (four sixes, four fours) lifted the spirits with an audacious use of his feet. But when he was fifth out, at 114, India still needed a major push to extend the Kiwis. This emerged in the form of Kapil (one six, four fours) and Kiran More (a protégé of the maharaja of the once princely state of Baroda, who employed his father) realizing 82 runs off the last 51 balls.

New Zealand batted safely and, so, didn't score swiftly enough. The experienced John Wright, laid low by a virus, was missing from the New Zealand line-up. This absence entrusted an onerous responsibility on Martin Crowe, the one man capable of stepping it up. But the left-arm spinner, Maninder (a Sikh like Bishan Bedi), one of three slow bowlers utilized by India, beat him in the air with a beauty. India won by 16 runs.

Toss: New Zealand
Man of the Match: N Kapil Dev
India 252/7 in 50 overs (Navjot Siddhu 75, Kapil Dev Nikhanj 72*, Kiran More 42*, Dipak Patel 3/36). **New Zealand** 236/8 in 50 overs (Ken Rutherford 75, Andrew Jones 64, Maninder Singh 2/40, Ravi Shastri 2/45).

17 October: Wankhede Stadium, Mumbai

In 1975, international cricket moved to the Wankhede Stadium (named after S.K. Wankhede, then Maharashtra state's finance minister and later a president of the BCCI, which staged a test against Lloyd's West Indies), following a quarrel between the Maharashtra Cricket Association, which Wankhede headed, and the Cricket Club of India, at whose comparatively upmarket Brabourne Stadium such matches used to be organized.

Zimbabwe elected to bat after winning the toss. But this decision boomeranged, as on a pitch with residual moisture—it being a dewy morning—Manoj Prabhakar, a Delhi all-rounder, swung the ball ebulliently, capturing four wickets off 17 balls. Andy Pycroft, with 61, at least ensured

Zimbabwe got to three figures. India, having bowled out their opponents well within the allotted overs, deliberately raced to victory, aware of the fact that a good run-rate could have a bearing on standings, in the event of a tight finish at the end of the group stage. Gavaskar's first 36 runs were all off boundaries. Dilip Vengsarkar (tagged 'colonel' by his teammates), then, collected runs with contemptuous ease. India won by eight wickets.

Toss: Zimbabwe
Man of the Match: M Prabhakar
Zimbabwe 135 all out in 44.2 overs (Andy Pycroft 61, Manoj Prabhakar 4/19, Maninder Singh 3/21). **India** 136/2 in 27.5 overs (Sunil Gavaskar 43, Krishnamachari Srikkanth 31, John Traicos 2/27).

22 October: Feroz Shah Kotla, New Delhi

Since international cricket could not ignore the capital of India after the country became independent in 1947, the Feroz Shah Kotla has been a test venue since 1948, with John Goddard's West Indians being the first visitors.

Here, Australia asked India to take first strike, but it was an easy batting wicket, with relatively short boundaries. Restricting the scoring was, therefore, a challenge. Consequently, with the ball coming on to the bat quite nicely from the Australian seamers, it was fairly cannon fodder for the Indian batsmen. Gavaskar and Srikkanth thus helped themselves to 50 off the first 10 overs, Sidhu recorded his third successive half-century and Vengsarkar and Azharuddin (who went to a Christian school, but was groomed in the Hyderabadi style of wristy, short-arm batsmanship) batted with assurance and class, rapidly knitting 65 in 10 overs.

Marsh and Boon (seven fours) replied with 88 in 18 overs, but the advent of the left-arm trundlers, Maninder and Ravi Shastri (whose family originated from the southern state of Karnataka, but had settled in Mumbai in Maharashtra), after 17 overs altered the tempo and the course of the match. Their accuracy, aerial control and spin were too much for the Australians to cope with. Steve Waugh was technically up to the task and also kept his head, but couldn't shake off the stranglehold as his side increasingly receded out of contention.

India prevailed by a convincing 56 runs and, with this win, the prospect of them finishing second in their group and, thus, having to play Pakistan at Lahore in the semifinal faded considerably.

Toss: Australia
Man of the Match: M Azharuddin
India 289/6 in 50 overs (Dilip Vengsarkar 63, Sunil Gavaskar 61, Mohammed Azharuddin 54*, Navjot Siddhu 51, Craig McDermott 3/61). **Australia** 233 all out in 49 overs (David Boon 62, Steve Waugh 42, Mohammed Azharuddin 3/19, Maninder Singh 3/34).

26 October: Ahmedabad

The western Indian city of Ahmedabad is a textile centre, where hypocritically prohibition exists on paper, but not exactly in practice. It also has an unfortunate history of Hindu–Muslim tension.

Here, Kevin Arnott, coming in at number three, batted patiently for 43 overs for his 60 after Zimbabwe were put in by India. With the Indians keen to avoid a semifinal in Pakistan, the scoring rate had become a pressing issue. But the Indian top-order were a bit strokeless on a slow pitch, notwithstanding the unruly, stone-throwing crowd disturbing their concentration. Gavaskar, in fact, utilized as many as 114 balls to get 50. But Kapil, promoting himself to number five, stole the thunder with a precipitate 41, which included three towering sixes. India won by seven wickets in the 42nd over. But they were in the tournament still at a cumulative run rate of 5.18 as compared to Australia's 5.20.

Toss: India
Man of the Match: N Kapil Dev
Zimbabwe 191/7 in 50 overs (Kevin Arnott 60, Andy Waller 39, Chetan Sharma 2/41, Kapil Dev Nikhanj 2/44). **India** 194/3 in 42 overs (Navjot Siddhu 55, Sunil Gavaskar 50, Peter Rawson 2/46).

31 October: Nagpur

At this commodities' hub, virtually at the geographical centre of India, New Zealand chose to bat first, but did so unconvincingly. Chetan Sharma, a Haryana state mate of Kapil, hit the timber in the last three balls of the

42nd over to record the first hat trick in World Cup history. Rutherford, Ian Smith and Ewen Chatfield comprised the dubious trio. Only a partnership of 39 between Martin Snedden and William Watson in the latter stages of the innings retrieved the situation somewhat.

The Kiwis' total of 221 meant India had to reach their destination in 42.2 overs, not impossible, but not easy either. In other words, to eclipse Australia on run-rate, India had to score at 5.25 runs an over. In Srikkanth, they had the perfect pilot. But amazingly, it was Gavaskar, reportedly, unwell on the eve of the match, who was in the most dashing form. After the pair helped themselves to 18 off the first two overs, the accumulator transformed into a Bombay bomber took 21 off Chatfield's third over as he struck the first two balls for sixes and the next two for fours. The 50 of the venture came up in the 8th over, the next 50 in another six overs. Srikkanth, not unknown to cause mayhem, lofted three sixes and clobbered nine fours in his 58-ball 75. Gavaskar, earning his 106th one-day cap for India and for whom the 1987 World Cup was his last appearance in limited-overs cricket, completed a timely maiden century in ODIs in 85 balls, adorned with three sixes and 10 fours. He recently moaned to the effect: "No one remembers this innings, which was the second fastest hundred in World Cup history at the time; every one remembers my first innings in the 1975 World Cup (when he infamously crawled to 36 not out in 60 overs)." India, helped by the knock, overhauled the New Zealand score with 10 overs to spare, and, as a result, qualified to meet England in the semifinals. It was a dazzling display. India won by nine wickets, with Gavaskar and Chetan Sharma sharing the Man of the Match award.

Toss: New Zealand
Men of the Match: SM Gavaskar and C Sharma
New Zealand 221/9 in 50 overs (Dipak Patel 40, John Wright 35, Chetan Sharma 3/51). **India** 224/1 in 32.1 overs (Sunil Gavaskar 103*, Krishnamachari Srikkanth 75, Mohammed Azharuddin 41*, Willie Watson 1/50).

Semifinal, 4 November: Gaddafi Stadium, Lahore

Opting for first use of the wicket, Australia were again rendered a good start by their openers. With Saleem Jaffer conceding 39 from his first five overs, Marsh and Boon put on 73 in 18 overs before Saleem Malik ran out the former with a direct hit from square leg. However, the stocky Tasmanian continued the good work with Jones (45 balls). They added another 82 until Pakistan removed them in consecutive overs—the 31st and the 32nd. Boon (four fours) was stumped by Javed Miandad, deputizing for Saleem Yousuf, who was struck on the face by a deflection from Jones' pad. Captain Allan Border and Michael Veletta, though, maintained the momentum with a partnership of 60. Now, Imran returned to snap up three for 17 in five overs; but at the 'death', Waugh boosted the total by a valuable 18 runs as he sent the hapless Jaffer soaring over long-on.

In contrast, Pakistan started catastrophically, losing three wickets by the 11th over. Rameez Raja could not recover his ground in the very first over, Mansoor Akhtar failed to impress and Saleem Malik front-edged the first ball of Waugh's spell to extra-cover. But Miandad and Imran, four fours apiece, maturely undid the damage with 112 off 26 overs. As a result, the target whittled down to 118 from 15 overs. Much rested on the mercurial Miandad. As long as he was in, his side had a chance. But after he left, playing across to the tall left-arm quick, Bruce Reid, in the 44th over, 56 runs were still needed, with only three wickets in hand. It was too much to ask for. McDermott polished off the tail with a fast and accurate spell and, in so doing, bagged the first five-wicket haul of the tournament. The defeat ruined the dreams of a nation that had aspired to match India's success of four years earlier.

For the third time, a World Cup final had eluded Pakistan's grasp at the semifinal stage. Australia, unfancied at the start of the competition, handled the pressure better to rightfully enter the final round. They won by 18 runs.

Toss: Australia
Man of the Match: CJ McDermott
Australia 267/8 in 50 overs (David Boon 65, Mike Veletta 48, Imran Khan 3/36). **Pakistan** 249 all out in 49 overs (Javed Miandad 70, Imran Khan 58, Craig McDermott 5/44, Bruce Reid 2/41).

Semifinal, 5 November: Wankhede Stadium, Mumbai

Kapil inserted England, expecting the ball to swing in the sweaty conditions and the swirling breeze of the Arabian Sea. His expectations were belied, though. Instead, the slow surface responded to turn. This suited India's strength, but Graham Gooch (11 fours) and Mike Gatting (five fours) skilfully blunted the spinners. Pulling and sweeping the two left-armers, Maninder and Shastri, against the tide, they stitched together 117 off 19 overs. Srikkanth dropped a difficult chance from the Essex opener when the batsman was 82. He finally departed caught at midwicket in the 43rd over. Gatting had exited two overs earlier. Allan Lamb, then, shepherded the lower half of the batting to add another 32.

India missed Vengsarkar, down with a tummy bug at his home ground. They received a further jolt when Philip DeFreitas uprooted Gavaskar's off stump early. Srikkanth and Sidhu, both heavy hitters, failed to produce a single boundary. Azharuddin and Chandrakant Pandit plundered 27 of Eddie Hemmings' first three overs. But Gooch was economical while his county teammate, Neil Foster, chipped in with another scalp—that of Pandit. Kapil launched a premature assault and paid the price, as Gatting, who had placed himself on the midwicket boundary, accepted the catch with a smug look on his face. In a 34-ball stint from here onwards, Hemmings captured four for 21, which included the crucial wicket of Azhar (seven fours). With five wickets in hand and a required run rate of five an over, India were still in the hunt. But with the Hyderabad artiste back in the hut, the calmness disappeared. It was largely left to Shastri to steer the steamer, but England's excellent catching, including a splendid running effort by Lamb to nip Chetan Sharma in the bud, ensured they did not relinquish the upper hand. England won by 35 runs.

Toss: India
Man of the Match: GA Gooch
England 254/6 in 50 overs (Graham Gooch 115, Mike Gatting 56, Allan Lamb 32*, Maninder Singh 3/54, Kapil Dev Nikhanj 2/38). **India** 219 all out in 45.3 overs (Mohammed Azharuddin 64, Eddie Hemmings 4/52, Neil Foster 3/47).

Final, 8 November: Eden Gardens, Kolkata

Kolkata was once the capital of British India and the second city of the Empire. Its Eden Gardens is the country's second oldest test venue after the Bombay Gymkhana (which hosted a one and only test in December 1933) and is the subcontinent's longest uninterrupted international venue, having staged its first test—India versus England—in January 1934.

On a smoggy morning, it was a full house at this, then the world's second largest cricket stadium (after the Melbourne Cricket Ground) virtually on the banks of the River Ganges, or the Ganga as it's called in Indian languages. DeFreitas and Gladstone Small's opening spell was wayward, which boosted Australia, who had decided to bat, to 52 in 10 overs. But Neil Foster corrected the profligacy by yielding only 16 runs in his first eight overs, which included the wicket of Marsh. Gooch, too, was steady until Border and Veletta (six fours) stepped it up by adding 73 in 10 overs after the fall of Boon, who, with his 75 (seven fours), posted his fifth half-century in six innings. The last six overs proved to be even more expensive for England as they resulted in another 65 runs.

So, Australia took the field requiring to defend a total of 253 and with the comforting thought that no side had compiled 254 to win a match in this World Cup. But England, 135 for two after 31 overs, were well on course, with the Australian wheel appearing to wobble. However, in a moment of madness, Gatting attempted to greet his counterpart's first ball with a reverse sweep. The left-arm delivery pitched on his leg stump took a top edge, glanced his shoulder, before ballooning into the wicketkeeper's gloves. With this, the scales tilted Australia's way. Tim Robinson found McDermott's pace too hot to handle. Bill Athey figured in three partnerships of 65 in 17 overs, 69 in 13 and 35 in eight with Gooch, Gatting and Lamb, respectively, before he was run out by Waugh while going for a third run. As England faltered in their run rate (and the asking rate of 75 from 10 overs became 46 off five), Waugh cleaned up Lamb in the 47th over. DeFreitas stirred excitement as he pummelled four, six and four in McDermott's second last over. But Waugh had him caught in the next over and also conceded only two runs in it. Seventeen runs were required in the final over; but McDermott kept his cool and Australia meritoriously lifted the Reliance World Cup.

Toss: Australia

Man of the Match: DC Boon

Australia 253/5 in 50 overs (David Boon 75, Mike Veletta 45*, Eddie Hemmings 2/48). **England** 246/8 in 50 overs (Bill Athey 58, Allan Lamb 45, Mike Gatting 41 (Steve Waugh 2/37, Allan Border 2/38).

The semifinals in Mumbai and Lahore held the subcontinent transfixed; though the outcomes dashed Indian and Pakistani hopes. Nevertheless, 70,000 spectators enthusiastically mushroomed for the final; and a sporting lot they were, too, as, not inappropriately, acknowledged by Border after the match.

In retrospect, Australia benefited from batting first in five of their six qualifying games, and in the semifinals and finals, too, on pitches that became slower and lower as a day wore on. To their credit, they appreciated this phenomenon early and also adhered to their strength—fast bowling. Besides, they didn't wilt in the heat.

Pakistan peaked too soon, winning their first five qualifying games, largely on the basis of some overwhelming bowling from Imran and Abdul Qadir, only for the dice to roll the other way in the semifinal.

India qualified for the last four without their bowling being really tested. Their batting was spectacular, though not always the most substantive. Immature crowds imploring big hits, rewards from a sponsor for exhibition of fours and sixes, were unnecessary distractions, while the dispute between some senior Indian players and the BCCI over insignia remained unresolved.

West Indies, not as high and mighty as in the past, were without Malcolm Marshall. New Zealand missed Richard Hadlee. The Sri Lankans and the Zimbabweans returned home without a win. But for sheer bravado, the innings of the World Cup was Zimbabwean David Houghton's 142 against New Zealand.

The Australians probably worked the hardest. As his teammates placed the glistening Reliance Cup in his hands and lifted him on their shoulders in their lap of honour around the Eden Gardens, it was a personal triumph for Border who had rebuilt Australia from one of their bleakest periods earlier in the decade.

THE 1992 WORLD CUP

Oddly, since it was meant to be a quadrennial event, the 5th World Cup, sponsored by Benson & Hedges, took place a year after it ought to have. This was because Antipodean cricket authorities, particularly the Australian

Cricket Board, were unwilling to abandon their regular calendar of test and one-day series, which generally covered the period from November to February; autumn (spring in the southern hemisphere) was weather-wise considered to be hazardous. But when the event did unfold a few months later, it was a further amplified occasion, jointly hosted by Australia and New Zealand. With the readmission of South Africa into the international fold, all eight test-playing teams were represented, plus Zimbabwe, who were then knocking on the door to gain full membership of the ICC. Thus, there were an unprecedented nine participants, and they were not divided into any groups. While the first two World Cups had constituted only 15 matches and the two thereafter, 27 apiece, the tournament in Australasia was enlarged to 39 fixtures—25 in Australia and the rest in New Zealand.

Besides, this World Cup fell in line with the practice initiated by Kerry Packer's World Series Cricket, in that players wore coloured clothing, white balls were used and some games were day/night affairs and, therefore, floodlit in the latter half. Such facets have become regulation since. It was again 50 overs a side, and each team played the others once before the top four in the qualifying table squared off in the semifinals. The rules governing rain-interrupted matches, though, were debatable.

The *Wisden Cricketers' Almanack* recorded:

'Recognizing the imperfection of a straight run-rate calculation when a second innings has to be shortened after rain, and unable to schedule spare days within the time-frame of the tournament, the World Cup committee adopted a scheme whereby the reduction in the target would be commensurate with the lowest-scoring overs of the side which batted first.'

The tournament was infused an early buzz when New Zealand tore up the form book to beat Australia, the holders and favourites, by 37 runs at Auckland. Martin Crowe's high-quality batting—he scored a hundred in the opener—aided by the power hitting of Mark Greatbatch (who got a look-in only because John Wright was injured) at the top of the order, not to speak of Dipak Patel's off-spin with the new ball, created an impressive run of victories in the Kiwis' first seven outings on their slow pitches.

Mohammed Azharuddin was now captain of India. His city of Hyderabad and its surroundings once had a princely ruler known as a Nizam. The one in the first quarter of the 20th century was reputedly then the world's richest person. Azhar wasn't a prince by birth, but was quite princely in his batting and fielding. A Muslim, he also illustrated a commendable trait in Indian cricket of non-discrimination against minorities in national selection. Before Azharuddin's long tenure, Ghulam Ahmed, a gifted off-spinner also from Hyderabad, and Tiger Pataudi for an extended term—had had the honour of leading India, as well. In fact, in 1946, a year before India's freedom, the latter's father, Nawab Iftikhar Ali Khan of Pataudi (whose maiden test appearance was in the 1st test at Sydney in the 1932-33 Bodyline series), was skipper for a tour of England.

22 February: WACA, Perth

England won the toss before a 13,000 attendance, but had difficulty coping with the pace of the wicket after playing on the slow pitches of New Zealand. Robin Smith, though, struck 91, with two sixes pulled to the long-leg boundary and Graham Gooch celebrated his 100th ODI with a half-century. Yet, England lost six wickets in five overs after Neil Fairbrother's departure, only to be saved by Ian Botham at his most irrepressible.

Thereafter, England bowled too short, which facilitated Krish Srikkanth firing on all cylinders, hitting seven fours in his 39. Contrarily, Ravi Shastri touched the fence only twice in two and a half hours. Philip DeFreitas then dropped him off his own bowling, but broke the stumps with a direct hit to subsequently run him out. This pattern became infectious as three more such dismissals followed. After Subroto Banerjee, a seamer from the eastern Indian state of Bihar, had capitalized with a six off Derek Pringle, India needed 11 runs to win in the last over. The prospects were 50:50. But with the effervescent Botham effecting the last of the run outs two balls later, the issue was settled in England's favour by nine runs.

Toss: England
Man of the Match: IT Botham
England 236/9 in 50 overs (Robin Smith 91, Graham Gooch 51, Manoj Prabhakar 2/34, Kapil Dev Nikhanj 2/38). **India** 227 all out in 49.2 overs (Ravi Shastri 57, Krishnamachari Srikkanth 39, Sachin Tendulkar 35, Dermot Reeve 3/38, Ian Botham 2/27).

28 February: MacKay (Australia)

An estimated 3000-strong crowd went home disappointed with a no-result. Start of play was delayed by five hours. Then, when Sri Lanka won the toss and the teams emerged for a 20-overs-a-side encounter, only two balls were possible before heavy showers submerged the ground.

1 March: Woolloongabba, Brisbane

In salubrious weather, Australia, electing to bat first, were propped up by an exquisite essay from Dean Jones after Kapil Dev and Manoj Prabhakar had pinned down some of the other Australians with penetrative line and length.

India, too, were subdued at the start, with Shastri hampered by a knee injury. But Azharuddin's artful 93 and Sanjay Manjrekar, son of Vijay and a worthy chip of the old block, with three fours and a six, carried the Indians to within striking distance. The lower order battled on spiritedly. Thirteen runs were required off Tom Moody's final over. Kiran More clipped the first two balls to the fine-leg boundary. The next bowled him. Prabhabhar took a single in the fourth, but was run out off the next. With four needed from the last ball, Javagal Srinath swung at it; Steve Waugh spilled it near the fence, but hurled it back to substitute wicketkeeper, David Boon. Venkatapathy Raju failed to make his ground while attempting a third run, which would have tied the scores. The 12,000-odd spectators, therefore, witnessed a nail-biting finish, which, to the delight of the majority, ended in the home side's favour. Rain clipped 15 minutes and three overs of play, when India were 45 from 16.2 overs. This reduced their target by two runs, taking into account Australia's three least fruitful overs.

Toss: Australia
Man of the Match: DM Jones
Australia 237/9 in 50 overs (Dean Jones 90, David Boon 43, Kapil Dev Nikhanj 3/41, Manoj Prabhakar 3/41). **India** 234 all out in 47 overs (Mohammed Azharuddin 93, Sanjay Manjrekar 47, Tom Moody 3/56).

4 March: Sydney Cricket Ground (Day/Night)

Before winning the toss, India rested Ravi Shastri and replaced him with youngster Ajay Jadeja to open the innings, who impressed in this slot. But quite the most charming innings came from Sachin Tendulkar, still only 18 and playing in his first World Cup, who contributed an unbeaten 54. Son of a Marathi professor and poet, this prodigious talent added 60 in eight overs with Kapil Dev.

When it came to Pakistan's turn to bat, Aamir Sohail was the dominant partner in an 88-run stand for the third wicket with Javed Miandad, who, uncharacteristically, took 34 overs to compile 40, thus stiffening the task for his teammates. This first World Cup clash between the South Asian rivals was made slightly unsavoury by a conflict between wicketkeeper More and Miandad. The former's enthusiastic shout for a leg-side catch provoked a verbal exchange and then a contemptuous response from Miandad. The umpires reported the matter to the match referee, who asked the respective team managers to resolve the issue. More, however, could look back with satisfaction at the cricketing aspect, having snapped up two catches, pulled off a stumping and run-out Imran Khan. India won quite easily as the last eight Pakistani wickets fell in a clatter for just 68 runs in front of over 10,000 people.

Toss: India
Man of the Match: SR Tendulkar
India 216/7 in 49 overs (Sachin Tendulkar 54*, Ajay Jadeja 46, Mushtaq Ahmed 3/59, Aaqib Javed 2/28). **Pakistan** 173 all out in 48.1 overs (Aamir Sohail 62, Javed Miandad 40, Manoj Prabhakar 2/22, Kapil Dev Nikhanj 2/30, Javagal Srinath 2/37).

7 March: Hamilton (New Zealand)

A crowd of about 1,500 waited patiently as rain devoured three hours of play in the morning. Then, India won the toss and Tendulkar starred in the 32 overs allocated to India. He hit eight fours and a six in his 81 and put on 99 in 15 overs with Manjrekar for the fourth wicket. The Indians thus set Zimbabwe a target of 204 to win. But with another downpour terminating the match after 19.1 overs, the contest was determined by the controversial rule on shortened innings. Unfortunate against Australia on this count, India were, perhaps, a trifle lucky on this occasion. Zimbabwe had rattled up 104 for one when the fatal showers ensued; while India had reached 106 for three at the same juncture. With Andy Flower going well, another 100 from 13 was not unattainable. There was, thus, some commiseration for Zimbabwe. India won by 55 runs after their total was revised to 158, as compared to Zimbabwe's to 103 on the basis of their highest scoring 19 overs.

Toss: India
Man of the Match: SR Tendulkar
India 203/7 in 32 overs (Sachin Tendulkar 81, John Traicos 3/35, Mark Burmester 3/36). **Zimbabwe** 104/1 in 19.1 overs (Andy Flower 43*, Ali Omarshah 31, Sachin Tendulkar 1/35).

10 March: Basin Reserve, Wellington

A gathering of more than 6,500 people saw India launch themselves encouragingly after winning the toss. Azharuddin was in fine fettle, though the diminutive Tendulkar was tied down by Curtly Ambrose's extra bounce. It was, however, Anderson Cummins who did the most damage. He took four wickets, the first of these being Azhar caught at long off in the 43rd over, when the Indians were 166. The advantage of having wickets in hand was completely squandered by India as seven wickets fell for only 31 runs.

The West Indies fairly flew off the block to reach 50 in six overs, with Brian Lara on 36. They were almost as dominant at 81 from 11 when the 20-minute interruption came. This disruption trimmed four overs and three runs off the innings. When play resumed, Lara left immediately and Simmons followed, victim to a falling catch by Tendulkar. Richie Richardson and Gus Logie didn't last long either. But Keith Arthurton and Carl Hooper steadied the ship and remained unseparated in an 83-run stand. The West Indies won by five wickets, their target having been reduced to 195 off 46 overs. They thus became the first side in the competition to trump a rain-adjusted target.

Toss: India
Man of the Match: AC Cummins
India 197 all out in 49.4 overs (Mohammed Azharuddin 61, Krishnamachari Srikkanth 40, Anderson Cummins 4/33, Curtly Ambrose 2/24). **West Indies** 195/5 in 40.2 overs (Keith Arthurton 58*, Brian Lara 41, Carl Hooper 34*, Javagal Srinath 2/23, Venkatapathy Raju 1/32).

12 March: Dunedin (New Zealand)

Anticipating rain, Azharuddin opted for first strike. Srikkanth holed out on the long-on boundary in the very first over and Jadeja pulled a hamstring, which forced him to retire. Such departures conjoined the captain with Tendulkar, who, together, realized 127 in 30 overs. Azhar then welcomed back Patel with a six, but in trying to repeat the stroke was brilliantly caught by Greatbatch. Tendulkar continued with Kapil, and the Indians reached a respectable total of 230. But Greatbatch, who had been batting in the tournament like a gunner on a roll, was not one to respect any score. He powered to 73 before being caught at square-leg mid-way through the venture, which put the New Zealanders ahead of the required rate. Four more wickets fell, including Crowe's, who was run out by More, scooting to gully to whip the ball back and knock down the stumps without even having a good look at them. But Andrew Jones then anchored the Kiwis to victory. New Zealand won by four wickets before nearly 10,000 fans. New Zealand's sixth win equalled West Indies' record run in the 1983 World Cup, and virtually barricaded India from further progress in the competition.

Toss: New Zealand
Man of the Match: MJ Greatbatch
India 230/6 in 50 overs (Sachin Tendulkar 84, Mohammed Azharuddin 55, Chris Harris 3/55, Dipak Patel 2/29). **New Zealand** 231/6 in 47.1 overs (Mark Greatbatch 73, Andrew Jones 67*, Manoj Prabhakar 3/46, Venkatapathy Raju 2/38).

15 March: Adelaide Oval

A cloudburst curtailed the match to 30 overs a side. South Africa then inserted India. After Srikkanth fell early to a one-handed catch by Peter Kirsten, Azhar, full of delicate strokes, added 78 with makeshift opener, Manjrekar, and followed this with 71 in eight overs with Kapil Dev, who produced a hurricane 42. The net result was a rapid run rate of six an over.

Yet, asked to open, Kirsten advanced at almost a run a ball, much to the appreciation of the 6,000-odd spectators, before he was yorked. He added 128 with Hudson, who registered his third fifty in four innings. Kepler

Wessels, then, completed the task of scoring 24 off four overs as South Africa stormed home by six wickets.

With this win, the South Africans were certain of a semifinal place, unless thwarted by political developments back home. The United Cricket Board of South Africa indicated they would feel obliged to withdraw from the tournament if a plebiscite of whites in South Africa two days later rejected constitutional reform to usher in a democratic, multiracial system of government. It would have been a breach of trust if it had happened, for South Africa's entry in the World Cup was accepted on an unwritten understanding that their politics would not revert to a *status quo ante*. An overwhelming vote for change, however, made the matter a non-issue.

Toss: South Africa
Man of the Match: PN Kirsten
India 180/6 in 30 overs (Mohammed Azharuddin 79, Kapil Dev Nikhanj 42, Adrian Kuiper 2/28, Allan Donald 2/34). South Africa 181/4 in 29.1 overs (Peter Kirsten 84, Andrew Hudson 53, Manoj Prabhakar 1/33).

This match was the last in which the omnipotent Kapil Dev would be seen in the World Cup. He had performed in four such competitions and enjoyed the singular honour of leading India to their 1983 conquest.

After retiring, he carried his buoyancy in cricket to his business activities. But to his chagrin, in 2000, aspersions were cast on him *vis-à-vis* match fixing during a spell as India's coach. He tearfully dispelled such insinuations in a television interview, but for some years deliberately distanced himself from the game—his new passion being golf. In September 2006, though, he succeeded Sunil Gavaskar as the chairman of India's National Cricket Academy in Bangalore, before his involvement with the Zee TV-sponsored Twenty20 Indian Cricket League in 2007 ruptured his relations with the BCCI.

Semifinal, 21 March: Eden Park Auckland

The day began with Martin Crowe being a bit prematurely—though perhaps not undeservingly—crowned Man of the Series for his batting and captaincy. He then proceeded to win the toss, bat first and demonstrate his pedigree with a quicksilver 91, which was decorated with three sixes. Greatbatch had typically given New Zealand an explosive start, hitting sixes off Wasim Akram and Aaqib Javed. But subsequently, Mushtaq Ahmed's leg-spin applied the brakes, before Crowe went into cruise control, adding 113 in 107 balls with Ken Rutherford. But as the batsmen crossed after the latter had skied a catch to Moin Khan, Crowe tragically pulled a hamstring. He continued with Greatbatch as his runner, but, in a comedy of errors, was run out by the latter. Nevertheless, Ian Smith and the tail sword-fenced their way to 262. This was no soft target and looked especially elusive half way through the Pakistani innings.

The Pakistanis needed 123 from 15 overs at 8.2 an over after Imran himself had failed to ignite. But this challenge was turned on its head by the precocious Inzamam-ul-Haq. He raced to 50 off 31 balls and then to 60, glittered with seven fours and a six, to forcibly snatch the game from the Kiwis. With Miandad, he added 87 in 10 overs. Indeed, when the rotund young man was run out, the target had eased to 36 in five. This was comfortably negotiated, as Wasim and Moin threw their bats at virtually every delivery and Miandad chugged along at just the right pace to remain undefeated on a half-century.

Pakistan, thus, qualified for their first World Cup final by getting the better of the previously unbeatable New Zealanders twice in four days. The fusillade of shots from Inzamam's bat paralysed the Kiwis. The strategy of opening the bowling in the tournament with Patel paid off again, as this off-spinner returned figures of one for 28 in his first eight overs; but his last two cost 22. Imran Khan rushed to embrace his heroes, as Crowe was reduced to a limp, as much metaphorically as physically, in accompanying his colleagues in a lap of thanksgiving to the 32,000-plus capacity crowd.

Toss: New Zealand

Man of the Match: Inzamam-ul Haq

New Zealand 262/7 in 50 overs (Martin Crowe 91, Ken Rutherford 50, Wasim Akram 2/40, Mushtaq Ahmed 2/40). **Pakistan** 264/6 in 49 overs (Inzamam-ul-Haq 60, Javed Miandad 57*, Willie Watson 2/39).

Semifinal, 22 March: Sydney Cricket Ground

England were unhindered by the morning conditions and, so, kept the scoreboard ticking. But the *pièce de résistance* came from a middle order gambit by Graeme Hick. This former Zimbabwean, after getting the benefit of the doubt in an lbw appeal and being caught off a no-ball before opening his account, went on to register 83 off 90 balls, adding 71 in 14 overs with Alec Stewart and 73 with Neil Fairbrother. Dermott Reeve then hurtled to 25 off 14 balls, which was helped by 17 of 18 pillaged in Alan Donald's final over.

Thrown down a gauntlet of 5.62 runs an over, South Africa erased 58 runs from their first 10 overs. Kirsten was handicapped by injury, but Andrew Hudson almost completed his fourth 50 of the tournament. Adrian Kuiper scorched three fours in a row off Gladstone Small, while Jonty Rhodes, hitherto more discernible for his fielding, now clicked with the willow. Such efforts compressed the 'ask' to 47 off five overs. Brian McMillan and David Richardson reduced this by 25 in 2.5 overs. But this is when rain intervened and sank South Africa.

The requirement of 22 runs from 13 balls before the shower was first revised to 22 from seven and then to an impossible 21 off one. McMillan could only manage a single off this Lewis delivery. The vanquished were shattered and the victors left morally encumbered, while the 35,000 crowd felt a little cheated. The South Africans, though, cheerfully did a round of the ground. They were just so relieved to have been welcomed back to the international fold after being completely ostracized for two decades.

Many trashed the Organizing Committee. Under the rules, a completely new match could be held the next day only if the team batting second did not face at least 25 overs. Others insisted it was nemesis at work: Wessels fielded first fully cognizant of the pitfall, not to mention the weather forecast. Besides, South Africa's over rate was torpid and this provoked a financial penalty.

Toss: South Africa
Man of the Match: GA Hick

England 252/6 in 45 overs (Graeme Hick 83, Alec Stewart 33, Meyrick Pringle 2/36, Allan Donald 2/69). **South Africa** 232/6 in 43 overs (Andrew Hudson 46, Jonty Rhodes 43, Adrian Kuiper 36, Richard Illingworth 2/46, Gladstone Small 2/51).

Final, 25 March: Melbourne Cricket Ground

Perhaps recognizing the savage consequences of rain and the fact that no side had won a World Cup final batting second, Imran opted for first use of the willow. Initially, this move seemed to be a mistake as Pringle had Pakistan in shaky straits at 24 for two in nine overs. But the veterans, Imran and Miandad, now dug in. Gooch dropped Imran when he was nine, but the duo slowly saw off the shine. Pakistan could only post 70 in 25 overs. Yet, by the 31st over, they had motored to 139. However, Miandad, batting with the aid of a runner, perished to a reverse sweep. And Imran was caught by Richard Illingworth off Botham. The bazookas, Inzamam (35 balls) and Wasim (18 balls), then, took over. Their 52 in six overs boosted the runs from the last 20 overs to 153 despite Pringle's last over costing just two runs and ensnaring both their wickets.

England suffered an early setback when Botham was adjudged caught behind. Stewart, though, was not shown the dreaded finger when Moin claimed another catch. Yet, the Surrey cricketer, son of Micky, who had toured India in 1963–64 as Mike Smith's vice-captain, failed to persevere. Mushtaq, thereafter, bamboozled Hick with a googly and also dislodged Gooch. With 181 needed from 29 overs, England faced a monumental task. But the battle-hardened Allan Lamb, selected ahead of Robin Smith, whose fitness was a question mark, put 72 of these on the board from 14 overs in association with Fairbrother, the left-handed Lancastrian nicknamed the 'finisher'. Wasim, the latter's county mate, was, now, re-introduced for a final burst. Fairbrother, who had run out of specialist batsmen as accomplices and was himself down to seeking the assistance of a runner, top-edged to the wicketkeeper. The others simply caved in. Pakistan won by 22 runs.

An attendance of nearly 90,000 witnessed a worthy climax to the tournament. Imran affirmed this was the most fulfilling and satisfying cricketing moment of his life. He described the victory as a triumph of youth over experience. He also attributed the success to the edge his aggressive specialist bowlers provided over Gooch's all-rounders.

Imran, Oxford-educated but an autocrat as captain, had practically hand-picked his squad. The absence of star pace bowler Waqar Younis, who suffered a stress fracture before the team left Pakistan, was a serious setback. They lost four of their first five matches (including their meeting with Zimbabwe), but went on to win the next five. They peaked perfectly, while England ran out of steam. The English won all their matches in New Zealand, but were less impressive on the faster Australian wickets they encountered in the knockout stage. 'It's not the end of the world', Gooch remarked after the match, 'but it is close to it.' He admitted England had been beaten fair and square. The three-figure stand between Imran and Miandad frustrated the Englishmen, while Wasim shattered their last hope by dismissing Lamb and Lewis with successive deliveries, one swinging in and then straightening and the other cutting in sharply.

Imran, then 40, and in the twilight of his career, beamed in delight as he held aloft the £7,500 Waterford crystal trophy. An iconic all-rounder in his country, he had by personal example inspired his younger colleagues through difficult patches in the competition. In such circumstances, they reacted, he said, like a cornered tiger. Earlier in the championship, he had described it as the worst organized of all the World Cups. He and Miandad (who became the highest overall run scorer) were the only ones to have played in all five tournaments.

So, Pakistan, hitherto thrice semifinalists, won the World Cup for the first time. England had now three times been within a match of a coronation, but never anointed kings. A limited-overs record crowd in Australia paid £880,000 to watch the final. Also, the international television audience—in 29 countries—ran into hundreds of millions.

Toss: Pakistan
Man of the Match: Wasim Akram
Man of the Series: MD Crowe (NZ)

Pakistan 249/6 in 50 overs (Imran Khan 72, Javed Miandad 58, Inzamam-ul-Haq 42, Wasim Akram 33*, Derek Pringle 3/22). **England** 227 all out in 49.2 overs (Neil Fairbrother 62, Allan Lamb 31, Mushtaq Ahmed 3/41, Wasim Akram 3/49, Aaqib Javed 2/27).

The Australians, disillusioned by the team's poor showing, started rooting for South Africa, led as they were by Bloemfontein-born former Australian batsman, Kepler Wessels. (A sizeable number of white South Africans who had migrated to Australia, supplemented, if not spearheaded, the support.) The South Africans had had only three matches in India—one of which they won—as previous experience of ODIs. Now coached by Mike Procter, a distinguished all-rounder for Gloucestershire during South Africa's isolation, with the quite expeditious Donald the lynchpin of their attack, they stepped seamlessly on to the world stage. Kirsten, who was left out of the original tour squad, was to average over 68 in the preliminary matches.

Defeated by New Zealand and Sri Lanka, the South Africans dramatically turned the tables on the West Indians and complemented this win with another over Pakistan at Brisbane, a match in which rain favoured the Proteas, formerly the Springboks (a change brought about to abandon an animal symbol of the apartheid era for the softer image of a flower). Rhodes, though, brought spectators to their feet with his gymnastic fielding, which included running out Inzamam-ul Haq while being airborne.

Across the Indian Ocean, the white minority who had discriminatingly ruled South Africa for decades, probably realized the value of scrapping their repugnant racism, as they saw live pictures from the eastern hemisphere of how warmly their cricketers had been accepted as a result of the promise of a conversion to civilized ways.

Bookmakers had quickly revised odds as the propensities of past winners, India and the West Indies, oscillated uncertainly. A new-look Caribbean side led by a slightly unsure Richie Richardson won their first match by making 221 without losing a wicket against Pakistan. They subsequently seemed to lose their way, though a young left-hander, Brian Lara, announced himself emphatically with four half-centuries. He, then, blossomed into an all-time great.

Sri Lanka successfully chased down 313 against Zimbabwe at New Plymouth in New Zealand. But the Zimbabweans upset England by nine runs, thanks to Eddo Brandes, after themselves being bowled out for a mere 134 on a lively pitch at Albury in Australia. England had, by this stage, already qualified for the last four, their previous run having included a comprehensive win over Australia.

The pool of umpires from the competing nations injected a flavour of internationalism, with Steve Bucknor and David Shepherd generally the most error free. Bouncers above the shoulder, though, were not no-balled with uniform strictness.

Akin to 1987, neither of the hosts reached the final. But the tournament gave rise to significant profits, struck many a chord and kept the cricketing world on tenterhooks.

However, far too many matches were decided somewhat artificially—by the rules governing stoppages caused by inclement weather. This left a slight unsavoury taste in the mouth. While India had only themselves to blame for their elimination in the league phase, their match with Sri Lanka was completely washed out and the ones with Australia, Zimbabwe, West Indies and South Africa settled by the aforesaid controversial method, albeit not always to India's disadvantage. In summary, India suffered from an unsettled opening combination and inadequate bowling and fielding.

THE 1996 WORLD CUP

All things considered, the sixth World Cup, sponsored by Wills, wasn't wholly memorable. The competition was clouded by an extended, at times uninteresting league stage and a knockout segment that whet the appetite, but was all too shortlived.

The imminence of spectator unrest finally surfaced with the scratching of a semifinal at Kolkata, following bottle throwing into the playing area and lighting of fires in the stands by some unruly elements among the spectators.

The scenario was in sharp contrast to the 1987 World Cup, which was generally acknowledged to be a success. Of course, that competition provided negligible profit, whereas the event now panned out to be an accountant's delight. The itineraries were inexplicable and the travel quite wearing.

Such rudimentary defects could have been dealt with by the ICC at source. But the governors of the sport adopted a hands-off policy, transferring all responsibility to the three-nation (India, Pakistan and Sri Lanka) Organizing Committee. The ICC have not repeated this mistake since and have increasingly strengthened their control over the World Cup.

The incorporation of three associate member countries in the draw was laudable. This enlarged the field to 12 teams. However, it also made the outcome of the league stage, divided into two groups of six sides each, rather a foregone conclusion. The tournament only spluttered to life from the quarter finals. The ICC could not be absolved of responsibility for such imbalance, either. Predictably, the three associate nations and the minnows of test cricket, Zimbabwe, were eliminated. Dispensing with the round of eight—with teams only progressing to the semifinals from the first phase—would have made the pre-quarter final segment more interesting. Patrons to a certain extent called the bluff, as the group games in Pakistan were poorly attended.

The decision to spread matches to various corners of India to keep associations affiliated to the BCCI in good humour was indefensible. Most of the 17 venues lacked infrastructure to host an international event. At the opening ceremony in Kolkata, a much-touted laser show malfunctioned and the master of ceremonies, the actor Saeed Jaffrey, sounded well fortified. A bemused 100,000 attendees wondered what on earth was going on.

It was egg on the face of the local chieftain, Jagmohan Dalmiya, later to become president of the ICC and one of the most powerful administrators in world cricket. Such embarrassment coincided with a fracas between, on the one hand, the organizers and, on the other, Australia and West Indies over their refusal to play at Colombo, following a bomb blast in the Sri Lankan capital a fortnight earlier. Positions being entrenched, the matches were forfeited, though it was a critique of the cosiness of the format that Australia and West Indies could make such sacrifices without seriously endangering their progress to the business end of the tournament.

The Sri Lankans had a smirk as well as a disconsolate look on their faces. They obtained four points by default and an automatic passage to the last eight, but had been denied the pleasure of hosting two of the best teams in the competition, especially when this island needed a respite from its gory civil war between the Sinhalese-dominated Central Government and Tamil separatists.

At 4 a.m. following the previous night's opening ceremony charade, four bleary eyed squads assembled in the lobby of Kolkata's Oberoi Grand Hotel to catch a 6 a.m. flight to Delhi, where they had to wait several hours before connecting with flights to their first-game destinations. Clearly, either no one cared or had not thought of arranging charter flights at decent hours.

18 February: Cuttack

While Azharuddin, retained as captain, became the seventh cricketer to win 200 ODI caps, all Kenyans were making their international debuts. Their batsmen, though, initially gave a good account of themselves. After being invited to bat, Steve Tikolo impressed with 65, hitting a six and six fours and putting on 96 with his skipper, Maurice Odumbe. But the middle order underestimated the accurate leg-spinner Anil Kumble, who, as a result, benefited with three wickets in four overs. India were, thus, set a target of 200.

Ajay Jadeja and Sachin Tendulkar erased 100 of these runs in 20 overs *en route* to compiling India's highest partnership for any wicket in the World Cup. But the former began to suffer from cramps and holed out on the boundary in the 33rd over. The special talent of Tendulkar was rewarded in that he scored his fifth ODI hundred, although he was stuck on 99 for nine balls. Neither Navjot Sidhu nor Vinod Kambli quite found his feet. They, too, succumbed in the deep. However, Tendulkar re-asserted control as he cruised to 127, with the assistance of 15 fours and a six. It was wicketkeeper Nayan Mongia, though, who hit the winning boundary. India won by seven wickets in this ancient, bustling city in the eastern state of Odisha on the Bay of Bengal.

Toss: India
Man of the Match: SR Tendulkar

Kenya 199/6 in 50 overs (Steve Tikolo 65, Anil Kumble 3/28, Venkatapathy Raju 2/34). **India** 203/3 in 41.5 overs (Sachin Tendulkar 127*, Ajay Jadeja 53, Aasif Karim 1/27).

21 February: Gwalior (Day/Night)

On a perfectly good batting pitch, it was hardly surprising that the West Indies opted for first strike. What was unforeseen was their performance thereafter. They lost two early wickets, but did not incur any further loss up to the half-way mark. At this point, captain Richie Richardson's exit prompted a collapse, from which the West Indians never recovered; indeed, later disintegrating a second time. Both times three wickets went down for eight runs in 12 balls. Of course, Brian Lara was rather unlucky to be adjudged caught behind off his fifth ball. But the West Indies were dismissed for 173, which was less than what the Kenyans had scored against the Indians.

India, too, lost a couple of wickets at the start of their venture, but remained unfazed. Again the resolute Tendulkar came to the rescue. He stroked his way to 70 off 91 balls, but was thereafter run out in a misunderstanding with Kambli, his friend from school days. Tragically for the West Indies, Courtney Browne had dropped a skier when Tendulkar was 22. Courtney Walsh returned for a mean spell, but the match had by this stage virtually slipped out of the West Indians' fingers. Indeed, Kambli made sure he finished the job. India reached their target in 40 overs to win by five wickets. This match was the first real challenge for both teams and India passed the test with flying colours. Some 30,000 spectators celebrated by lighting torches and setting off firecrackers, which smokily diffused the floodlights in this erstwhile seat of the princely state of Gwalior (now a part of Madhya Pradesh state). The maharaja (albeit officially de-recognised) at the time, Madhavrao Scindia, who went to Oxford and was also a Congress party politician, had been president of the BCCI. He died in an air accident in September 2001.

Toss: West Indies
Man of the Match: SR Tendulkar
West Indies 173 all out in 50 overs (Richie Richardson 47, Shivnarine Chanderpaul 38, Anil kumble 3/35, Manoj Prabhakar 3/39, Javagal Srinath

2/22). **India** 174/5 in 39.4 overs (Sachin Tendulkar 70, Vinod Kambli 33*, Roger Harper 2/34, Curtly Ambrose 2/41).

27 February: Wankhede Stadium, Mumbai (Day/Night)

It was the first-ever floodlit international in India's commercial capital; and the batsmen responded with a correspondingly dazzling display. Mark Taylor sprinted to 59 as Australia posted 103 for the first wicket at five an over after winning the toss. They seemed set to score 300. A bit overshadowed in this partnership, Mark Waugh now blossomed to become the first to score back-to-back centuries in a World Cup. His composition was engraved with three sixes and eight fours. But the spinners, Venkatapathy Raju and Kumble, chipped away and the last seven wickets fell for just 26—four of them in the final over.

Yet, India failed to transmit this momentum to their batting. In six overs they conceded two wickets to Damien Fleming, while Glenn McGrath sent down three maidens. Then, Tendulkar decided not to disappoint his home crowd. He hit three fours in McGrath's fifth over and hurried from 12 to 56 off 25 balls, planting seven fours and a six. He took a breather after Fleming cleaned up Azhar, but still managed an explosive 90 off 84 deliveries, with seven more boundaries. India remained in the hunt until he was stumped off a wide from Mark Waugh, toying with off-spin. Sanjay Manjrekar and Nayan Mongia persevered, notwithstanding Shane Warne's accuracy. India, though, were short of wickets to successfully conclude the chase. Australia won by 16 runs, with two overs to spare. Fleming finished with a five-wicket haul.

Toss: Australia
Man of the Match: ME Waugh
Australia 258 all out in 50 overs (Mark Waugh 126, Mark Taylor 59, Venkatapathy Raju 2/48, Venkatesh Prasad 2/49). **India** 242 all out in 48 overs (Sachin Tendulkar 90, Sanjay Manjrekar 62, Damien Fleming 5/36, Steve Waugh 2/22).

2 March: Feroz Shah Kotla, Delhi

The nerve centre of political power in India for centuries, Delhi, old and new, has many attractions. But the cricket ground controlled by the unsuitable Delhi and District Cricket Association at the otherwise alluring setting of Feroz Shah Kotla (inner citadel of the fourteenth-century settlement of Ferozabad, now in ruins) is not one of them. Its historically substandard facilities for players and the public alike are not exactly endearing.

Here, India seemed to be psychologically smitten after being sent in to bat by their southern neighbour. Play was delayed by a quarter of an hour because of a dew-laden outfield, following which the hosts initiated their innings in light mist and struggled to get their eye in. But 100 in 25 overs represented a considerable recovery. Indeed, after a brief shower, the last 11 overs fetched 105. Tendulkar blasted his way to 137—his second century of the tournament. Launching into five sixes and eight fours, he realized 175 with Azhar, which improved on India's all-wicket record in the World Cup established in the same tournament in the Kenya match. Ravindra Pushpakumara's last over resulted in a bountiful 23 for India as they coasted to 271 for three.

But Sri Lanka immediately replied in kind. It was a blitzkrieg from Sanath Jayasuriya and Romesh Kaluwitharana as they smashed 42 in the first three overs and Manoj Prabhakar yielded 11 and 22 in his first two. The 50 came up in the fifth, but Kumble now took an excellent catch off medium-pacer Prasad's bowling to dismiss Kalu as he attempted his seventh four. The wrist spinner, then, proceeded to capably contain the Sri Lankan middle order. But Jayasuriya galloped on, lashing nine fours and two sixes in his 79, although the latter phase of his effort was leisurely in comparison to the early riot. Indeed, having set off at double the needed pace, Sri Lanka lost three quick wickets—Kumble completed a run-out of Gurusinha and then removed Jayasuriya and Aravinda de Silva. So, Sri Lanka fell behind the required rate. Another specialist spinner might have served India better. They had instead opted for a four-man seam attack. In essence, Arjuna Ranatunga and Hashan Tillekeratne repaired the damage, adding 131 for the 5th wicket and Sri Lanka won with eight balls to spare. The victory ensured them first place in their group. In the final analysis, it was India's unsure start when they batted that cost them the match.

Kapil Dev, captain of the 1983 World Cup winning side, during his iconic innings of 175 not out against Zimbabwe at Tunbridge Wells.

Mohinder Amarnath: Player of the Tournament in the 1983 World Cup.

Roger Binny: the highest wicket-taker in the 1983 World Cup.

Sachin Tendulkar: the highest run-getter in World Cup history being lifted on the shoulders of his teammates after his sixth and final triumphant appearance in the tournament.

Sourav Ganguly: led India to the final in the 2003 World Cup.

Rahul Dravid: had the misfortune of leading India in the 2007 World Cup.

Mahendra Dhoni, skipper of the 2011 World Cup winning team, seals victory with a six in the final against Sri Lanka.

Yuvraj Singh: Player of the Tournament in the 2011 World Cup.

Zaheer Khan: joint highest wicket-taker in the 2011 World Cup.

Mohammed Shami: performed with consistency in the 2015 and 2019 World Cups.

Virat Kohli: batted with authority in the 2011, 2015 and 2019 World Cups, without matching aggregates.

Shikhar Dhawan: reliable as an opener in the 2015 and 2019 World Cups.

Toss: Sri Lanka
Man of the Match: ST Jayasuriya
India 271/3 in 50 overs (Sachin Tendulkar 137, Mohammed Azharuddin 72*, Kumar Dharmasena 1/53, Ravindra Pushpakumara 1/53). **Sri Lanka** 272/4 in 48.4 overs (Sanath Jayasuriya 79, Hashan Tillakaratne*, Arjuna Ranatunga 46*, Anil Kumble 2/39).

6 March: Kanpur

This industrial hub, with its polluted air and poor urban development, nestling on the banks of the river Ganges, regarded as holy by religious Hindus, persists as an international cricketing venue after it generated India's first-ever test victory over Australia in 1959. Jasu Patel, an off-spinner with a sharpish action, not much recognized before or since, took 14 wickets in the match, including nine for 69 in one innings, to send Richie Benaud's side headlong to defeat. Prior to this, tests had been played here on matting wickets. Patel exploited an underprepared pitch better than the Aussies, including the leg-spinner Benaud.

Now, there were no apparent devils in the pitch. Quite simply, Zimbabwe preferred to chase rather than set a target. India, however, were seriously jolted when they lost three wickets for only 32 by the 13th over. Heath Streak disfigured Tendulkar's stumps, while Manjrekar and Azharuddin were both caught at midwicket. The crisis, though, was an opportunity for Sidhu and Kambli to impress; neither had been in the limelight in previous games. They seized this chance by adding 142 in 29 overs. Kambli, a rugged left-hander, was the more aggressive, reaching his 50 a ball ahead of Sidhu, despite giving the Sikh a 22-run start. He was fortunate to be let off twice, but recorded 106, with 11 fours, before being consumed in the deep. Then, Ajay Jadeja plundered 19 off Charles Lock's last over. With this contribution, India reached 247 for five.

For Zimbabwe, Grant Flower and Andrew Waller dashed to 50 in 11 overs, but the introduction of the spinners halted the progress and sharply altered the course of the match. Flower departed in Raju's first over and Waller in Kumble's second. After 25 overs, Zimbabwe had been 92 for two, to India's 85 for three, but three wickets in successive overs thereafter put paid to the Zimbabweans' World Cup campaign. India won by 40 runs.

Toss: Zimbabwe
Man of the Match: A Jadeja
India 247/5 in 50 overs (Vinod Kambli 106, Navjot Siddhu 80, Ajay Jadeja 44*, Charlie Lock 2/57). **Zimbabwe** 207 all out in 49.4 overs (Grant Flower 30, Heath Streak 30, Venkatapathy Raju 3/30, Ajay Jadeja 2/32).

The quarter final line-up was, therefore, England versus Sri Lanka, South Africa versus West Indies, Australia versus New Zealand and a high-voltage showdown between India and Pakistan.

Quarter final, 9 March: Chinaswamy Stadium, Bangalore

In this city, now the Silicon Valley of the East, India decided to bat; but, in spite of limited venom on the part of the Pakistani bowlers, their top order failed to capitalize. Tendulkar was off-colour in scoring 31, while Sidhu missed his hundred when beaten by a top-spinner from Mushtaq Ahmed, though he charted India to an imposing 168 for two. Vitally, though, the scoring rate was barely 4.5 an over until Jadeja, with the cooperation of the lower order, corrected this trend. He himself raced to 45 (four fours and two sixes). Then with the tail in harness, 51 runs were lambasted off the last three overs. Waqar Younis bore the brunt of this bombardment, costing 40 in just two overs—as opposed to 27 in his first eight. When he finally smothered Jadeja's explosion, he became only the fourth bowler to capture 200 wickets in ODIs.

A slow over rate reduced Pakistan's allocation to 49 overs, the only instance of such a penalty being imposed in the competition. Their openers were, however, undaunted. Saeed Anwar breezed to 48 in 32 balls, which included a bracelet of two sixes, before he skied a catch to Kumble off Srinath's bowling. Aamir Sohail, standing in as skipper for an injured Wasim Akram, reached 55 with the help of a six, when he cut injudiciously at Venkatesh Prasad. Pakistan took full advantage of the first 15 overs, scoring 113 for two, which put them markedly ahead of India at the same juncture. But Prasad snatched a couple of more wickets and, steadily, the run rate slipped downwards. Rashid Latif, with two towering sixes in his 26, kept the fight alive but Kumble, first, had him stumped and then polished off the tail.

When Javed Miandad, unable to force the pace, was run out, this was journey's end for a long and lustrous career. With typical rebelliousness, he laced the announcement of his retirement with a frontal attack against the Pakistani team management for not treating him with due importance. More importantly, it was curtains for the defending champions' campaign.

This face-off sparked intense emotions. In Pakistan, a fan, reportedly, sprayed his television set with bullets before shooting himself. Others burned Wasim's effigy. Speculation was rife he might have pulled out of the match without cause. He vehemently denied this charge. The previous year's allegations of match fixing against him didn't help. But the truth is, the match was keenly fought and a delightful cliffhanger.

Toss: India
Man of the Match: NS Sidhu
India 287/8 in 50 overs (Navjot Siddhu 93, Ajay Jadeja 45, Mushtaq Ahmed 2/56, Waqar Younis 2/67). **Pakistan** 248/9 in 49 overs (Aamir Sohail 55, Saeed Anwar 48, Venkatesh Prasad 3/45, Anil Kumble 3/48).

Semifinal, 13 March: Eden Gardens, Kolkata (Day/Night)

In day/night circumstances, conventional wisdom pointed to batting first. But Azharuddin did otherwise. There was, of course, little criticism when Jayasuriya and Kaluwitharana, Sri Lanka's audacious openers, both holed out at third man in the very first over. Asanka Gurusinha did not last long either; but Aravinda de Silva threw caution to the winds and adhered to the predetermined tactics of going for shots in the early overs, when fielding restrictions applied. Prasad suffered, giving away 22 off his first two overs. Indeed, when de Silva was bowled in the 15th over, he had accumulated 66, studded with 14 fours; and Sri Lanka had 85 on the board. Thereafter, Arjuna Ranatunga and Roshan Mahanama (who was later constrained by cramps) maintained a steady five-an-over run rate.

A target of 252 was by no means beyond India's reach. But Tendulkar was stumped and, seven balls later, Azharuddin was caught and bowled by Kumar Dharmasena. The estimated 100,000 spectators plunged into shocked silence. Soon, this soundless atmosphere turned into a boisterous and disruptive outburst as seven Indian wickets tumbled for a mere 22 runs. Indian supporters in an enclosure adjacent to the pavilion hurled glass bottles on to the field and set seats ablaze. Match referee, Clive Lloyd, who probably had nightmares of the 1967 New Year's Day riot at the same ground, when he was a young member of the West Indies side under Sir Garry Sobers, at first ordered the teams off the field for 15 minutes. He, then, attempted a resumption, before declaring Sri Lanka winners by default.

The difference between 1967 and 1996 was that the earlier unrest was caused by blatant overs-selling of tickets by corrupt elements in the Cricket Association of Bengal, while this time it occurred because the complexion of the crowd at the Eden Gardens had changed drastically in the 1990s as compared to previous decades. Whereas in the past generally people acquainted with cricket attended international matches at the Eden Gardens, following the craze for one-day cricket triggered by India's victory in the 1983 World Cup, the spectators now were mainly those who could muscle their way into the ground with money power. This transformation translated to little knowledge of the game; and worse, a tendency to place bets on matches—the centre of such unlicensed activity being a locality in the city called Burrabazar (or big market).

Lloyd's was a fair interpretation, as India required a Herculean 132 runs from 15.5 overs. He rightly deemed it was impossible for play to continue after Aashish Kapoor's exit to a running catch in the deep by de Silva. The BCCI would have preferred the match to be awarded to Sri Lanka on the basis of their better run rate. Jayasuriya compensated his batting failure by capturing three for 12 in seven overs in addition to taking two catches and executing a run-out.

Bizarrely, the presentation ceremony proceeded amidst smoking stands. Post-match interviews were carried out in the same atmosphere. It was an unnerving sight for folks from outside the subcontinent, whether at the ground or watching on TV.

The riot, not Sri Lanka's splendid recovery after an awkward start, hogged the headlines. Genuine cricket lovers in Kolkata squirmed in embarrassment. Others were furious over the failure of their players. Sadly, Azhar had to be given armed security at his Hyderabad residence.

Toss: India
Man of the Match: PA de Silva
Sri Lanka 251/8 in 50 overs (Aravinda de Silva 66, Roshan Mahanama 58 retired hurt, Javagal Srinath 3/34, Sachin Tendulkar 2/34). **India** 120/8 in 34.1 overs (Sachin Tendulkar 65, Sanath Jayasuriya 3/12).

This became Siddhu's last World Cup appearance for India. A few months later, he walked out of a tour of England after a spat with Azharuddin, never to return to international cricket. Said to be a loner as a cricketer, he recoined himself as a talkative TV personality and wit. His comic yet creative use of language was a concealed talent he has consequently revealed. He also remained in the limelight by getting elected to the Indian Parliament from the city of Amritsar, which houses Sikhdom's holy of holies, the Golden Temple. In 2014, though, he was denied a ticket to seek re-election.

Semifinal, 14 March: Punjab Cricket Association Stadium, Mohali

At this splendid facility on the outskirts of Chandigarh, Punjab and Haryana states' common capital and a city planned by a French architect, Le Corbusier, the match appeared to be over when Australia after 40 minutes were 15 for four on a pitch with a lining of grass on it. It seemed like the worst decision in the tournament by a captain after winning the toss. Ambrose and Bishop had blasted out the Waughs twins, Ricky Ponting and Taylor for a total of four runs. But hereafter it was runs not ruins, as Stuart Law and Michael Bevan at first defended steadfastly and then ventured into shots to realize 138 in 32 overs. This endeavour boosted the score past 200, which seemed unreachable after the initial rout.

But even after Warne removed Courtney Browne with his first ball, the target looked well within the West Indies' grasp. Indeed, they were 165 for two, requiring a mere 41 from the last nine. Lara had departed but Shivnarine Chanderpaul appeared to be closing in on a century and Richie Richardson on a-happier-than-envisaged ending to his captaincy. However, as soon as the Guyanese left-hander—hamstrung by cramps—left, incredible panic set in. Stroke players Roger Harper and Ottis Gibson were sent in to finish the job, but their short-lived stays only augmented the pressure. Jimmy

Adams and Keith Arthurton soon fell. Australia were now in the reckoning for the first time, and they strengthened their hold when Warne took three for six off his next three overs. Richardson, though, was still unbeaten and the one to face Fleming as he started the final over. He despatched the first ball for four, so West Indies needed six from five deliveries, with two wickets in hand. But he now set off for a thoughtless single, which not only ran out Ambrose, but also left Walsh with the strike. Walsh attempted a cross-batted heave to be bowled. The last eight wickets, thus, capitulated for a motley 29 runs, and the West Indies snatched an exceptional defeat from the jaws of victory. In contrast, Taylor had marvellously kept his cool. He later generously admitted West Indies had won 95 per cent of the match.

Toss: Australia
Man of the Match: SK Warne
Australia 207/8 in 50 overs (Stuart Law 72, Michael Bevan 69, Curtly Ambrose 2/26, Ian Bishop 2/35). **West Indies** 202 all out in 49.3 overs (Shivnarine Chanderpaul 80, Richie Richardson 49*, Brian Lara 45, Shane Warne 4/36, Glenn McGrath 2/30).

Final, 17 March: Gaddafi Stadium, Lahore (Day/Night)

The province of Punjab was vivisected when British-ruled India was partitioned into today's India and Pakistan. The state, therefore, falls on both sides of the border between the two countries, with the bigger slice and the capital of the undivided region—Lahore, the pride of Punjabis—falling under Pakistani jurisdiction.

It was the first day/night international to be played in Pakistan.

Conditions in this northern part of the country were cool and there was hardly any sunlight, following overnight storms. The dampness notwithstanding, the Australians would have batted first. But Ranatunga's decision to field was made in quest of some early wickets from his seamers. He also backed his batsmen to chase down a target rather than set one.

But the show didn't quite go according to plan. The generally accurate Chaminda Vaas pitched too short, although Sri Lanka did succeed in removing the dangerous Mark Waugh with the new ball as he flicked a half-volley to square-leg. Not that this made a vast difference, for Taylor and Ponting carried the score to 137 by the 27th over, before the captain mistimed a sweep and his partner missed a cut. De Silva, the successful bowler, in fact, produced five overs of off-spin for two wickets, conceding just 19 runs.

Hence the newcomers to the crease were exposed to a quartet of spinners, who increasingly made the ball bite off the track. Such bowling was indeed discomfiting. The incoming batsmen were hard put to pierce the in-field, let alone sound the boundary boards. Where Taylor had struck eight fours and a six, his colleagues managed only five fours between them; and not one such stroke materialized from the 24th to the 49th over, other than Law pulling a six. The balance, therefore, shifted quite dramatically and only 178 runs were registered by the 40th over, not to mention the loss of five wickets. The wily Ranatunga had implacably tightened his grip over the match.

The gritty Australians fought back, though, by taking two early wickets. By the sixth over, Jayasuriya had been run out and Kaluwitharana had spooned a pull to square-leg. Law, then, spilled Gurusinha at deep midwicket when he was 53 and three half-chances also went down. The evening dew also made it harder for the spinners, Warne and Mark Waugh, to grip the ball.

Gurusinha rubbed salt into the wound by hitting Warne for four to long-on and six over long-off from successive deliveries. Such activity triggered acceleration at both ends, as de Silva settled in with characteristic elan. After Gurusinha departed to an indiscreet slog, the portly right-hander retreated to taking singles and only punishing the bad ball so as to enable the new man, Ranatunga, to get his eye in. Once this was accomplished, they took a dozen off a Mark Waugh over. Sri Lanka needed 51 from the last ten overs, after the required rate had risen to almost a run a ball. This figure became a mere 10 off five as de Silva completed a masterly hundred, only the third three-figure knock in a World Cup final (after Clive Lloyd in 1975 and Viv Richards in 1979)—and signed off with 107, which included 13 meticulous fours.

Australia had run out of answers in their third searching encounter in a week. And a side batting second had won for the first time in six World Cup finals. Sri Lanka had controlled the match almost throughout. Their batting was more adept at handling spin; their spinners froze the opposition after the medium pacers conceded 72 runs in the first 13 overs; and their catching and fielding were faultless. Only in the pace department did the Aussies have an edge.

Toss: Sri Lanka
Man of the Match: PA de Silva
Man of the Series: ST Jayasuriya
Australia 241/7 in 50 overs (Mark Taylor 74, Ricky Ponting 45, Aravinda de Silva 3/42, Muttiah Muralitharan 1/31). **Sri Lanka** 245/3 in 46.2 overs (Aravinda de Silva 107*, Asanka Gurusinha 65, Arjuna Ranatunga 47*, Damien Fleming 1/43, Paul Reiffel 1/49).

The rain returned as soon as Prime Minister Benazir Bhutto presented the Wills World Cup to Ranatunga, playing his fourth such competition. The crowd sympathy lay with Sri Lanka. The Australians had earlier not exactly charmed Pakistanis by expressing reservations about Saleem Malik, who had been suspected of taking bribes. A well-organized climax was watched by a stadium bursting at the seams, although the official capacity was no more than 23,826.

The adoption of pinch-hitters to take advantage of the first 15 overs, when fielding restrictions applied, was in evidence in the tournament. The better batting wickets of the subcontinent lent themselves to such innovation. Sri Lanka, through their bombardiers, Jayasuriya—later to be heralded the Most Valued Player of the Tournament—and Kaluwitharana, took over from where Mark Greatbatch of New Zealand had left off in 1992. As the outcome proved, none of the others did it better.

As a sidelight, Taylor's sportsmanship, in refusing to claim a slip catch at a pivotal stage against the West Indies, was laudatory. The brilliant batting of Mark Waugh and Tendulkar also made a big impression. Besides, the catch by Kenya's beefy, bespectacled and none-too-nimble wicket-keeper, Tariq Iqbal, to dismiss Lara testified a spirit that took Kenya to victory by 73 runs over the West Indies. Here was a great upset of the World Cup; and a bad portent for West Indian cricket. For their part, Kenyans embraced the big stage without inhibition.

Defeat, however, acted as a tonic and the West Indies rallied to reach the last eight—lifted by a 93 not out from their beleaguered captain, Richie

Richardson, against Australia at the league stage—and then proceeded to get the better of South Africa in the quarter final. The South Africans had, in fact, played impressive cricket before this fixture.

The tournament achieved one aim, that of increasing the profile of cricket through television coverage on a technically impressive but slightly uncritical scale. It also generated unprecedented income, much to the satisfaction of the organizers and the participating boards. But, perhaps, the most lingering memory of this World Cup was the unbridled joy of its unexpected winners, Sri Lanka.

THE 1999 WORLD CUP

The aberration of the 1992 World Cup in Australia being held five and not four years after the previous competition was corrected in 1999, when the event, returning to England after 16 years, took place three, not four years after the 6th edition. In effect, the tournament was restored to the quadrennial frequency as envisaged at its inception in 1975.

For this latest edition, the England and Wales Cricket Board (ECB) divided the 12 participants into two groups, with the top three in each group qualifying for a Super Six face-off, while retaining the points they had obtained from the two teams that had also made the cut from their group. They then met the qualifying teams from the other group, with the top four on points cumulatively, entering the semifinals.

The format was complicated, and it backfired. Teams on equal points after the Super Six phase were to be separated by who won between them. There were, though, three-way ties in both qualifying groups; and New Zealand and Zimbabwe, fourth and fifth in the Super Six, had shared the one washed-out game of the tournament. So, to resolve dead heats one had to fall back on net run rate, which meant a reliance on calculators rather than cricket.

In other words the tournament boiled down to technical knockouts, with even a semifinal, which ended in a tie, being decided on net run rate in the Super Six stage. Earlier, Zimbabwe had topped their group to make it to the Super Six. They had beaten teams that went through with them, but lost to the two that were eliminated. Such complexities rather befuddled followers of the tournament and converted a potentially exciting encounter at the group level—Australia versus the West Indies—into a ludicrous affair, as both teams attempted to manipulate the system to their advantage.

The West Indians would have gone through if they had won in a more business-like manner against Bangladesh, whereas England's demise was due to a lack of vigilance about the pitfalls created by their own officials. The England dream was the World Cup would reignite affection for cricket in the hearts of their youngsters, who had become disillusioned as a result of losing the Ashes—all-important in the English psyche—six times running.

Administratively, the 1999 World Cup looked doomed from the start. The ECB had rejected the hitherto accepted concept of a sole sponsor and wanted eight commercial partners, who would be entitled to utilizing all prime advertising space. To their dismay, they got commitments from only four, two of whom (NatWest and Vodafone) were already firm sponsors of English cricket; the others were Pepsi and Emirates Airlines, the latter paying half its contribution in the form of air passages instead of cash.

Besides, the tournament got underway in mid-May, generally too early for international cricket in England. Indeed, a drizzle spoilt the opening ceremony. As it is, a grand, Olympic-style unveiling was eschewed; only a modest fireworks display was in evidence.

15 May: Hove

The setting and the 6,000 spectators created a fairground atmosphere at the dwelling of Sussex County Cricket Club—whose colours Ranji, Duleep and the junior Pataudi had worn with distinction from the late 19th century to the 1960s. But this ambience and a fitting finish were darkened by the unethical conduct—certainly against the spirit of the game—of the South Africans. Hansie Cronje and Allan Donald were wired up with earphones in a three-way live radio link with coach, Bob Woolmer, who, sitting in the dressing room, enjoying the benefit of TV close-ups and without the pressure of having to think on his feet, was happily rendering advice. With sticking plaster over the earpieces, the captain and premier pace bowler had even attempted to camouflage the instruments (and perhaps also to prevent these from falling off). Such subterfuge prevailed for an hour before referee, Talat Ali, scrutinizing the TV pictures, put a stop to the nonsense. It was baffling that India did not lodge a serious protest. It was also pathetic that the ICC took no meaningful action against South Africa. They meekly proscribed the practice for the rest of the tournament.

While much has strenuously been argued to the contrary, the incident bespoke a character lacuna in Cronje, not that the other two were any less innocent. It was, therefore, unsurprising he was later convicted of match fixing (credit for identifying such involvement went to Delhi's police). As K. K. Paul, the detective (later police commissioner) who unearthed the conspiracy, revealed to me, this was by accident, as they were intercepting phone calls for a different purpose when they stumbled on a clinching conversation between Cronje and an illegal bookmaker.

Where others may have escaped the net in a murky phase in world cricket, thanks to officers like Paul, Cronje did not. Other countries pontificated aplenty on the subject of corruption, but most failed to deliver up until several Pakistani cricketers were imprisoned for taking bribes to under-perform in England in 2010.

India, batting first, lost Sachin Tendulkar during the South African remote conferencing—not that this element was necessarily to blame for the exit. The little master had promised much only to disappoint. Sourav Ganguly and Rahul Dravid, though, persevered to realize 130 between them. The former, playing in his 100th one-day international, was in good touch. But the duo failed to drive home their dominance in the face of a characteristically restrictive Donald. The Kolkata left-hander took the high risk of testing Jonty Rhodes' arm.

Mysorean Javagal Srinath, genuinely fast, removed Gary Kirsten and Herschelle Gibbs early. But an unruffled Jacques Kallis steered his side to within 27 runs of victory, with 26 balls to come. After he was run out by Venkatesh Prasad, Lance Klusener bludgeoned his first three deliveries for four. The rest was easy. As the fielders headed back to the pavilion, a spectator got too close to Azhar and Dravid for comfort. This prompted the Indian captain to call for greater security.

Toss: India
Man of the Match: JH Kallis
India 253/5 in 50 overs (Sourav Ganguly 97, Rahul Dravid 54, Lance Klusener 3/66). **South Africa** 254/6 in 47.2 overs (Jacque Kallis 96, Jonty Rhodes 39*, Mark Boucher 34, Javagal Srinath 2/69).

19 May: Leicester

4,000 excited fans, a noticeable number of them East African Gujaratis settled in this East Midlands city, watched the closest contest of the tournament up to this point. India won the toss and invited Zimbabwe to bat. But other than when Andy Flower and Alistair Campbell were at the crease, the Zimbabweans failed to make sufficiently brisk progress. Undisciplined Indian bowling, though, gifted 51 extras, a fifth of the total. Consequently, the over rate was also so badly affected that four overs were deducted when India batted. Zimbabwe were no great shakes either on this front: they permitted 39 sundries, which created a World Cup record for a match, but one which was to survive only for a day. Nayan Mongia, with five dismissals, equalled the ODI record for a wicketkeeper, held by among others his compatriot Syed Kirmani.

India started smoothly, rattling up 44 in the seventh over before Dravid departed. Left-handed Sadagopan Ramesh, replacing Tendulkar who had flown back to Mumbai to attend his father's funeral, and Ajay Jadeja added 99 before Ramesh skied to mid-on. The middle order kept up the pace. Srinath, then, produced two massive sixes, and India needed only nine runs from two overs. Now, Henry Olonga was reintroduced. He had been quite wayward in his previous spell, which cost 17 runs in three overs. This time, Robin Singh holed out to cover off his second ball, Srinath was yorked by his fifth and Prasad was lbw to the last. Zimbabwe triumphed by three runs. They had played two matches and won as many; whereas India had lost both their outings.

Toss: India
Man of the Match: GW Flower
Zimbabwe 252/9 in 50 overs (Andy Flower 68*, Grant Flower 45, Javagal Srinath 2/35, Venkatesh Prasad 2/37, Anil Kumble 2/41). **India** 249 all out in 45 overs (Sadagopan Ramesh 55, Ajay Jadeja 43, Henry Olonga 3/22, Heath Streak 3/36).

23 May: Bristol

Kenya sought to improve their chances by putting India in. Indeed, the game was still in the balance with India on 92 for two when Tendulkar, back from his father's cremation the day before, entered the fray. An 8,500 crowd at this headquarters of Gloucestershire County Cricket Club thunderously greeted his advent. In an emotionally charged environment, he responded with a resounding display. He began cautiously, but soon stepped on the pedal to acquire 50 off 54 balls and then 100 in 84. He concluded by clipping the last ball of the innings for six over midwicket—his third over-boundary in addition to 16 fours. His 140 came off only 101 balls. It was his first ODI hundred not as an opener and a fairytale return after a personal tragedy. It went unnoticed that at the other end, Dravid, too, produced a sublime century and the pair added a World Cup record-breaking 237 in 29 overs. This partnership surpassed the 207 by the Waugh brothers, also against Kenya in 1996.

Kenya were shell-shocked by the Tendulkar-led assault. Their first boundary did not materialize until the 10th over. Still, Steve Tikolo and Kennedy Otieno stitched together 118. Anil Kumble and Venkatesh Prasad were injured and missing from the Indian attack, but Debasis Mohanty, from Orissa, markedly bending the ball both ways, compensated for their absence. The lasting memory, though, was of Tendulkar's ton. He dedicated his highest World Cup score to his late father. After two defeats, it revived India's hopes of making the short-list for the Super Six. India won by 94 runs.

Toss: Kenya
Man of the Match: SR Tendulkar
India 329/2 in 50 overs (Sachin Tendulkar 140*, Rahul Dravid 104*, Martin Suji 1/26). **Kenya** 235/7 (Steve Tikolo 58, Kennedy Otieno 56, Debasis Mohanty4/56).

26 May: Taunton

Nearly 7,000 assembled at this old-fashioned west country ground (made famous by Ian Botham, Vivian Richards and Joel Garner), home of Somerset County Cricket Club. Arjuna Ranatunga won the toss and sent India in, possibly anticipating some assistance for his quicker bowlers.

When Chaminda Vaas cut one back to dislodge Ramesh's off-stump, it seemed he may have got it right. But the wicket was of consistent bounce and the straight boundaries relatively short. Consequently, Ganguly and Dravid dished out an exotic exhibition to establish a clutch of ODI records. Their staggering stand of 318 in 45 overs was the highest in any ODI, eclipsing the previous record of 275 notched up by Azharuddin and Jadeja against Zimbabwe in 1997–98. Ganguly clobbered 183 off 158 balls, then the fourth-highest ODI score, with seven sixes and 16 fours. In World Cups, this was second only to Gary Kirsten's 188 not out against the United Arab Emirates in 1996. India's 373 for six was the highest versus test opposition in the World Cup, although behind Sri Lanka's 398 for five against Kenya also in 1996. The left-hander–right-hander combination worked to perfection. Ganguly, reminiscent of another Bengal left-hander, Ambar Roy, timed the ball beautifully; his century came off 119 deliveries. He then demonstrated what a good striker of the ball he was by collecting the rest of his runs in 39 balls. (Presumptuously nicknamed 'Maharaj', he has, by a section of his fellow Bengalis, been adoringly tagged with the epaulette of 'Prince' of his city of Kolkata after the former England opener, now commentator, Geoffrey Boycott referred to him as such. In circumstances where his state of West Bengal has produced few regular incumbents in the Indian side, his success has been a dizzying experience for such Bengalis, including much of Kolkata's overwhelmed media.) Dravid was less spectacular, yet he posted virtually a run-a-ball hundred—his second in successive matches. Even the wondrous Muttiah Muralitharan was at his wits' end.

Sri Lanka reinstated Romesh Kaluwitharana as opener. But both he and Sanath Jayasuriya, great successes in 1996, were back in the dressing room within five overs. The game then petered out into an inevitable defeat for the Sri Lankans. And with it, dissipated their hopes of retaining the title.

Toss: Sri Lanka
Man of the Match: SC Ganguly
India 373/6 in 50 overs (Sourav Ganguly 183, Rahul Dravid 145, Pramodya Wickramasinghe 3/65). **Sri Lanka** 216 all out in 42.3 overs (Aravinda de Silva 56, Arjuna Ranatunga 42, Robin Singh 5/31).

29–30 May: Edgbaston, Birmingham

On a lovely, sunny morning, before a capacity 20,000 crowd, Alec Stewart won his fifth toss of the tournament and elected to field. The pitch was a slow seamer, and the English bowlers exploited it well by not allowing any liberties to the Indian batsmen. Ganguly was unfortunate to be run out when Dravid's straight drive touched bowler Mark Ealham's fingertips before hitting the non-striker's stumps. But this setback was offset by Tendulkar escaping a run-out and a catch before he eventually hit Ealham down midwicket's throat. So, Dravid's 82-ball 53 became the highest score for the Indians.

An ominous cloud cover came to preside over play when England batted. Such conditions were ideal for Mohanty's swing bowling. Stewart and Graeme Hick were out to him off consecutive legal deliveries (as the one in between was a wide). Nasser Hussain then succumbed in deteriorating light, before a torrential downpour halted play. England were 73 for three in 20.3 overs, with Graham Thorpe, quite the most skilful of the English batsmen, unbeaten on 36. The match resumed the next morning—the only group tie in the tournament to spill over into the reserve day. To England's disappointment—and English media unduly fretted over this decision—Thorpe was ruled leg before wicket by umpire Javed Akhtar. Neil Fairbrother tried to keep the score ticking, but without much support. England were, consequently, eliminated at the preliminary stage of a World Cup for the first time; and calamitously, this debacle occurred at home.

England had arrived at Birmingham reasonably certain of a Super Six place. But Zimbabwe's giant killing of South Africa meant they had no alternative to beating India. When the weather was no longer a factor—on the second day—their batsmen crumbled to pressure. Also, contributing to the exit was their defeat at the hands of South Africa and the lackadaisical approach in their three victories. For young Andrew Flintoff, a conspicuous failure in the tournament, the final insult was having his bat nicked from the dressing room.

Toss: England
Man of the Match: SC Ganguly

India 232/8 in 50 overs (Rahul Dravid 53, Sourav Ganguly 40, Mark Ealham 2/28, Darren Gough 2/51, Alan Mullally 2/54). **England** 169 all out in 45.2 overs (Graham Thorpe 36, Nasser Hussain 33, Sourav Ganguly 3/27, Javagal Srinath 2/25, Anil Kumble 2/30).

Super Six, 4 June: The Oval, London

India invited Australia to bat, but an excellent team effort, spearheaded by Mark Waugh—who got 83—set the Indians 283 to win, a target never achieved in a 50-over ODI in England.

Then, in four impeccable overs, McGrath emphatically ensured history would not be created. With remarkable accuracy and movement off the wicket, he constricted India to an unenviable 17 for four. He removed Tendulkar for a duck—a prized wicket since this Mumbai maestro had scored hundreds in his last three appearances against the Aussies—and the others just caved in. Jadeja and Robin Singh rallied to realize 141 for the fifth wicket, with the former posting three figures—so far the fifth in the competition, all by Indians. It was a brave but fruitless endeavour, for the result was never in doubt once McGrath had sliced through the top order. Twenty-one runs in Warne's 6th over, though, brought a cheer from the sizeable Indian supporters among the 18,000 attendees. Australia eventually won by 77 runs.

Both teams had made it to the Super Six without any points, or wins against other qualifiers, from their respective groups. The reverse for India, therefore, reduced their chances of advancing to the semifinals. Interestingly, speculation about the suitability of the white ball in English conditions (used for one-day cricket, as opposed to the traditional red leather in test matches) increased after this match. The debate was generated by a proliferation of wides in the tournament, which insinuated difficulty on the part of bowlers to control the ball. Now, it was suggested that it was hard to keep track of in gloomy light.

Toss: India
Man of the Match: GD McGrath
Australia 282/6 in 50 overs (Mark Waugh 83, Steve Waugh 36, Robin Singh 2/43). **India** 205 all out in 48.2 overs (Ajay Jadeja 100*, Robin Singh 75, Glenn McGrath 3/34, Steve Waugh 2/8, Damien Fleming 2/33).

Super Six, 8 June: Old Trafford, Manchester

With 22,000 animated spectators made up of Indians, Pakistanis and indigenous folks packing the stands on a sparkling day, India won the toss, but made heavy weather with the bat. Tendulkar took off momentarily, and held the stage initially to cross 8,000 ODI runs. But Dravid struggled to penetrate the gaps in the field and got rather bogged down. Skipper Azharuddin, though, proficiently farmed the strike and, as the overs started to run out, rose to a crescendo. During his innings, he added 60 in nine overs with Robin Singh.

The destination for Pakistan was 228; and the classy Saeed Anwar made light of this journey with a barrage of half-a-dozen fours. But the pacy Srinath started the rot before transferring the baton to Prasad, his Karnataka teammate. The latter, cutting the ball off the wicket as was his wont, scalped Saleem Malik, Anwar, Moin Khan, who briefly threatened to take the game away from the Indians with his 34, Inzamam, untypically out of touch during his 30-over stay, and Wasim Akram, playing at his adopted home of Lancashire, caught on the square-leg boundary trying to force the pace. Prasad's figures of five for 27 were an authentic reflection of his incisiveness. In course of his career, he rendered yeoman service to Indian cricket as a seamer; his leg-cutters being particularly effective. On this occasion, his compatriots on and off the field were ecstatic.

While widely acknowledged to be the better one-day side in the 1990s, Pakistan had, now, lost all three encounters to their arch-rivals in the World Cup—in 1992, 1996 and now. And Azhar and Tendulkar had been members of the Indian team in all such successes.

The clash between India and Pakistan, whose armies were then locked in combat in the freezing Himalayan heights of Kargil in Jammu and Kashmir state, had caused concern about resultant tension spilling over to England. Security in and around the ground and in sensitive South Asian neighbourhoods elsewhere was especially tight. But in the end, three arrests, nine ejections and one flag-burning (of the Indian tricolour) incident during a fracas between rival groups were less alarming than apprehended. Indeed, the lively behaviour of the fans—flag waving, whistle blowing and drum beating—introduced an almost unprecedented spectacle to a cricket match in England.

Toss: India
Man of the Match: BKV Prasad
India 227/6 in 50 overs (Rahul Dravid 61, Mohammed Azharuddin 59, Sachin Tendulkar 45, wasim Akram 2/27, Azhar Mahmood 2/35). **Pakistan** 180 all out in 45.3 overs (Inzamam-ul-Haq 41, Saeed Anwar 36Moin Khan 34, Venkatesh Prasad 5/27, Javagal Srinath 3/37, Anil Kumble 2/43).

Super Six, 12 June: Trent Bridge, Nottingham

India were fortunate with the coin, but the pitch proved to be less dependable than envisaged. Their batsmen misjudged the track by being flamboyant where a little watchfulness might have paid dividends. They looked stylish, but their stay in the middle was temporary. The only one who seemed to understand the trick was Jadeja. He showed patience, particularly during the middle overs, before cashing in later. Circumspection was demanded against Geoff Allott, who was constantly threatening and became the first bowler to bag 20 wickets in a solitary World Cup. Less caution may have been justified against the other New Zealand bowlers.

The Kiwi openers set off at close to five an over and the run rate always hovered around this rate. Mathew Horne was asked to anchor the innings and did so dutifully. In the context of the match, this performance was priceless, though his 74 was nothing special in terms of batsmanship. Roger Twose, on the other hand, was demonstrating the hardiness of an Antipodean from the outreaches of the southern hemisphere. With 58 runs required off as many balls, rain stopped play for over an hour. This interruption could have played havoc with a batsman's concentration. It didn't in his case. New Zealand won by five wickets. It was a victory of temperament over talent.

Even a win would not have elevated India to the semifinal. Only once in 12 matches prior to this had a target of 250 proved inadequate—that was when India lost to South Africa in the opening game. It emphasized the point that India's bowling was quite harmless in less-than-helpful situations. In the run-up to the tournament, it had been marketed as a carnival. But when Azhar and Steve Waugh strongly objected to the post-match field invasions, the organizers clamped down to the extent of scolding Indian supporters among the over 14,000 spectators at this match for being too noisy. Unsurprisingly, they were not amused.

Toss: India
Man of the Match: RG Twose
India 251/6 in 50 overs (Ajay Jadeja 76, Chris Cairns 2/44). **New Zealand** 253/5 in 48.2 overs (Matt Horne 74, Roger Twose 60*, Debasis Mohanty 2/41).

The match proved to be Azharuddin's last hoorah in the World Cup. He continued to turn out for India in ODIs as well as tests until 2000, when the BCCI, quite sensationally, found him guilty of match fixing and banned him for life from all cricket under their auspices. Uniquely, he blazed hundreds in his first and last tests; but was denied further distinction. He was left stranded one short of 100 appearances.

Jadeja, too, followed Azhar into oblivion for the same reason, but his suspension was revoked by a court order in 2005; and he, therefore, returned to first-class cricket.

Mongia also got the chop. He, too, was suspected of match-fixing.

Semifinal, 16 June: Old Trafford, Manchester

The most valuable partnership in New Zealand's innings against Pakistan, after they won the toss, stemmed from Stephen Fleming and Twose, who put on 94. But Shoaib Akhtar was at his fastest and he sent Fleming's stump cartwheeling with a spectacular yorker. Indeed, in his allotted overs, spread over three spells, he made a stunning impact. As his captain commented after the match, pace does matter in one-day cricket. All the same, the Kiwis compiled a fighting total of 241, albeit helped by 47 extras carelessly contributed by the Pakistanis.

The New Zealand effort was, however, made to look ridiculous by an opening essay of 194 runs between Anwar and Wajahatullah Wasti—a World Cup record for the first wicket. Indeed, they looked like completing the assignment on their own when the latter made his exit in the 41st over. Anwar continued to record a hundred in consecutive matches—his 17th in ODIs, which brought him level with Desmond Haynes, with only Tendulkar ahead of him. Ijaz Ahmed joined the party to crack 28 off 21 balls. Some overexcited Pakistani supporters among the 22,000 spectators ran on to the field when their side were still six runs short of victory. This intrusion held up play for 10 minutes. When play resumed, Twose could not attempt to catch what was awarded as Anwar's match-winning stroke—a lofted off-drive—as the crowd invaded the green. The two runs needed were never actually completed as the players raced to the pavilion for safety. It was an explosive entry into the final in more ways than one, with their fans setting off firecrackers the way people in Pakistanis in tribal areas fire machine guns in the air to mark celebration. Security was lax; Fleming appealed for stricter measures, fanning demand for the hitherto unthinkable in England—fencing off of spectators.

Toss: New Zealand
Man of the Match: Shoaib Akhtar
New Zealand 241/7 in 50 overs (roger Twose 46, Chris Cairns 44*, Stephen Fleming 41, Shoaib Akhtar 3/55, Abdul Razzaq 2/28, wasim Akram 2/45).
Pakistan 242/1 in 47.3 overs (Saeed Anwar 113*, Wajahatullah wasti 84, Chris Cairns 1/33).

Semifinal, 17 June: Edgbaston, Birmingham

The match glittered with shining performances. South Africa sent Australia in. Shaun Pollock, striking form, which had eluded him earlier in the tournament, was marvellously penetrative. His comrade-in-arms, the fast and furious Donald, picked up a pair of wickets in as many overs. Kallis, despite nursing an injury on his waist, bowled with speed and accuracy. But Steve Waugh and Bevan crafted a recovery, which initially indicated restraint, thereafter scientific hitting.

Kallis led the chase with an unruffled 50. Then, Shane Warne skittled Herschelle Gibbs' stumps with a prodigiously turning leg-break. His first eight overs cost only 12 runs. He grabbed three more wickets. However, Man of the Tournament Klusener's hefty hitting motored South Africa to the brink of victory. He had been quite unstoppable in the tournament; now he pummelled 31 runs off 14 balls, converting a tough target into a cakewalk. At the non-striker's end was Donald, if not anything else, a seasoned campaigner. It was a re-run for Damien Fleming, who had bowled the last over in the semifinal against the West Indies four years before, which Australia won. This time, though, Klusener despatched the first two balls of the over for fours. Only one run was required off four balls, with the brawny left-hander facing the bowling. Steve Waugh predictably tightened the ring of fielders saving the single. Klusener drove the next ball straight. Donald, taking too much of a start, would have been run out had Darren Lehman's throw been more accurate. The following delivery, Klusener drove to mid-on and then dashed off for a single. Donald, who had stayed put inside his crease, in a late reaction dropped his bat and set off in response. Mark Waugh returned the ball to Fleming, who in a piece of quick thinking, rolled it to Gilchrist, who whipped off the bails to run out Donald. South Africa had choked. The match had dramatically ended in a tie.

This was not just *the* match of the tournament, but one of the most memorable ODIs ever played. The outcome meant South Africa were ousted because of the critical fact that Australia had finished higher than them in the Super Six table by virtue of a better net run rate. Many among the 20,000 odd spectators were left bewildered.

Toss: South Africa
Man of the Match: SK Warne
Australia 213 all out in 49.2 overs (Michael Bevan 65, Steve Waugh 56, Shaun Pollock 5/36, Allan Donald 4/32). **South Africa** 213 all out in 49.4 overs (Jacques Kallis 53, Jonty Rhodes 43, Shane Warne 4/29).

Final, 20 June: Lord's, London

Wasim Akram chose to bat and this was probably the right decision, for the wicket looked amenable to a decent total. Anwar struck three fours at the expense of Fleming, who rather sprayed it around. But that was the end of the purple patch for Pakistan. Wasti flirted with a ball from McGrath that deviated and jumped and Mark Waugh flung himself to his right to bring off a classic slip catch with both hands. For Australia, the wheels were now in motion.

Anwar played on. For a while, Abdul Razzaq and Ijaz Ahmed looked comfortable, although the former got a reprieve when he was spilled at long-off. The escape, though, was short-lived as soon afterwards Steve Waugh made no mistake at extra cover. With the Pakistanis wobbling at 69 for three after 21 overs, Waugh introduced Warne. This virtually settled the issue. The leg-spinner conjured amazing turn to get rid of Ijaz, who had been resisting tenaciously. The ball pitched around leg and hit off. It veritably unnerved the rest of the Pakistani batting. They counterattacked, but for every boundary hit, a stroke was clipped into the safe hands of an Australian fielder. To add insult to injury, Inzamam was given out caught behind by umpire David Shepherd off the batsman's pad. The Sultan of Multan stared in disbelief and walked off somewhat reluctantly. When Wasim skied a catch, Warne pocketed four wickets, which boosted his tally for the tournament to 20, a joint record for the World Cup with Allott of New Zealand. McGrath wrapped up the innings when Ponting maintained his team's dizzy standard of catching with a take at third slip. Pakistan were bundled out for 132 in the 39th over.

In reply, Adam Gilchrist set off like the French TGV. Shoaib was a bit unfortunate when his first delivery was snicked by Gilchrist and fell perilously close to long-leg. Thereafter, the ball thudded into the boundary boards with a rapidity that dashed all hope of any twist or turn relieving Pakistan. Gilchrist's 50 transpired off 33 balls. He was, in fact, back in the dressing room by the 11th over. It took only another 10 overs for Australia to accomplish their task, in course of which Mark Waugh crossed 1,000 World Cup runs. Australia had utilized only 121 balls when Lehman unleashed the winning stroke.

The victory paired the Aussies with the West Indies in winning the World Cup a second time. This, the 200th World Cup match, had been decided in less than 60 overs. The first World Cup final at Lord's 24 years almost to the day had consumed nearly twice as many overs and lasted all of ten hours.

Those who, reportedly, paid touts £2,500 for a ticket may have felt cheated, unless they were rich Australians. Pakistan, who had earlier seemed promising, had been thoroughly exposed. It was, as the cliché went, always a question of which Pakistani side would turn up. In the event, the wrong one did. Uniquely for Lord's, to control a secton of the crowd, announcements were made in Urdu, Pakistan's national language. This precaution, though, did not deter overrunning of the outfield. Akram later remarked Pakistan could have defended 180. Such a claim seemed unrealistic.

The crowd of 28,000 was, however, replete with bored bystanders. The involvement and exuberance appeared to be greater outside the perimeter of the premises. Dozens of Pakistani fans stood atop a building site with a bird's eye view of proceedings. But the police soon evacuated the vantage point and expelled the enthusiasts from that area.

Australia regained the World Cup after 12 years and, thereby, the best test team in the planet also became the world one-day champions. In short, they emerged as the undisputed champions of cricket, an honour held by the West Indies in the late 1970s and early 1980s. The West Indies surrendered their unqualified dominance when India beat them—at this very ground 16 years earlier.

Toss: Pakistan
Man of the Match: SK Warne
Player of the Tournament: L Klusener (SA)
Pakistan 132 all out in 39 overs (Ijaz Ahmed 22, Shane Warne 4/33, Glenn McGrath 2/13, Tom Moody 2/17). **Australia** 133/2 in 20.1 overs (Adam Gilchrist 54, Mark Waugh 37*, Saqlain Mushtaq 1/21).

When Australia embarked on their final group match, they were in serious danger of early elimination. It was an equally close call during their last Super Six match. But having made it to the final by the skin of their teeth, they redeemed themselves when it mattered the most.

Indigenous Englishmen understandably lost interest after England's early exit. But the English of South Asian descent happily failed the Tebbit test—of loyalty to the United Kingdom, once advocated by a British cabinet minister Norman Tebbit—by supporting countries of their origin.

All 18 English county headquarters staged at least one match. The other three were outside the beaten track—Edinburgh, Dublin and Amstelveen in Holland.

Fortunately, the despised (though sometimes necessary) Duckworth/Lewis method of determining weather affected matches (devised by Frank Duckworth and Tony Lewis, the latter a Welshman and former captain of England) was never employed. It was generally believed that the team batting second had an advantage because of morning moisture. But among the teams batting first, 19 won and 21 lost, thus throwing up a hung jury. Of course, captains more frequently opted to field after winning the toss in May than June, when it was warmer.

The lacquered white ball was reckoned to be harder than its red counterpart. It seemed to swing more, including in reverse, which the bowlers couldn't always control, thus conceding 979 wides. But bowlers, reduced to cannon fodder in the 1996 World Cup, competed on equal terms with batsmen. Often, the 15th over passed with little change in the close-in cordon.

Jayasuriya, pinch-hitter *par excellence* in 1996, scored only 82 in five matches this time. The defending champions were a shadow of their former selves. Their captain Arjuna Ranatunga was duly sacked, as was his English counterpart Stewart.

The great shock was Bangladesh's defeat of Pakistan, who had already qualified for the Super Six, in the final fixture of the preliminary stage at Northampton. English bookmakers had offered 33-1 on a Bangladesh win. Inevitably, such odds led to an assumption the match was fixed. Wasim did not help contradict this impression by being beside himself with laughter on the pavilion balcony every time a Pakistani wicket fell and remarking after the match his side had only lost to their Muslim 'brothers'. However, there was no evidence to establish any wrongdoing. It was just a major upset. Bangladesh, who had served notice on their coach Gordon Greenidge the previous evening, were without his services in the second half of the match after he left the ground prematurely. There were joyful scenes at London's East End, where tens of thousands of British Bangladeshis reside.

Bangladesh also beat Scotland, and so finished a respectable fifth in the Group B table. But the remaining associate members of the ICC or the non-test-playing sides taking part in the tournament merely made up the numbers.

Rahul Dravid, once considered to be too slow for one-day cricket, was the leading scorer of the tournament, amassing 461 runs. His parents were downcast when the demands of cricket compelled him to discontinue his pursuit of a masters degree in business administration. They have had no regrets since.

Australian politicians jostled with each other to fete their players. In Pakistan, postmortems began. Quite unfairly, talk of bribery returned to haunt Pakistani cricket, instead of an acceptance that they had been beaten fair and square in the final.

CHAPTER FIVE

2003
Hope

IN 1994, SOUTH AFRICA HELD ITS FIRST ELECTIONS ON THE basis of universal suffrage. Its new rulers, led by the charismatic Nelson Mandela, proclaimed the new nation as a 'rainbow' republic or as a beautiful integration of the different colours of its people. This, multiracial South Africa, after decades of seclusion, spearheaded the staging of the 2003 World Cup, with Zimbabwe and Kenya as its partners.

The three African countries were keen to promote themselves as attractive tourist destinations; hence an extravagant opening ceremony in Cape Town could well have been mistaken for a travel commercial.

On the eve of Australia's opening encounter, Shane Warne, their Man of the Match in the 1999 World Cup semifinal and final, was sent home after reports confirmed he had taken performance-enhancing drugs during the Victoria Bitter (VB) Series in Australia the previous month. He was, thereafter, banned for a year, quite a light sentence considering the seriousness of the offence. Warne admitted wrongdoing, but gave a story that suggested he had committed this offence unknowingly. Acceptance of this explanation was either naivety or not in the spirit of sport. Previously, Australian authorities had taken a lenient view of Mark Waugh and Warne's confessions that they had accepted money from a bookmaker in Sri Lanka to offer their views on matches!

However, all-rounder Andy Bichel reflected Australia's depth of talent and paceman Brett Lee their incisiveness. The latter finished with 22 wickets to Chaminda Vaas' 23—a World Cup record. 'Lee is not a match winner,' taunted Shoaib Akhtar. The Pakistani bowled the fastest ball of the tournament: a 100-mph delivery against England. But despite the needling, Lee proved to be more of a match winner.

Conflicts between the World Cup's sponsors and existing contracts of players, particularly when it came to the Indians, provoked the ICC to threaten member boards with damages. In turn, the BCCI issued warnings to their players over endorsement of rival products. In the end, the ICC withheld the BCCI's share of revenue till the issue was resolved.

Meanwhile, matters extraneous to cricket, such as whether it was safe to play in Kenya and morally right to do so in Zimbabwe, given the violent and repressive nature of President Robert Mugabe's regime, afflicted the event.

The 14 teams were segregated into two groups in the first stage. In one group, New Zealand refused to play in Nairobi; in the other, England desisted from visiting Harare. The ICC awarded the matches to the hosts, which threw the tournament out of gear. Had England gone to Harare and avoided defeat, they, rather than Zimbabwe, would have reached the second phase. By winning four of the five pool matches they actually played, New Zealand reached the Super Six anyway, but the forfeiture enabled Kenya to go through at the expense of the improving West Indies and eventually qualify for the semifinal.

The ICC withheld $3.5 million from England's share of revenue and $2.5 million from New Zealand's.

Two prominent Zimbabwean players, Andy Flower and Henry Olonga, one white, the other black, took the field against Namibia in Harare wearing black armbands after issuing a statement 'mourning the death of democracy in our beloved Zimbabwe'. The ICC asked them to abstain from making political gestures. Flower said he was not making a political statement but a humanitarian plea. For what turned out to be Zimbabwe's next match—against India nine days later—the pair wore black wristbands; Olonga in his capacity as twelfth man, he having been dropped in what looked like an act of retaliation.

As the tournament continued, it appeared that the selection of Zimbabwe's team had become highly politicized, with preference given to those not critical of Mugabe's regime. Andy Pycroft, a selector, resigned after being told the team was 'non-negotiable'. It was also clear that Flower and Olonga's days as Zimbabwe players were numbered. For Flower, at 34, this prospect posed little hardship; indeed, he had already arranged to play professionally for Essex and South Australia in domestic competition in England and Australia, respectively. But in the case of Olonga, only 26, it was a considerable loss.

Public expectations of a home victory were sky high long before South Africa's opening encounter with the West Indies—graced by an accomplished hundred from Brian Lara—which the former lost by three runs. The outcome for the hosts could hardly have been worse. They failed to beat any major opposition or progress beyond the first phase of the tournament. They were trounced by New Zealand in a rain-affected match in Johannesburg, and the elements also had a say in their do-or-die affair with Sri Lanka in Durban. With South Africa needing 269 under lights, the contest was on a knife-edge when it started to rain. The dressing room sent word to the batsmen, Mark Boucher and Lance Klusener, that the Duckworth/Lewis target at the end of the following over—the 45th—was 229, provided they lost no more wickets. Boucher attained this target by hitting the fifth ball from Muttiah Muralitharan for six and then blocking the last.

But the rain had intensified and the umpires took the players off, never to return. A score of 229 actually tied the match, as Duckworth/Lewis clearly stated. While a tie was fine for Sri Lanka, it wasn't for South Africa. So, for the second World Cup in a row, South Africa lost a bit synthetically. The South African camp were justly criticized for misreading the Duckworth/Lewis Chart. But the fact remains had the electronic scoreboard at Kingsmead carried the par score, the mistake would probably not have occurred.

However, an African team, Kenya, did make it to the semifinal. Indeed, they enjoyed the greatest giant-killing run in international cricket. Yet, had they played and lost to New Zealand, they would not have made the second phase. The enthusiasm of their players, coached by Sandeep Patil, a member of the World Cup-winning Indian squad in 1983, and of their red-white-and-green-painted supporters, were a delightful sight.

Though they later lost to South Africa by 10 wickets, Kenya defended a score of 210 against Sri Lanka in Nairobi. Collins Obuya, who was inspired to bowl leg-spin by watching Mushtaq Ahmed on television in the 1996 World Cup, took five for 24 against a team normally accomplished at playing slow bowling. The Kenyans confirmed a Super Six place with an altogether less surprising victory over Bangladesh. The points from the New Zealand 'win' were carried forward to the second stage, meaning that Kenya began the Super Sixes second only to Australia, and they sealed a semifinal spot with a victory over Zimbabwe, their third over test opposition.

12 February: Paarl

It was a dream day for Holland's Tim de Leede, who had previously frequented several English county 'second XIs', but collected Sachin Tendulkar as his first World Cup wicket and proceeded to take three more. During his knock of 52, Tendulkar surpassed Javed Miandad as the highest run-getter in World Cups. (This was the Indian's fourth World Cup as compared to the Pakistani having partaken in six.) Yuvraj Singh and Dinesh Mongia, then, prevented what could have been an embarrassing total after the Indians, considered to be a dazzling batting line-up, had opted to bat first.

Of course, early wickets bagged during the Dutch reply averted any awkward moments for India. But Holland's tail did wag; and it was not until the second-last over that the winners wrapped up their opponents' innings. Daan van Bunge, a student from The Hague, scored 62. Anil Kumble, by passion a wildlife conservationist, returned career best figures in the World Cup. A wrist spinner of a faster variety, who bowls more googlies and top-spinners than leg-breaks, his wicket taking in one-day cricket in general had up to this point not been as abundant as in tests. India won by 68 runs.

Toss: India
Man of the Match: TBM de Leede
India 204 all out in 48.5 overs (Sachin Tendulkar 52, Dinesh Mongia 42, Yuvraj Singh 37, Tim de Leede 4/35, Adeel Raja 2/47). **Netherlands** 136 all out in 48.1 overs (Daan van Bunge 62, Javagal Srinath 4/30, Anil Kumble 4/32).

15 February: SuperSport Park, Centurion

India's decision to bat first was jettisoned by a swinging ball. Their batsmen failed to cope; the top six in their order scoring just 51 among them. There was no colourful strokeplay so characteristic of the Indians. That is, not until Harbhajan Singh briefly fluttered in the pressureless situation of a lost cause. Glenn McGrath's nagging line and Lee's whiplash pace created considerable uncertainty. But it was Jason Gillespie who broke the Indian backbone. Introduced as first change, he operated with unerring accuracy. Indeed, he sent down his entire quota of 10 overs without a break, finishing with three for 13. He removed Tendulkar with a mesmerizing slower off-cutter. This dismissal smothered India's last chance of erecting a respectable total.

Australia expended a mere 22.2 overs to overhaul this lowest-ever Indian total in the World Cup. Adam Gilchrist and Mathew Hayden briefly delighted the 18,000-odd crowd, who clearly didn't get their money's worth from a match hyped as one of the most alluring early encounters of the tournament. Australia trotted to victory by nine wickets.

Toss: India
Man of the Match: JN Gillespie
India 125 all out in 41.4 overs (Sachin Tendulkar 36, Harbhajan Singh 28, Jason Gillespie 3/13. Brett Lee 3/36). **Australia** 128/1 in 22.2 overs (Adam Gilchrist 48, Matthew Hayden 45*, Anil Kumble 1/24).

19 February: Harare

Sourav Ganguly's side's rather flat start to the tournament provoked angry public protests back in India, and among Mumbai lobbyists—keen to see Tendulkar back at the helm—a desire for the sacking of the skipper. However, the Mumbaikar and Delhi's Virender Sehwag, after India were sent in, responded with a thumping opening stand of 99. The later order, though, was restricted by Grant Flower's steady left-arm spin. First, he tied Dinesh Mongia in knots before having him caught in the deep. Then, he deceived Tendulkar with one that came in with the arm and then straightened. He was thereafter withdrawn from the attack because of a finger injury, and India reached 255, which was more than what was earlier expected.

In any case, Zimbabwe soon found themselves in the woods. Javagal Srinath swiftly removed the openers, and the best endeavour of Andy Flower to disturb the bowlers had little effect. Indeed, a captain's bowling effort thereafter virtually emasculated the Zimbabweans. Ganguly ensnared three wickets for two runs in six balls. At 87 for six, Zimbabwe's primary objective was to save face before their 6,000-odd supporters and not suffer too much in terms of their net run rate. As India won by 83 runs, it was later revealed that a sporadic check by the ICC had discovered that bats belonging to players on both sides were marginally wider than permitted by the laws of cricket.

Toss: Zimbabwe
Man of the Match: SR Tendulkar
India 255/7 in 50 overs (Sachin Tendulkar 81, Rahul Dravid 43*, Virender Sehwag 36, Grant Flower 2/14). **Zimbabwe** 172 all out in 44.4 overs (Tatenda Taibu 29*, Guy Whittall 28, Sourav Gabguly 3/22, Javagal Srinath 2/14).

23 February: Pietermaritzburg

It was a comparatively minor engagement, but on momentous soil, for it was at this railroad junction in 1893 that an Indian barrister, Mohandas Karamchand, later 'Mahatma' (Great Soul) Gandhi, was ejected from a first-class compartment of a train (although he held a perfectly valid ticket) for the colour of his skin by a white conductor. This one, supercharged incident probably changed the course of world history, starting with the liberation of India and decolonization of the rest of the subjugated world. Before the match, the Indian cricketers had, appropriately, participated in the unveiling of a plaque to the memory of the apostle of non-violence at the aforementioned railway station.

On the field, Tendulkar paid his tribute with his 34th ODI hundred and picked up his second successive Man of the Match award. As the ground reverberated to chants of 'Sachin, Sachin' from the 5,000-strong crowd, he effortlessly posted 152, after Namibia, who had opted to field first, had the mortification of grassing him on 32. Ganguly was, perhaps, in even better form, as he smote sixes and fours with superb timing. In tandem, they realized 244—their third partnership of over 200 in ODIs. India's batting had at last clicked, albeit against a non-test-playing team.

Jan-Berrie Burger then embarked on an adventurous reply, hitting four fours and a six; and Namibia batted out 42 of their 50 overs. India's 181-run win was their biggest in the World Cup. But there was a casualty in that Ashish Nehra—who was more in rhythm than any other Indian bowler—retired after damaging his ankle early in his spell.

Toss: Namibia
Man of the Match: SR Tendulkar
India 311/2 in 50 overs (Sachin Tendulkar 152, Sourav Ganguly 112*, Rudi van Vuuren 2/53). **Namibia** 130 all out in 42.3 overs (Jan-Berrie Burger 29, Deon Kotze 27, Yuvraj Singh 4/6, Dinesh Mongia 2/24, Zaheer Khan 2/24).

26 February: Kingsmead, Durban (Day/Night)

Justifying their decision to bat first, India treated the 18,000-plus attendance to a riotous start, with 75 emanating from 11 overs. But Andrew Flintoff now applied the brakes. Sehwag, the new swashbuckler in the Indian squad, was caught off a front edge and Tendulkar, continuing his crimson touch, holed out at point. Rocked back, India only managed 21 in the next 10. The Lancastrian all-rounder, accurate and of extra bounce, conceded just nine runs in his first eight overs. But Rahul Dravid and Yuvraj Singh could not be silenced. They compensated with a run-a-ball stand of 62, although England, thereafter, resurrected themselves, capturing four wickets from the last four balls.

Nick Knight paid the penalty for underestimating Mohammed Kaif's athleticism and was run out in the second over of the Englishmen's reply; Marcus Trescothick mishooked to make his exit. Both openers were thus back in the hut in quick time. With the ball wobbling in the clamminess of a South African summer evening, Michael Vaughan was lucky to survive a hypnotic spell from Zaheer Khan. But it was Nehra, his ankle strapped after hurting it in the previous match, who made inroads. In his third and fourth overs, he extracted a bottom edge from Nasser Hussain, had Alec Stewart plumb in front with an in-swinger and Vaughan caught behind with a virtually unplayable delivery. The top six had flopped for 62; only

Flintoff, in pristine form in this match, averted utter disgrace. To be fair, England probably fell foul of the toss; but they also had an inspired Nehra to contend with, as India won by 82 runs. Bowling at around 90 miles an hour and with admirable control, this left-armer from Delhi grabbed six for 23. His career record before this fixture was 30 wickets in 32 ODIs. His two most flattering World Cup figures were both posted at the bowling paradise of Headingley, Leeds. This effort was his third-best.

Toss: India
Man of the Match: A Nehra
India 250/9 in 50 overs (Rahul Dravid 62, Sachin Tendulkar 50, Yuv raj Singh 42, Andy Caddick, Andrew Flintoff 2/15). **England** 168 all out in 45.3 overs (Andrew Flintoff 64, Ashish Nehra 6/23, Zaheer Khan 2/29).

1 March: SuperSport Park, Centurion

The much awaited, frenetically discussed clash—between India and Pakistan—now took place. Large segments of the cricketing world, including millions in the subcontinent, were glued to this face-off. The arch-rivals were meeting for the first time in three years. In boiling weather and with virtually all the 20,000 seats in the stadium taken up, the cricket was not an anti-climax.

Pakistan won the toss and made good use of a flat wicket. Saeed Anwar, all wrist and placement, led the way with a hundred. His contribution was invaluable despite there being only seven fours in it. Indeed, it took a golden yorker from Nehra, continuing to impress in the tournament, to uproot him. Younis Khan, later in the innings, exhibited a puckish flurry of strokes.

However, it was Tendulkar who really emblazoned the occasion by dishing out a riveting display—perhaps the innings of the tournament. Targeting 274 against a star-studded pace attack, with Shoaib Akhtar at his fastest, he was three musketeers rolled into one. His cut for six, a highly unorthodox stroke, as much silenced as thrilled the audience. He swirled one into the leg side, pushed another down the ground; all in Akhtar's first over. India's 100 came up in the 12th over. Tendulkar, granted a life on 32 and suffering from cramps, finished on 98 off 75 balls. Kaif's contribution after two quick wickets fell went almost unnoticed. But after the thunder and lightning, Dravid and Yuvraj guided the ship safely to shore. Pakistan conceded 28 extras. But this was no indictment of Taufeeq Umar, substituting for Rashid Latif, who was struck on the helmet and could not keep wickets. It was a case of the Pakistani bowlers trying too hard and thereby erring in line.

Thus, India's 100 per cent record against their neighbours in the World Cup remained intact, with four wins in as many meetings. The six-wicket victory also ensured India's advance into the Super Six.

Toss: Pakistan
Man of the Match: SR Tendulkar
Pakistan 273/7 in 50 overs (Saeed Anwar 101, Younis Khan 32, Rashid Latif 29*, Zaheer Khan 2/46, Ashish Nehra 2/74). **India** 276/4 in 45.4 overs (Sachin Tendulkar 98, Yuvraj Singh 50*, Rahul Dravid 44*, Waqar Younis 2/71, Shahid Afridi 1/45).

Super Six, 7 March: Newlands, Cape Town (Day/Night)

Kenya played to their carefully cultivated strengths—good fielding, paceless bowling and the will to bat through 50 overs.

It was a liberally disposed crowd of around 18,000. Success with the coin gave Kenya an opportunity to bat in dry, afternoon conditions, when the wicket was at its best. Besides, they were assisted by some abysmal Indian catching as three simple chances were floored in the first hour—all off the persistent, yet hapless, Nehra. Kennedy Otieno escaped in two such instances to post a patient 70—the top score for his side.

Then, sustained swing bowling in a helpful environment and a brilliant catch by Tony Suji off a well-timed clip from Tendulkar depressed India to 24 for three in the 10th over. However, Ganguly found an ally in Dravid and, more tangibly, in Yuvraj. The last mentioned, by swinging with the spin, stepped up the run rate, while his captain made sure he stayed till the end. With this 21st ODI hundred, Ganguly swept past Saeed Anwar to reach the second spot in the all-time list, which was, as one would expect, headed by Tendulkar with 34 centuries. The skipper's contribution helped India cross another barrier—by six wickets. It was only the second time in eight day/nighters in the tournament that a team had won chasing in the dewy circumstances under lights. It was a hard-earned victory for a side considered on paper to be much superior. After the match, Ganguly was asked if India had considered throwing the game in order to devise meeting the Kenyans in the semifinals. The answer was emphatically in the negative. As South Africa's experience had demonstrated, it's a folly to complicate matters with calculators.

Toss: Kenya
Man of the Match: SC Ganguly
Kenya 225/6 in 50 overs (Kennedy Otino 79, Maurice Odumbe 34*, Ravi Shah 34, Harbhajan Singh 2/41, Javagal Srinath 2/43). **India** 226/4 in 47.5 overs (Sourav Ganguly 107*, Yuvraj Singh 58*, Rahul Dravid 32, Thomas Odoyo 2/27).

Super Six, 10 March: Wanderers, Johannesburg

To the 23,000 spectators, Sanath Jayasuriya, with a dodgy thumb and an injured forearm, represented a soldier just back from a battlefront. After he inserted India on a decent pitch, he was tormented by a huge headache. With the exception of Chaminda Vaas, Sri Lanka's faster bowlers were all over the place. Tendulkar and Sehwag pounced on such aberrance to pile up 153 for the opening wicket. It was their best effort in 10 innings together and their third three-figure partnership. Tendulkar treated Vaas with due respect and peered at Muttiah Muralitharan probingly; but brushed aside the rest imperiously. He, unfortunately, missed a second hundred in 10 days, but crossed 500 runs in a World Cup for the second time in a row. Sehwag, the destroyer from Delhi, displayed a more sensible approach than he was reputed to have, before the last of a crescendo of shots concluded at long-on.

From a Sri Lankan standpoint, 293 was a demoralizing target. By the fourth over during their pursuit, this had become even more distant, as Marvan Atapattu, Jehan Mubarak, Mahela Jayawardene and Aravinda de Silva all departed without troubling the scorers. Mubarak seemed a misfit at number three and Jayawardene looked desperately out of nick. Then, a handicapped Jayasuriya hoisted Srinath to cover, which resulted in one of four catches for the agile Kaif, a World Cup fielding record. Srinath, Kapil's successor as India's primary pace bowler, had justified the faith reposed in him by captain Ganguly, who had coaxed him out of retirement for the event. India won by a record margin of 183 runs. Their mounting dash and dexterity clinched them a place in the last four. Sri Lanka could at this juncture also have got there; but the road had become a trifle labyrinthine.

Toss: Sri Lanka
Man of the Match: J Srinath
India 292/6 in 50 overs (Sachin Tendulkar 97, Virender Sehwag 66, Sourav Ganguly 48, Muttiah Muralitharan 3/46, Chaminda Vaas 2/34).
Sri Lanka 109 all out in 23 overs (Kumar Sangakkara 30, Javagal Srinath 4/35, Nehra 4/35).

Super Six, 14 March: SuperSport Park, Centurion

New Zealand were in difficulty no sooner had the crowd of 16,000 settled into their seats. After India won the toss, Zaheer Khan, left-arm, fast-medium from the western Indian city of Baroda in Gujarat state, sent Craig McMillan and Nathan Astle packing in the very first over. At the non-striker's end, Stephen Fleming looked like a trainer whose lightweight wards had been punched by a heavyweight. Every move Ganguly made thereafter was richly rewarded. Only the lower half of the Kiwi batting provided any resistance.

India's main worry had been the express pace of Shane Bond. Predictably, Sehwag snicked his sixth ball to slip and Ganguly was yorked by sheer speed. Tendulkar, then, skied Daryl Tuffey after lashing him for three successive fours. There, thus, arose a glimmer of hope for New Zealand; and a murmur of a match in hand among the 16,000 in the galleries. But Dravid was let off by the keeper and this proved too costly a mistake. He and Kaif then showed the New Zealanders a clean pair of heels to complete a seven-wicket victory with nine overs to spare. The latter wrapped up proceedings with two fours off Scott Styris. India—already guaranteed a place in the semifinal—won their seventh game in a row in a show of increasing confidence. It was also a mentally restorative result after their drubbing in New Zealand only a few weeks earlier. The Kiwis now could only hope Zimbabwe would get the better of Sri Lanka.

Toss: India
Man of the Match: Z Khan
New Zealand 146 all out in 45.1 overs (Stephen Fleming 30, Zaheer Khan 4/42, Harbhajan 2/28). **India** 150/3 in 40.4 overs (Mohammed Kaif 68*, Rahul Dravid 53*, Shane Bond 2/23).

Semifinal, 18 March: St George's Park, Port Elizabeth

In an era in which sportsmanship has been overtaken by career compulsions, Adam Gilchrist, rather refreshingly, walked even after umpire Rudi Koertzen's decision had gone in his favour. He got a faint touch in attempting a sweep that ricocheted off his pads. (As he later so eloquently emphasized with his demeanour in India in 2004, when captaining Australia in the absence of Ricky Ponting, this is the estimable way he plays his cricket.) His nobility, though, led to a crisis as Ponting's was only a brief stay. This opened the shutter for Sri Lanka after they had lost the toss, but they squandered the ray of light. Kumar Sangakkara muffed an easy stumping chance off Jayasuriya when Symonds was on 33; the Australian didn't look back, adjusting well to another slightly awkward pitch at this coastal venue. Jayasuriya later dismissed Lehmann and Bevan off consecutive deliveries; but Symonds stayed put in a watchful rather than a forceful manner.

Sri Lanka required 213 to win. The in-touch Atapattu was floored by Brad Hogg at cover when he was 14, but his off stump was knocked back by the very next delivery from Brett Lee, timed at 99.4 mph. Jayasuriya replied with a six off this speedster only to be soon consumed at square leg off McGrath. Then Bichel got into the act. He fielded a defensive push from Sangakkara on his follow-through, swivelled and broke the stumps at the batsman's end to beat a doddering de Silva. It was an unfitting end to a fine career as this stocky Sri Lankan artiste faded into the sunset.

A late-afternoon downpour interrupted Sri Lanka's first healthy partnership—47 for the eighth wicket between Sangakkara and Vaas. So, the match was decided on the Duckworth/Lewis rule—Australia winning by 48 runs, without any protests from the 14,500 onlookers. With this win, the Australians qualified for their fifth World Cup final and their third sequentially.

Toss: Australia
Man of the Match: A Symonds
Australia 212/7 in 50 overs (Andrew Symonds 91*, Darren Lehmann 36, Chaminda Vaas 3/34, Aravinda de Silva 2/36, Sanath Jayasuriya 2/42).
Sri Lanka 123/7 (Kumar Sangakkara 39*, Brett Lee 3/35, Brad Hogg 2/30).

Semifinal, 20 March: Kingsmead, Durban (Day/Night)

Captaining India for the 99th time in a one-day international, Ganguly himself took charge after deciding to bat. With a contemptuous innings, he laid the foundation of an august if not unassailable total. Leg-spinner Obuya bowled two economical overs. Ganguly then danced down the track to hit the first ball of the next for six and repeated the stroke before the end of the over. Obuya was taken off after six overs lest he became too expensive. A century from Tendulkar appeared to be on the cards before he pulled Steve Tikolo to deep midwicket. Ganguly, however, pressed on to equal Mark Waugh's 1996 record of three hundreds in a World Cup, heralding the landmark with his fifth over-boundary, which had laziness written all over it. Bat and helmet raised, he soaked in the applause.

Ganguly's counterpart, Tikolo, was also the highest scorer in course of the Kenyan response. But all Ganguly had to do was to unleash his fast-medium trio to record a 91-run victory. With this eighth win on the trot, India matched their record of consecutive successes, established in the "World Championship of Cricket" in Australia in 1985. They had become professional enough not to be complacent against unfancied opposition. As for the Kenyans, though there was no fairytale ending, they happily acknowledged the cheers from an 18,000 plus attendance, their spot in history books secured.

Kenya's romantic journey brought huge benefits. The ICC earmarked more than £1 million for their development. Moreover, the players, who had threatened strike action over pay before the tournament began, picked up $530,000 in prize money, having at one stage anticipated a mere fraction of this sum.

Toss: India
Man of the Match: SC Ganguly

India 270/4 in 50 overs (Sourav Ganguly 111*, Sachin Tendulkar 83, Peter Ongondo 1/38, Thomas Odoyo 1/45). **Kenya** 179 all out in 46.2 overs (Steve Tokolo 56, Zaheer Khan 3/14, Ashish 2/11, Sachin Tendulkar 2/28).

Final, 23 March: Wanderers, Johannesburg

Ganguly amazed many by inserting Australia. It had, obviously, been a collective decision, but he as captain was the final arbiter. His critics immediately attributed this decision to his fear of facing Australia's fast bowlers. But there was some life in the pitch for India's quicker bowlers, though the seamers, hitherto promising, now crumpled under pressure.

Zaheer took 10 balls to complete his first over, conceding 15 runs; and that set a trend. Gilchrist and Hayden took full advantage, albeit a little chancily, and after nine overs, Australia were 74 without loss. Ganguly switched to spin in the next over and Harbhajan, who had terminated the Kangaroos' unbeaten run in tests in 2001 to be dubbed 'turbanator' by Australian media, succeeded in repatriating both openers back to the pavilion.

But history didn't deter the Aussies. Ponting and Damien Martyn proceeded to raise a partnership of 234, which was a record for Australia in ODIs for any wicket. So was their total. Martyn's showing was the more noteworthy, since he had skipped the semifinal with a finger injury and was not thought to have recovered. His batting was cerebral; he read the circumstances to precision and was unselfish. He gave a six over handicap to Ponting, but reached his fifty first.

Ponting was just into starters, though. His 50 took 74 balls to Martyn's 46 and contained a solitary four. But his next 47 balls gave rise to 90 runs, with eight leg-side sixes (the highest number of over-boundaries in any World Cup innings, beating the seven by Viv Richards and Ganguly) and three more fours.

A shift in strategy was signalled by Harbhajan's reintroduction in the 39th over. Ponting blasted him out of the attack with two consecutive sixes over midwicket. Nehra had a go; but he, too, was greeted by a spectacular one-handed slog-sweep off a low full toss, which also sailed over midwicket. Off the second-last ball of the innings, the Aussie skipper lofted Srinath for a towering six over long-on. His 140 was the highest personal contribution by any player in a World Cup final. Australia's change of gear had been awe-inspiring: 109 came off the last ten overs, and 64 off the last five. Srinath haemorrhaged 87 runs, the most profuse in a World Cup final.

The phalanx of Indian supporters in a capacity crowd of 32,000 had lost their verve, and their spirits were irreversibly deflated when Tendulkar made his exit, top-edging McGrath to be caught and bowled off the fifth ball. Sehwag survived a catch on account of a no-ball, and bravely kept India ticking with a run-a-ball innings, which was embroidered with ten fours and three sixes. But he was caught napping by a direct throw from Lehmann at deep midoff, which terminated a blossoming partnership of 88 with Dravid.

Showers briefly promised Indian fans the prospect of a replay. Sensing Australia had to bowl a minimum of 25 overs to secure a result, Ponting employed his spinners, Hogg and Darren Lehman, at both ends. India cashed in by flaying them to all parts of the ground. Bichel and McGrath were brought back as the lights were switched on, but the rain became so intense that the players were compelled to leave the field, with India on 103 for three. When they returned, 25 minutes later—without any reduction in overs—Australia consummated a 125-run victory, their third triumph in a World Cup and their 17th successive one-day win. It came under threatening skies and to the accompaniment of thunderclaps. The Australians took home US $2 million as winnings. Tendulkar, though, was declared the Man of the Tournament.

Toss: India
Man of the Match: RT Ponting
Player of the Series: SR Tendulkar
Australia 359/2 in 50 overs (Ricky Ponting 140*, Damien Martyn 88*, Adam Gilchrist 57, Harbhajan Singh 2/49). **India** 234 all out in 39.2 overs (Virender Sehwag 82, Rahul Dravid 47, Glenn McGrath 3/52, Andrew Symonds 2/7, Brett Lee 2/31).

South Africa's early exit contributed to the event failing to capture the imagination of the country's majority. A broadening of cricket's appeal had been one of the aims of the Organizing Committee. To this end, sponsor companies were required to have a black empowerment element and 50,000 tickets were reserved for black children to attend games. However, a survey revealed that only a small minority of black South Africans expressed interest in the event.

The programme was criticized in some circles as being too elaborate and too long. Participants had been increased from 12 in 1999 to 14, the number of games to 54 and the duration to over six weeks.

There were no reserve days at the pool stage, which cost the West Indies dear. Their game with Bangladesh was rained off when they were in a dominant position. Had it been completed, the West Indies, and not Kenya, would have gone through to the Super Six. The staging of day/night matches in the seaside cities of Durban and Cape Town was questioned. The ball seemed to swing more for the sides bowling second, though the results were not unduly skewed.

The umpiring was generally good. And the biggest security operation mounted by the ICC led by the former police commissioner of London, Lord Paul Condon, head of the ICC's Anti-Corruption Unit, declared the tournament—the first World Cup since the Cronje scandal—clean.

Two days after England's game against Australia, Nasser Hussain, exhausted by an arduous winter, was making his resignation speech as one-day captain. He and Pollock were not the only leaders to jump or fall. In the, now-customary post-World Cup captaincy clearance, Sanath Jayasuriya, Carl Hooper of the West Indies, Waqar Younis of Pakistan and Khaled Masud of Bangladesh, too, lost their jobs.

The Pakistanis were the biggest disappointment. They won no match of consequence. Against Australia, Waqar was ordered out of the attack for bowling two beamers. Gilchrist subsequently brought a racial abuse charge against Rashid Latif, which was, however, turned down by match referee Clive Lloyd. Shahid Afridi was suspended and fined by his own board for sledging during the politically sensitive match against India.

On the other hand, John Davison, Canada's 32-year-old Australian recruit, smashed the fastest century in World Cup history against the West Indies only four days after his team had been dismissed for 36. Then, there was Namibia's Jan-Berrie Burger applying his beefy blade to England's attack in Port Elizabeth and the exemplary glove work of Jeroen Smits, the Dutch keeper who conceded only five byes in six matches.

Shoaib Akhtar of Pakistan swung his way to the highest score by a number 11 batsman in one-day internationals. The West Indian Ramnaresh Sarwan returned from hospital after being felled by a bouncer to take the field to a standing ovation. And Aasif Karim, a 39-year-old from Kenya, bowled maiden after maiden to Australia.

But the *pièce de résistance* was of the Canadians, made up of amateurs, beating the game's newest test nation, Bangladesh, by 60 runs. Until the warm-up games, the Canadian players had not played together for five months.

In financial terms, with profits of US $194 million representing a huge increase on the $51 million made in 1999, the 8th World Cup was the most successful yet.

CHAPTER SIX

2007 Disaster

INDIA HAD NOT QUALIFIED FOR THE SEMIFINALS IN FOUR of six World Cups outside the subcontinent. At the same time, they compensated for their shortcomings in 1992 and 1999 by respectably entering the final in 2003. Arguably, a trained coach in John Wright made a difference.

But India were, now, under new leadership and management. Sourav Ganguly, captain in 2003, was in 2005 unceremoniously unhinged to the extent of being excluded from the squad. His long-serving deputy, Rahul Dravid, was in the hot seat. Wright had been succeeded by Greg Chappell, the former Australian skipper and master batsman. Dravid was likeable, uncontroversial, unselfish and the side's most dependable batsman. Chappell's was a razor-sharp cricketing brain, ruthless and technology-savvy.

The Ganguly Affair

While his critics said he was asking for it, the BCCI's treatment of Ganguly is indefensible. Any cricketer deserves courtesy if he is to be omitted from the national side, especially if he's been the country's most successful skipper ever (which he was at that point).

The East Zone have historically been one of the backwaters of Indian cricket. Indeed, Bengal, the leading Ranji Trophy side in this region, had, since India's maiden appearance in tests in 1932, produced only two regular test players—Pankaj Roy, an opener in the 1950s and early 1960s, and

Dilip Doshi, a left-arm spinner, in the late 1970s and early 1980s. Ganguly became the third.

Ganguly was un-parochial. Practically none of the players successfully drafted in or recalled during his tenure was from his part of the country. He had a hunch that Harbhajan Singh would serve him well. The Sikh responded by capturing 28 wickets in two tests against Australia as India stormed to victory in 2001. Only Mahendra Singh Dhoni hailed from Ganguly's zone, but not from his state of Bengal. Few will argue against this choice, for this Jharkhand batsman-wicketkeeper's eruptive strokeplay has added a new dimension to India's batting and calmness as captain in limited overs cricket.

In an email message to the BCCI in 2005, Chappell alleged Ganguly was manipulating team selection to protect his increasingly insecure place in the side, because of indifferent form.

However, in his autobiography published in 2014, Sachin Tendulkar describes Chappell's attitude towards Ganguly as "astonishing". He goes on to say: "Chappell seemed intent on dropping all the older players and in the process damaged the harmony of the side."

Notwithstanding Chappell's charge, the selection committee could have, in a civilized manner, conveyed to Ganguly that he no longer figured in their plans. It was suspected in some quarters that relations between Kiran More, chairman of selectors, and Ganguly were a bit strained.

Ganguly's exclusion created a furore in political circles in India. His state of West Bengal was on the verge of elections. Its Marxist chief minister, Buddhadeb Bhattacharyya, astoundingly, twisted his side-lining to be an injustice against Bengal and Bengalis by India's central cricketing establishment. The provincial president of his rival Congress party, Pranab Mukherjee (also then the union defence minister and later the president of India), too, demanded Ganguly's reinstatement. Neither had much knowledge of cricket. Therefore, they were shamelessly indulging in naked populism.

Street demonstrations rocked Kolkata, the capital of West Bengal and Ganguly's home city, protestors burnt effigies of Chappell and More and there was widespread talk of conspiracy against Bengal's favourite son. The politicians were only too happy to fan such flames.

The incumbent president of the BCCI, Sharad Pawar, food and agriculture minister at the centre and therefore a cabinet colleague of Mukherjee, was also only remotely familiar with cricket. His closest link to the sport was the fact that his father-in-law, Sadashiv Shinde, a leg-spinner, appeared in seven tests for India and once captured eight wickets in a match against England at Delhi in 1951, including six for 91 in the first innings.

In the BCCI's quixotic constitution, their president has the final say in the selection of a contingent for an overseas tour. From all indications, Pawar, a shrewd public figure, subtly but patently invoked such powers to re-induct Ganguly in the squad for Pakistan in the winter of 2005–06. Pawar, meaningfully, dined with the selectors on the eve of their meeting to pick the side. Ganguly battled to notch up 34 and 37 in a losing cause at Karachi, but was, thereafter, again peremptorily exiled. But he was on the basis of a creditable showing in ODIs thereafter selected in the squad for the 2007 World Cup.

Dravid and Chappell managed to arrest India's slump in one-dayers since 2003 by thrashing higher ranked Sri Lanka and Pakistan and drawing with South Africa (they also beat lower placed England). But the Indians met their match in the unfancied West Indians, who beat them 4–1 in the Caribbean. Having recorded their success on flat, un-seaming wickets in the subcontinent, India's batsmen were unsettled by the tennis-ball type bounce in the Caribbean. Accustomed to hitting on the 'up', they either mistimed or played too early. They also held the wooden spoon in a triangular series with the Windies and Australia at Kuala Lumpur.

For the World Cup, India hired the West Indian sports psychologist, Rudi Webster, to assist their campaign. Chappell considered him to be among the best he has ever interacted with. Webster had briefly worked with the Indians in the Caribbean in 2006. The caress of the whip, though, only works on thoroughbreds!

In 2007, the field was enlarged to 16 participants from 14 in 2003. They were divided into four groups—A, B, C and D. The winners and runners-up from each would constitute a Super Eight—another league stage—prior to the semifinals and final on a knockout basis.

India were drawn in Group B with Sri Lanka, Bangladesh and Bermuda.

I covered the 2007 World Cup for *The Tribune* of Chandigarh, *Daily News & Analysis* (DNA) of Mumbai and *Indo-Asian News Service* (IANS). Here are extracts from selected despatches:

Kingston, 13 March 2007

The seconds are out of the ring; pugilism of a cricketing kind and partying Caribbean style is about to begin. The first pair scheduled to enter the arena are the hosts, the West Indies, and Pakistan tomorrow. The setting: the historic Sabina Park, now renovated but still nestling below the island's majestic Blue Mountain, after which the Jamaican coffee is branded.

If most recent evidence is of any relevance, the West Indians, winners in 1975 and 1979, would be worried about the capitulation to India in the warm-up game; and in contrast, Pakistan, champions in 1992, should be elated with their victory over South Africa, currently number one in the ICC rankings, on the same day.

But as history reveals, such results are often immaterial, more so in the limited overs format, where the luck of the draw and the form on the day count considerably.

Hosts have never won the World Cup, other than Sri Lanka (who were joint organisers with India and Pakistan) in 1996. Yet, few forecasters ignore home advantage. On paper, the West Indians, to start with, have less of a chance of wearing the crown than South Africa had four years ago.

Erstwhile West Indian fast bowler Andy Roberts, who has been supervising pitch preparation for the World Cup, has contested claims that wickets in the competition will be slow turners. Indeed, he expects "sporting" surfaces at Barbados and Antigua, with an even bounce and decent "carry" to the wicket-keeper. But he's unsure about Guyana, where India are slated to play South Africa, if both qualify for the last eight.

Port of Spain, 15 March

Indian captain Rahul Dravid exhorted his teammates not to lower their guards against Bangladesh in their opening World Cup match on Saturday. "We saw what they did against New Zealand; we have to give respect to them, we cannot be complacent," Dravid said. Bangladesh had overcome dark horses New Zealand in their first warm-up game.

Dravid added: "We are expected to do well in the tournament. I want my boys to put out a clinical performance." He emphasised that performance on the day and not rankings matter in ODIs.

Port of Spain, March 16

Amerindians from South America, who were the first to settle in Trinidad, christened it the "Land of the Humming Bird". There is certainly a buzz in this island every time Indian cricketers set foot on it. From the East Indian taxi driver to the traders in this capital city's high streets, persons of Indian origin, who constitute nearly 50 per cent of the population, excitedly enquire about Rahul Dravid's team's prospects.

Even the money changer at the airport, a polite Afro-Caribbean, was not immune to the chatter of his colleagues of Indian descent.

Quite simply, Queen's Park Oval, venue of India entering the stage in the current World Cup today, is India's happiest hunting ground in the West Indies. They have won three Test matches here and lost only on a solitary occasion.

The record in one-day internationals, though, is less inspiring, including defeats in both bi-laterals last year. The Indians, therefore, have to banish any negative thoughts arising from previous displays if they are to stake a serious claim in the tournament.

The assignment for India since the opening ceremony on Sunday has been to adjust to the different pitch condition here as compared to Jamaica, where the wickets in the warm-up encounters were comparatively faster.

While the facilities and stands at the Queen's Park Oval have undergone a massive makeover, the pitches and the outfield remain unaltered, except that the square has endured endless rolling and the rest of the turf more manicuring in recent months.

The nature of clay in the eastern Caribbean, other than in Barbados and perhaps to a certain extent in Antigua, render wickets to be soft and slow by Caribbean standards; and yet, the ball bounces as if pitched on a foam mattress. The heavy rolling, though, may have reduced the sluggishness.

India have undertaken four days of practice before tackling Bangladesh for the first time in a World Cup. They cannot afford to experience an off-day, despite the odds on India's eastern neighbours varying between 100-1 and 200-1.

The Bangladeshis had an unenviable experience at this level four years ago. They have also beaten India only once in 14 meetings. But their defeat of Australia at Cardiff in 2005 and success over New Zealand last week suggest they are steadily improving and are not incapable of upsetting a more fancied side.

In the 1990s, their totals against India never reached 200; yet, they have crossed this mark five times in seven matches in the current decade. Besides, they appear to be quite comfortable when chasing targets.

Shahriar Nafees is averaging over 40 in ODIs; and captain Habibul Bashar and Mohammad Ashraful (who recorded a hundred in the famous victory over Australia) cannot be underestimated.

Mashrafe Mortaza is a lively fast-medium bowler, while Mohammad Rafique is a seasoned left-arm spinner. To cap these, they have a skilful coach in Dav Whatmore.

India are likely to repose their faith in the recently non-performing Virender Sehwag (this is a little harsh on Robin Uthappa) and Irfan Pathan, who boasts impressive statistics against Bangladesh, in an endeavour to haul them back to form. It is not insensible to adopt such a ploy against weaker opposition than versus Sri Lanka.

Perhaps, only one spinner will play. The surface in Wednesday's Sri Lanka-Bermuda match was by no means a turner; and there was moisture for quicker bowlers in the first hour.

Queen's Park Oval, Port of Spain, 17 March

India won the toss and elected to bat on what proved to be a helpful wicket for quicker bowlers. Mashrafe Mortaza's produced one of his better spells with the new ball—which ultimately reaped a reward of four wickets for 38 runs. Unwatchful, the Indians were soon in dire straits at 40 for three, before Sourav Ganguly and Rahul Dravid put up a resistance.

But Dravid fell on 14; so it was left to two left-handers—Yuvraj Singh having joined his former captain at the crease—to realise 85 runs for the fifth wicket, which carried India to 157. But the fall of five wickets for two runs thereafter frittered away the pair's efforts. India collapsed from 157 for four to 159 for nine in the space of 15 balls.

Left-arm spinners Abdur Razzak and Mohammad Rafique aided Mortaza in the later overs.

The total of 191 was India's worst against Bangladesh, inferior to their 214 in Dhaka in 2004. The man Chappell would have excluded from the squad top scored with 66; but it wasn't a vintage Ganguly innings.

The only other meaningful contribution was Yuvraj's 47. But for the spirited partnership between Zaheer Khan and Munaf Patel of 32 runs for the tenth wicket the situation would have been even more embarrassing for the Indians.

In contrast, it was a fine all-round performance in the field by Bangladesh. And they rounded this off by reaching their target with five wickets and nine balls to spare. Left-handed Tamim Iqbal (51) got them off to a flyer. Subsequently, the all-rounder Shakib al Hasan (53) and the diminutive wicket-keeper Mushfiqur Rahim (unbeaten on 56) finished the job.

India 191 all out in 49.3 overs (Sourav Ganguly 66, Yuvraj Singh 47, Mashrafe Mortaza 4/38, Mohammad Rafique 3/36, Abdur Razzak 3/38). **Bangladesh** 192/5 in 48.3 overs (Mushfiqur Rahim 56*, Shakib Al Hasan 53, Tamim Iqbal 51, Virender Sehwag 2/17, Munaf Patel 2/39).

18 March: Port of Spain

"I looked at the wicket in the morning and felt it was a lot drier than we had come to expect in the Caribbean," remarked Rahul Dravid after the match. "We thought it would get progressively slower and become useful to spinners which it did actually," he ventured to add.

He revealed other members of the team didn't feel differently. "We all felt that it could be difficult in the first 40-50 minutes of batting, then help the batsmen; but it was a lot damper."

"Our batting was bad throughout," he stressed.

He complimented Bangladesh, especially the man-of-the-match Mortaza and the 17-year-old Iqbal, whose 51 runs came off a mere 53 balls.

19 March: Queen's Park Oval, Port of Spain

Bermuda, an island off the north American coast, making their debut in a cricket World cup, invited India to bat, having observed Bangladesh's success in bowling first. This, though, backfired as Dravid's side registered a World Cup record total of 413 for five, surpassing the previous best of 398 compiled by Sri Lanka versus Kenya at Kandy in 1996.

Batting at first drop, Sehwag, lately found wanting against stiffer examination, struck a blistering 87-ball 114—his first ODI hundred in nearly two years. He and Ganguly, who hit 89, put on 202 for the second wicket after Uthappa became a victim of a brilliant catch by Dwayne Leverock, a bulky 19-stoner and policeman by profession, at slip off a bouncing ball.

Yuvraj unfurled a whirlwind 83 off 46 balls and Tendulkar was unbeaten on 57 not out. The two posted a rapid 122 runs for the fifth wicket. The last 10 overs grossed 136 runs as the Indians ran amok against ordinary opposition. Tendulkar heaved seamer David Hemp for six over square leg to eclipse Sri Lanka's feat as well as record a 400-run total for the first time in a World Cup match.

India, then, skittled out Bermuda for 156 in 43.1 overs. In effect, the 2003 runners-up won by an unprecedented margin of 257 runs. Four years earlier, Australia had beaten Namibia by 256 runs at Potchefstroom.

India 413/5 in 50 overs (Virender Sehwag 114, Sourav Ganguly 89, Yuvraj Suingh 83, Sachin Tendulkar 57*, Delyone Borden 2/30). **Bermuda** 156 all out in 43.1 overs (David Hemp 76*, Ajit Agarkar 3/38, Anil Kumble 3/38, Zaheer Khan 2/32).

22 March: Port of Spain

After practicing yesterday at a location 40 miles from the Trinidadian capital, the Indian cricketers today returned to the nets at the Queen's Park Oval for a final session of fine tuning before Friday's all-important match with Sri Lanka in Group B of the World Cup.

The clash will occur on one of the central and so far unutilised pitches. This wicket is one of the surfaces used in an India-West Indies ODI last year, but is expected to be more settled, with a higher and more even bounce than before.

Greater lift off the wicket is, theoretically, to India's advantage, though the Sri Lankans are more accustomed to the seaside atmosphere.

After two outings by both sides, India are two points behind the Sri Lankans, who have an unblemished record, having comprehensively beaten Bermuda and Bangladesh; whereas India lost to the Bangladeshis in their first fixture, before putting up a record breaking performance against the Bermudans. India are also markedly behind Sri Lanka on net run rate—2.51 to 4.49.

However, if the Indians beat Sri Lanka—and thereby draw level on points—it's highly unlikely that Bangladesh (who are -2.00 on net run rate) will sufficiently improve their net run rate to challenge India, even if they defeat Bermuda in the last fixture of the Group on Sunday.

In theory, India can succumb to Sri Lanka and still qualify. But for this to happen, Bangladesh (now on equal points with India) would have to surrender to Bermuda and continue to have an inferior net run rate to India.

Overall, India have a superior one-day record (94 matches played, 49 won and 36 lost) against Sri Lanka. But this needs to be viewed with caution, as in the first decade and a half of competition between these two countries, the Sri Lankans were in their formative years as a cricketing nation. In fact, Sri Lanka boast favourable statistics in the World Cup cumulatively.

In 1979, the Sri Lankans, then still not granted official test status, surprised India at Old Trafford, Manchester. In 1992, at Mackay, in Australia, the match was washed away. Four years later, Sri Lanka won both at the preliminary stage in Delhi and in the semifinals in Kolkata. Admittedly, India have thrashed Sri Lanka in their last two encounters—at Taunton in 1999 and at Johannesburg in 2003—but the win:loss ratio is still 3:2 in the Sri Lankans' favour.

India, of course, may draw comfort from the fact that eight of the last 10 completed ODIs between the two have ended in their favour. But again, they must treat this carefully. All such matches have been on slower Indian pitches; and Sri Lanka were without their trump cards Chaminda Vaas and Muttiah Muralitharan in the series last month.

One-day cricket, being a single innings affair, provides limited room for recovery. Consequently, form on the day often prevails. In India's case, their batting, which is their main strength, must click; and the bowling must simply concentrate on off-stump and not give the Sri Lankans room to free their arms. There is very little the Indians can do about their fielding, other than not be worse than what they are.

After being bitten by Bangladeshi cubs, Rahul Dravid may be wary of batting first. But India have no choice other than to take chasing or defending in their strides.

23 March: Queen's Park Oval, Port of Spain

It was a good toss to win; and Dravid not unexpectedly inserted Sri Lanka. The Indian seamers contained the Sri Lankan batsmen to start with, but the latter cut lose in the second half of their innings.

Typically, India held their own in the field until giving way in the slog overs. Significantly, the only over boundary of the Sri Lankan venture did not surface until the 48th over.

Chamara Silva and Tillekaratne Dilshan put up a stand of 83 for the fifth wicket, after Upul Tharanga laid the foundation with a cautious and chanceless 64 off 90 balls. The left-hander steadied the ship after the early exits of the formidable trio of Sanath Jayasuriya, Mahela Jayawardene and Kumar Sangakkara.

There was life in the pitch for quicker bowlers; and Zaheer Khan and Ajit Agarkar capitalised on this. Dravid turned to his part-time swing bowler Ganguly, who removed Sangakkara in his second over when the left-hander didn't middle a lofted straight drive.

Indeed, another occasional bowler—Tendulkar—captured the important wicket of Tharanga, when he trapped him leg before wicket.

But Silva and Dilshan arrested the slump, partly with aggressive running between the wickets. The former's half-century was his third in as many World Cup matches.

Harbhajan Singh was expensive with none for 53 as was Tendulkar. The Indians bled 54 runs in the last six overs. The bowlers conceded 27 extras. Sri Lanka benefited overall to the tune of 256 for six.

In reply, India fell like nine pins barring a valiant 60 from Dravid and 48 from Sehwag. They were bundled out for 185 in the 44th over, losing by 69 runs. Left-arm medium pacer Chaminda Vaas and off-spinner Muttiah Muralitharan lured the Indians to their doom.

India are, in effect, out of the World Cup, having earlier gone down to Bangladesh. Any glimmer of entering the Super Eight stage depends on an unlikely defeat of Bangladesh by minnows Bermuda in the last Group B tie on Sunday.

India's disastrous display follows Pakistan's elimination in Group D after they lost to debutants Ireland.

Sri Lanka 254/6 in 50 overs (Upul Tharanga 64, Chamara Silva 59, Tillekaratne Dilshan 38, Zaheer Khan 2/49). **India** 185 all out in 43.3 overs (Rahul Dravid 60, Virender Sehwag 48, Muttiah Muralitheran 3/41, Chaminda Vaas 2/39).

24 March: Port of Spain

Rahul Dravid blamed his batsmen for India's defeat to Sri Lanka. "I thought it (255) was a good score to chase, we had the batting, we had an extra batsman, but we kept losing wickets," he said.

The Indian skipper did not think the pitch played a role in the outcome. "It was a good wicket to bat on. There was a little bit of spin, but then (Muttiah) Muralitharan turns the ball on any surface," he stated.

24 March: Port of Spain

The bottom line is India bowled in favourable conditions, batted in equally opportune circumstances, yet they lost to Sri Lanka. It's a tale of incredible incompetence.

Even after seven years of international exposure, Zaheer Khan cannot bowl a correct line on big occasions. Harbhajan Singh, who was wrongly picked (Anil Kumble should have selected), failed to capture any wickets. He was, moreover, the most expensive Indian bowler.

Robin Uthappa established he was unripe for the big stage. Sourav Ganguly can be excused for failing after a fairly consistent trot following his return to ODIs. But he overlooked the fact that mid-off had been stationed deeper than usual to attend to his penchant for the lofted drive.

Sachin Tendulkar was, admittedly, beaten by a beautiful delivery. But would he not have blocked this in his prime? Yuvraj Singh attempted a suicidal run, but these things occur under pressure.

The Indians should not have allowed the pressure to accumulate in the first place. Mahendra Dhoni was for the second time in three innings caught napping going back and across—this time trapped plumb in front.

At least Rahul Dravid got one thing right that Virender Sehwag is a man for the big occasion. As long as the latter and the skipper were at the crease, the target against Sri Lanka looked achievable. But the Delhiite ought to have been vigilant about the conjurer's "doosra".

While it was a lost cause, Dravid unnecessarily ventured into a lofted off-drive off the back foot, forgetting the Queen's Park Oval's expansive outfield. Besides, as captain, he could have set a more aggressive field with the new ball against Sri Lanka.

For decades, the most unsuitable people have administered cricket in India.

Ever since Kapil Dev's team won the 1983 World Cup, the BCCI have systematically undermined India's potential by going berserk with one-day cricket, forgetting or being unaware that the aim has got to be to become the world's best in Test cricket.

The Indian corporate sector, too, riding piggyback on the game, has rendered incalculable harm. Has it occurred to the one-day-wallas what could befall Indian cricket once the ageing triumvirate of Tendulkar, Ganguly and Dravid lay their bats to rest?

Australia, clearly the world's leading cricketing nation, aspire to produce complete cricketers who are capable of excelling at the highest level, namely Test cricket, thus taking into account the lesser examination of one-day cricket.

India will never achieve that as long as politicians, civil servants and businessmen run the sport in a so-called honorary capacity, as if it's acceptable to operate an organisation with an income of $400 million with part-timers!

Greg Chappell is an astute cricketing mind but he can be abrasive as well. He also originates from a vastly different culture from a majority of current-day Indian players. Some benefit from his approach, but others may have been unsettled by it.

India were one of the weakest fielding sides in the tournament. It is the lack of grass root ethics in the BCCI's system that pays no attention to basics. Bluntly put, today's Indian cricketers are overpaid under-performers.

27 March: Port of Spain

"I take full responsibility for the fact that we haven't progressed to the next round," Rahul Dravid told media.

On continuing as skipper, he asserted: "I was appointed captain till the World Cup. So I am not even the captain at this point of time, it's not my decision to make."

He explained: "We have not batted anywhere near our potential. We picked what was the best batting line-up in the conditions but I guess we were the best batting line-up in India, and we did not bat well enough in these two games." He added: "It is definitely something to think about."

(Meanwhile, a Press Trust of India [PTI] report from India claimed Chappell was not happy with the composition of the Indian cricket team for the World Cup, it was revealed today.

Before leaving for the West Indies, Chappell, in a text to an Indian journalist Rajan Bala, reportedly, messaged: "Even in the last selection meeting, I fought for youth. The senior players fought against it and the chairman went with them out of fear of media, if youth did not perform."

The SMS was said to have been sent on 17 February or the day of an ODI against Sri Lanka at Visakhapatnam.

"The problem with Yuvraj is that he believes he is a star when he is only a rising one," Chappell confided to Bala, an old friend of mine, adding: "Suresh Raina is a must. But he was not wanted.")

England ruin Lara party

It was meant to be a last rendition of Lara's theme. But it was much too short and it ended in tragedy. A capacity crowd at Barbados' first world facility—the new Kensington Oval—had mushroomed to bid farewell to Brian Charles Lara, master batsman for 17 long years. There were tears in their eyes as they left the ground in fading light.

The music throbbed, the conch shells blew in a true reflection of a West Indian carnival. To the delight of the spectators, Lara promoted himself to number three in the batting order. The England team greeted him with a guard of honour.

The high, unfurling back lift together with that whiplash descent of the willow was immediately in evidence. Gliding the ball with strong but supple wrists, the maestro was on his way. Soon a trademark square drive rebounded from the blade, piercing the packed off-side field to the fence. An excited murmur spread through the ground. "We are in for a treat", was the consensus.

But it terminated in a most cruel fashion. Marlon Samuels stroked the ball to mid-on and called Lara for a run, only to send him back. It was too late. Kevin Pietersen swooping on the leather, flicked it back underarm to shatter the non-striker's stumps. A stunned silence, an utter helplessness enveloped the attendance. Then everyone exploded into a standing ovation as Lara raised his bat for the last time and made an emotional exit as a batsman from an international match. Though the Jamaican right-hander compensated with a crisp 50, Lara fans were in no mood to forgive him.

The Trinidadian had tormented England more than any other side, piling two record-breaking individual scores in tests of 375 and 400 not out on them. The first time he achieved this, he lowered another eminent left-hander, Sir Garfield Sobers' 365 not out against Pakistan in 1958, which had stood for 36 years. The Barbadian all-rounder, arguably the greatest the game has known, ran on to the field to embrace Lara on that day in Antigua.

Now, he enigmatically looked on from the VIP enclosure as the most recent legend in West Indian cricket soaked in the generous appreciation of cricket lovers.

Semifinal, 24 April: Sabina Park, Kingston

Sri Lankan captain Mahela Jayawardene led from the front. He opted to bat after winning the toss and then proceeded to peg 115 not out, thereby helping his side to an impressive total of 289 for five, notwithstanding a couple of umpiring errors.

It was Jayawardene's maiden World Cup century. He accurately assessed the pace of the pitch to strike 10 fours and three sixes in a 109-ball essay. His late flourish saw Sri Lanka accumulate 102 runs off the last 10 overs for the loss of a solitary wicket.

Earlier, the consistent opener Upul Tharanga recorded a run-a-ball 73 after the experienced Sanath Jayasuriya and Kumar Sangakkara had failed to trouble the scorers too much. Left-arm medium pacer James Franklin collected both wickets and was, otherwise, the most economical of the New Zealand bowlers.

Tharanga handled Shane Bond intelligently, using the latter's speed to deflect him backward of square on the onside. He danced down the pitch to hoist the left-arm spinner Daniel Vettori for six over extra cover. But he left his stumps unprotected in an attempt to sweep to be bowled by the same bowler.

The veteran Sri Lankan spinner Muttiah Muralitharan, then, had the Kiwis in sixes and sevens. He finished with four for 31, including three wickets in six balls.

The New Zealanders had been softened up by a blitzkrieg with the new ball by the round-arm Lasith Malinga. Sri Lanka won by 81 runs to enter the final, where they await the winners of the Australia-South Africa match.

The losers folded up in 41.1 overs. It was the fifth time New Zealand had stumbled at the semifinal stage.

Sri Lanka 289/5 in 50 overs (Mahela Jayawardene 115*, Upul Tharanga 73, James Franklin 2/46). **New Zealand** 208 all out 41.4 overs (Peter Fulton 46, Scott Styris 37, Jeetan Patel 34, James Franklin 30*, Muttiah Muralitharan 4/31, Tillekaratne Dilshan 2/22, Sanath Jayasuriya 2/57).

Semifinal, 25 April: Beausejour, St Lucia

South Africa chose to bat. But were dismissed for their lowest total in a World Cup, that of 149 in 43.5 overs. South Africa's previous worst was 184 against Bangladesh earlier in the tournament in a match they lost.

Justin Kemp's 49 not out off 91 deliveries was the highest individual score; while Herschelle Gibbs obtained 39. He was, though, a trifle lucky to survive an appeal for a catch behind the wicket when he was four. The rest of the South African batting simply didn't show up.

A combination of injudicious shots by the batsmen and incisive bowling by speedster Shaun Tait (four for 39) and the fast medium Glenn McGrath (three for 18) was responsible for the one-sidedness.

Captain Graeme Smith was bowled by Nathan Bracken. The same fate befell Jacques Kallis in the face of McGrath. Both departed cheaply. A B de Villiers, opening the innings, lasted slightly longer, but was caught by the wicket-keeper off Tait, who worked up disconcerting pace.

In reply, Australia completed their assignment in the 32nd over with seven wickets in hand. Michael Clarke posted an unbeaten 60 and Mathew Hayden struck 41.

Thus, Australia entered their fourth successive World Cup final and sixth altogether. The defending champions are now in quest of a hat-trick of World Cup titles, hitherto unaccomplished by any side. Their opponents in the final will be the same as in 1996—Sri Lanka.

South Africa 149 all out in 43.5 overs (Justin Kemp 49*, Herschelle Gibbs 39, Shaun Tait 4/39, Glenn McGrath 3/18). **Australia** 153/3 in 31.3 overs (Michael Clarke 60, Matthew Hayden 41).

Final, 29 April: Kensington Oval, Bridgetown

Many a great has graced the podium of a World Cup final. None has quite provided the breathtaking display Adam Gilchrist rendered at this cradle of West Indian cricket yesterday. It was murder at midday! But as Australia won by 53 runs through the Duckworth-Lewis method to record their fourth triumph, a truncated final and Sri Lanka having to battle the elements as much as the mightiest force in cricket history made it a controversial climax to a tortuous tournament.

(Eventually, referee Jeff Crowe and umpires Steve Bucknor, Aleem Dar, Rudi Koertzen and Billy Bowden were punished by the ICC for their incorrect conduct of the final. They were excluded from the panel of officials for the inaugural World Twenty20 championship in South Africa in September 2007.)

Gilchrist's stunning 104-ball 149 was the highest individual score compiled in a World Cup final. It not only roughed up the Sri Lankan bowlers; but by the time he was caught at midwicket, it had all but settled the issue. No matter how hard Sri Lanka toiled—and they made a valiant attempt—the target of 282 at over 7.4 runs an over was an unenviable one.

On a beautiful batting wicket, Gilchrist calculatedly clattered the fence and terraces, permanent and temporary, with 13 fours and eight sixes. It testified to Australia's ability to raise their game at will, after the curtailment of overs gave a theoretical advantage to the chasers.

Kumar Sangakkara was conspicuously short of runs in this competition. But entering at first drop, he raced to a run-a-ball fifty, only to pull Brad Hogg down midwicket's throat. In one over of Glenn McGrath, in particular, he demonstrated his class, with a six to long-on, followed by an inside-out drive past extra cover and a textbook hook to midwicket for fours.

As passing showers and fluctuating light conspired against Sri Lanka and eventually invoked the Duckworth-Lewis method, Sanath Jayasuriya battled on. Having scored 63 off 67 balls, though, he swung impatiently at Michael Clarke to be bowled. Ricky Ponting's switch to Clarke's part-time spin not only dried up boundaries but also fetched him two invaluable wickets.

Earlier, a glance at the advertisements on the boundary boards clearly reflected it was a party Indian corporates had overwhelmingly sponsored. But the sea of yellow shirts in the packed stands suggested a majority Australian presence, which was confirmed by the loud cheer when Ponting won the toss and elected to bat.

Ironically, in one of the sunniest parts of the world, rain intervened as never before in a World Cup final to delay the start by two and three-quarter hours. A grand occasion—enhanced by throbbing music, even hits from Hindi movies, conch shells and drums—was, thus, reduced to a 38-overs-a-side encounter.

After a few watchful overs, Gilchrist embarked on a brutal, calculated assault. Crucially, there was no swing for Chaminda Vaas, whom he, first, flicked for four and then stepped out to loft to long-on for six. This prompted Jayawardene to move wicketkeeper Sangakkara up to the stumps, which restricted the Australian to the crease, but did not restrain his strokeplay.

Rather expensively, Dilhara Fernando dropped Gilchrist off his own bowling, when the batsman was 31. The next ball, a full toss, was whipped away for four, the following one driven missile-like to the sightscreen and the succeeding delivery smashed to long-on for a massive six.

Muttiah Muralitharan restored some sanity, but at the other end, Tillakaratne Dilshan was despatched for two sixes in one over to the Worrell-Weekes-Walcott Stand by the irrepressible Western Australian. He heralded the hundred of the Australian innings with another boundary, this time to long-off, at the expense of Fernando. Even Murali did not escape punishment, as Gilchrist slog-swept the off-spinner for a six to midwicket.

Postponement of the second power-play to the 21st over made no difference. Lasith Malinga, bowling within himself with the new ball, but with excellent economy, was now off-driven for four by Gilchrist to complete his awesome century. Sangakkara gave him a second life off the very next ball. Indeed, throughout the Australian innings, there were several miscues, but fortune favoured the brave.

Eventually, the slingy paceman removed Matthew Hayden, who had struggled to discover his timing, brilliantly caught at extra cover. But the first-wicket partnership had produced a pulverising 172 runs at 7.5 an over.

Australia 281/4 in 38 overs (Adam Gilchrist 149, Matthew Hayden 38, Ricky Ponting 37, Lasith Malinga 2/49). **Sri Lanka** 215/8 in 36 overs (Sanath Jayasuriya 63, Kumar Sangakkara 54, Michael Clarke 2/33).

So, Australia not only established a pioneering hat-trick of World Cup wins, but subdued the domination of this championship by the West Indies in the 1970s.

The Wisden Almanack summarised: "Victorious in all their 11 matches, Australia plundered over 300 whenever they batted first on their way to the final—where they amassed 281 for four from their weather shortened 38 overs. They never yielded more than six wickets and won by more than 200 runs three times, more than 100 once more. Four of their batsmen featured in the top ten run-scorers, four of their bowlers in the top seven wicket-takers."

Hayden was the highest run-getter in the tournament and 37-year-old McGrath captured the most wickets to be declared Player of the Tournament.

But it was an ill-fated event. The first misfortune arose six days into the competition. Pakistan's coach and former England batsman Bob Woolmer was discovered dead in his Kingston hotel room hours after his side's surprise elimination.

Four days later, the Jamaican police shockingly announced that Woolmer had been murdered. Pakistani players unfairly came under suspicion. It was only three months later that suspicions of death by strangulation or poisoning were debunked. Woolmer, a diabetic with heart problems, died of a cardiac arrest.

India and Pakistan's premature departures affected sponsors and television networks from the sub-continent. It also impacted on airline, hotel and ticket bookings. The much anticipated Super Eight clash between the South Asian rivals was disappointingly replaced by Bangladesh versus Ireland.

Brian Lara, too, was a loser, as bookings for parties at his attractive plantation house in Barbados were cancelled once India were dumped at the Group stage.

Tickets for matches were too expensive for locals. Even for the West Indies versus Australia Super Eight match at Antigua, only half the 20,000 seats were occupied.

The 47-day duration of the tournament was far too long. Towards the climax, though, with strictures relaxed, a festive atmosphere was evident.

South Africa's Herschelle Gibbs bludgeoned six sixes in an over from Netherlands' Dan van Bunge. He, thus, became the first man to achieve this in international cricket. (India's Yuvraj Singh was to replicate the feat in the World Twenty20 later in the year at the expense of Stuart Broad.)

"I never thought about getting six in a row, but if it's your day, it's your day," Gibbs was quoted as saying. He expanded: "After the first three, I thought I was in with a chance. But I decided I wasn't going to charge him; I'd wait to see what he does and luckily they fell into the right slot."

Hayden marked the fastest hundred in World Cup history off 66 balls. This, against South Africa at the Super Eight stage.

India's poor exhibition predictably cut short Greg Chappell's career as this country's coach.

Tendulkar claims in his book: "Just months before the World Cup, Chappell had come to see me at home and, to my dismay, suggested that I should take over the captaincy from Rahul Dravid." He adds: "I rejected his proposition outright."

More intriguingly, he goes on to disclose: "A few days after Greg had come to my house, I suggested to the BCCI that the best option would be to keep Greg back in India and not send him with the team to the World Cup. I also said that we as senior players could take control of the side and keep the team together. That's not what happened, of course, and the 2007 campaign ended in disaster."

Duncan Fletcher (who re-surfaced as India coach in 2011) and Bennett King, too, lost their jobs with England and the West Indies respectively.

Inzamam-ul-Haq of Pakistan and Stephen Fleming of New Zealand vacated their one-day stewardships. Both soon lost the test captaincies, as well.

Meanwhile, Andrew Flintoff capsized a pedalo in the sea in the wee hours. The all-rounder was duly sacked as vice-captain and suspended for a match.

CHAPTER SEVEN

2011
Triumph

THE HONOUR TO HOST A WORLD CUP HAS GOT TO BE distributed by rotation to International Cricket Council (ICC) member countries or regions. That said, there is no good reason to be partial towards such an event being staged in the Indian subcontinent as compared to any other part of the world. In South Asia, the facilities, other than good hotels in most of the cities and improved outfields, are often not exactly world class, while the hysterical public following is not necessarily reflective of genuine appreciation or affection for the game. It is, in fact, largely partisan.

As an aircraft descends on Mumbai, one is shocked by the sprawling, unsightly slums. Admittedly, in the past decade, airports in some of the bigger cities in India have attained higher standards. But the coach travel from the aerodrome to one's allotted abode is often in terms of the quality of the vehicle, roads and the scenes *en route* nothing to write home about.

Internal flights to destinations beyond the major metropolises can be challenging, for air terminals at such places are yet to be upgraded, not to mention hotels at such venues not being up to the mark.

The state associations affiliated to the Board of Control for Cricket in India (BCCI) have benefited from considerable largesse from the parent body and consequently created new stadiums or renovated existing ones. Yet, barring plastic bucket seats replacing concrete benches or terraces, creature comforts have hardly been enhanced. The toilets can be filthy;

availability of food and beverages is limited or not conducive to the stomach. Corporate boxes are either absent or an apology for it. Some of the pavilions and dressing rooms are downright tacky. Practice areas lack attention. If it rains, an indoor option could well be missing. The wickets are variable, when consistency is called for in limited overs cricket.

The design and architecture of stands at, for instance, the Feroz Shah Kotla, is tasteless, given they mushroomed only a few years ago. Centres such as Ahmedabad, Nagpur, Kanpur—the list is endless—do not seem to emit a cricketing culture. In some cases, the governing association is directly or indirectly controlled by anti-social elements. Allocation of ties in a sub-continental World Cup is all about disbursement of favours in *lieu* of votes at the Annual General Meeting. The BCCI at least used to hold an AGM annually. One or two others don't even bother.

Australia and New Zealand were provisionally designated as hosts of the 2011 World Cup. But persuasive money talk on the part of Sharad Pawar, as head of BCCI and then the International Cricket Council (ICC), not merely snatched the privilege away from their grasp, but ensured that the capital of his home state of Maharashtra, Mumbai—not undeservingly, though—would stage the final. This required flattening of the Wankhede Stadium built in 1974 and construction of a new arena from scratch. It was the third time the subcontinent was the scene of a Cricket World Cup, only one less than England, and arguably, disproportionately ahead of particularly Australasia, which had had the honour only once.

In a bygone era, the first three World Cups were held in England. India's unexpected victory in the last of these earned India its first hosting right in 1987, albeit with a compromise of doing so jointly with Pakistan. With India especially going crazy about one-day cricket after 1983, corporate advertisers and sponsors went overboard in their pursuit of attracting eyeballs. Therefore three of seven such competitions have since been held in South Asia.

Apart from other objectives, a calculation behind organising a World Cup is—legitimately—to facilitate within reason familiar and friendly playing conditions for host country players, so as to advantageously tackle opposition from beyond one's shores. For India, this did not work in 1987 and 1996. But they were third time lucky!

Following Australia's invincibility in 2007, the 2008 edition of the Wisden Cricket Almanack could not visualise such dominance not being sustained in 2011. But four years is a long time in sports; and so it proved to be.

After the financial catastrophe of 2007—when India were ejected before the Super Eight stage—the 2011 format was engineered to avoid a repeat. Cricket remains Australia's number one sport; but this is a thinly populated country with modest economic might. In England, football has far outstripped cricket in terms of popularity and turnover. Thus, the cricketing cosmos is dependant on Indian TV channels and their advertisers and sponsors who underwrite them.

Other amendments from 2007 included trimming of the number of competitors from 16 to 14, with two ICC associate member countries getting the chop. Instead of four groups of four sides in each, there were now only two groups of seven teams in each. At the end of the round robin exercises, the top four in the respective clusters would proceed to the quarter-finals.

Group A comprised of Australia, Canada, Kenya, New Zealand, Pakistan, Sri Lanka and Zimbabwe. Group B consisted of Bangladesh, England, India, Ireland, Netherlands, South Africa and the West Indies. And the line-up for the last eight emerged as Pakistan versus the West Indies, India versus Australia, New Zealand versus South Africa and Sri Lanka versus England.

India, gradually a more confident nation after its 1991 economic reforms, possessed greater mental strength than their neighbours. And their batting line-up was the most durable of all on the easier paced Indian wickets.

Despite the slow pitches, a record number of totals in excess of 300 were registered in the league stage; but none thereafter, indicating perhaps the greater intensity of inter-locking in the knockout segment.

Pakistan's Shahid Afridi, now more a guileful wrist spinner than a reliable run-getter, captured the highest number of wickets in the tourney jointly with Indian left-arm medium pacer Zaheer Khan, but played one fewer match than him. That a slow bowler and one of a quicker variety topped the wickets tally bore testimony to the squares generally rewarding mettle.

Express bowlers South African Dale Steyn and Australian Brett Lee and otherwise Pakistan's fast-medium exponent Umar Gul were, in fact, among the successes.

India's left-handed Yuvraj Singh was declared the Player of the Tournament for his tangible contribution as a middle order batsman and left arm spinner. The night before the kick-off match against Bangladesh, Sachin Tendulkar invited him to his room for dinner, because he felt the all-rounder was a little down in the dumps. "I encouraged him to set some targets and concentrate on meeting them," recalls Tendulkar. "We really needed a fully focussed Yuvraj and I am delighted to say that's what we got from him all the way through the tournament."

Ireland's upset of England was unexpected; and justified inclusion of so-called minnows in the competition. For the former, Kevin O'Brien posted a whirlwind 133 off 63 balls to help the Irish cross their opponents' total of 327. The Englishmen recovered, though, to sensationally tie with India, only to subsequently go down to Bangladesh. It was inexplicable inconsistency.

At the same time, the quarter-final line-up was in accordance with the formbook. South Africa, though, once again slightly underperformed, losing to the plucky New Zealanders in the last eight.

With several of the stars of 2007—notably Mathew Hayden and Glenn McGrath—no longer in their party, Australia were no more unbeatable. But skipper Ricky Ponting kept them in the hunt in an honourable defeat to India.

Since the advent and ascent of Twenty20 and the immediate success of the World T20 championship in 2007, doubts had arisen about the future of the 50 over game. But India being the financial hub of cricket in the 21st century, their triumph in the 2011 World Cup rekindled the faltering format, just as much as their 1983 triumph had induced the entry of bigger money in ODI cricket.

19 February: Mirpur

This was the curtain-raiser. After they felled India in the preliminary stage of the 2007 edition, there was understandably great expectation in Bangladesh of an encore, especially since they enjoyed home advantage. India batted first—after Bangladesh won the toss. And from Virender Sehwag punching the first ball of the match off the back foot through the covers for four, the Indians looked determined not to slip up a second time.

He typically continued in that fashion to peg 175 off 140 balls, hitting 14 fours and five sixes, before being bowled by the Bangladeshi captain Shakib Al Hasan. Sachin Tendulkar—who was run out—and Gautam Gambhir only briefly partook of the plunder. Virat Kohli, though, making his debut in a World Cup, did not miss out, demonstrating his growing maturity and promise with an unbeaten hundred. Indeed, the mammoth Indian total of 370 for four fairly quietened an initially raucous crowd.

Sehwag, latterly with the aid of a runner, and Kohli—preferred in place of the more experienced Suresh Raina—realised 203 runs for the third wicket. The latter delightfully stretched his front foot to the bounce of the ball to drive piercingly off both pace and spin. If anyone pitched short, he powerfully pulled off the backfoot to midwicket. The batting powerplay produced nearly 10 runs an over.

But if the India batsmen indicated how they could bully average attacks on a relatively flat sub-continental pitch, their bowlers showed they were, perhaps, the weak link. Imrul Kayes, Tamim Iqbal (who had also tormented India at Port of Spain four years earlier) and Shakib exposed the limitations of the Indian users of the leather.

Admittedly, the evening dew made it harder for a bowler to grip the ball and additionally made it come on to the bat quite nicely. But Sreesanth was all over the place; and was rightly punished. Bangladesh made a game attempt; but the target was far beyond their reach.

Besides, Munaf Patel, Zaheer Khan and Harbhajan Singh duly controlled the flow of runs, with the first mentioned with his medium pacers capturing four wickets.

India won by 87 runs. "The 2007 defeat had been avenged and we were off to the start we had hoped for," was Tendulkar's feeling.

The previous 12 day-night matches at this Sher-e-Bangla (Bengal Tiger) stadium had been won by sides chasing. History was, however, not to repeat itself.

Toss: Bangladesh

Man of the Match: Virender Sehwag

India innings (50 overs maximum)		R	M	B	4s	6s	SR
V Sehwag	b Shakib Al Hasan	175	198	140	14	5	125.00
SR Tendulkar	run out (Shakib Al Hasan/†Mushfiqur Rahim)	28	46	29	4	0	96.55
G Gambhir	b Mahmudullah	39	49	39	3	0	100.00
V Kohli	not out	100	113	83	8	2	120.48
YK Pathan	c †Mushfiqur Rahim b Shafiul Islam	8	10	10	0	0	80.00

Extras: (b 1, lb 2, w 16, nb 1) 20

Total: (4 wickets; 50 overs) 370 (7.40 runs per over)

DNB: Yuvraj Singh, MS Dhoni*†, Harbhajan Singh, Z Khan, S Sreesanth, MM Patel

FoW: 1-69 (Tendulkar, 10.5 ov), 2-152 (Gambhir, 23.2 ov), 3-355 (Sehwag, 47.3 ov), 4-370 (Pathan, 49.6 ov)

Bowling	O	M	R	W	Econ	0s	4s	6s	
Shafiul Islam	7	0	69	1	9.85	15	8	1	(1nb, 2w)
Rubel Hossain	10	0	60	0	6.00	22	4	0	(5w)
Abdur Razzak	9	0	74	0	8.22	20	6	3	(1w)
Shakib Al Hasan	10	0	61	1	6.10	23	4	1	(3w)
Naeem Islam	7	0	54	0	7.71	8	4	1	
Mahmudullah	7	0	49	1	7.00	15	3	1	(3w)

Bangladesh innings (target: 371 runs from 50 overs)		R	M	B	4s	6s	SR
Tamim Iqbal	c Yuvraj Singh b Patel	70	136	86	3	1	81.39
Imrul Kayes	b Patel	34	33	29	7	0	117.24
Junaid Siddique	st †Dhoni b Harbhajan Singh	37	66	52	1	1	71.15
Shakib Al Hasan*	c Harbhajan Singh b Pathan	55	65	50	5	0	110.00
Mushfiqur Rahim†	c sub (SK Raina) b Khan	25	39	30	2	0	83.33
Raqibul Hasan	not out	28	44	28	0	1	100.00
Mahmudullah	b Patel	6	6	6	0	0	100.00
Naeem Islam	lbw b Patel	2	8	8	0	0	25.00

Abdur Razzak	lbw b Khan	1	6	5	0	0	20.00
Shafiul Islam	run out (Harbhajan Singh)	0	1	1	0	0	0.00
Rubel Hossain	not out	1	4	6	0	0	16.66

Extras: (lb 10, w 13, nb 1) 24

Total: (9 wickets; 50 overs) 283 (5.66 runs per over)

FoW: 1-56 (Imrul Kayes, 6.5 ov), 2-129 (Junaid Siddique, 23.1 ov), 3-188 (Tamim Iqbal, 32.1 ov), 4-234 (Shakib Al Hasan, 39.4 ov), 5-248 (Mushfiqur Rahim, 42.3 ov), 6-261 (Mahmudullah, 44.3 ov), 7-275 (Naeem Islam, 46.3 ov), 8-279 (Abdur Razzak, 47.6 ov), 9-280 (Shafiul Islam, 48.3 ov)

Bowling	**O**	**M**	**R**	**W**	**Econ**	**0s**	**4s**	**6s**	
S Sreesanth	5	0	53	0	10.60	11	7	0	(1nb, 1w)
Z Khan	10	0	40	2	4.00	35	2	0	(4w)
MM Patel	10	0	48	4	4.80	37	3	2	
Harbhajan Singh	10	0	41	1	4.10	26	1	0	(1w)
YK Pathan	8	0	49	1	6.12	12	3	0	(2w)
Yuvraj Singh	7	0	42	0	6.00	15	2	1	(1w)

27 February: Bangalore

This match had originally been allocated to Kolkata's Eden Gardens. But the failure of the Cricket Association of Bengal to meet the ICC's deadline for preparedness, led to a forfeiture and a transference of the opportunity to the Chinnaswamy Stadium in Bangalore.

In India's first home game in the competition, the everlasting Tendulkar warmed the hearts of his countless compatriots with an exquisite century after India decided to bat. His better than a run-a-ball 120 was juxtaposed with a 134 run second wicket partnership with Gambhir and paved the way for the middle order to boost the total to an imposing 338. He stroked 10 fours and five sixes in course of a 47th ODI ton; a superbly calculated knock.

Tendulkar entered the fray with a much repaired and restored favourite bat of his, one which he had been using from the previous season. But when a full-blooded square cut did not travel fast enough, the Mumbai maestro summoned a new willow, which he had knocked in—in case he needed it. But such can be the emotional bond between a batsman and a bat which has rendered yeoman's service, that Tendulkar records: "While I felt a little sad sending the old bat back to the pavilion, I did score a century with the new one." His association with the new one, though, didn't last too long; he broke it in same the tournament.

James Anderson, master swing merchant, conceded 9.25 runs per over, dubiously the most expensive by an English bowler in the World Cup. His less regarded colleague and medium pacer Tim Bresnan compensated with figures of five for 48 in his allotted 10 overs.

Andrew Strauss was gifted a ragged opening spell by Khan. He also benefitted from India not appealing for a snick off the same bowler in the cacophonous arena. Meanwhile, Kevin Pietersen, promoted to open the innings with him, raced to 31 from 22 balls, before being caught and bowled at the second attempt by Patel.

Strauss, businesslike, found an ally in Ian Bell to uncoil a defining partnership of 170 runs for the third wicket, which took England to the verge of victory. Bell, who contributed 69, survived a referral of an appeal for lbw by Yuvraj, when umpire New Zealand's Billy Bowden controversially but lawfully rejected Hawkeye's recommendation on the grounds that the batsman had been struck on the pad more than 2.5 metres from the stumps.

He was also dropped by Kohli off leg-spinner Piyush Chawla just before holing out to extra cover in the batting powerplay. Khan's very next ball, a yorker, trapped Strauss lbw to terminate his Herculean effort of 158 in 145 deliveries, with 18 boundaries and one over the ropes. Strauss' sixth ODI hundred was at the expense of an unimpressive Indian bowling. It was the highest score ever by an England batsman in the World Cup.

Indeed, with the Englishmen on 280 for two and eight overs still to come, India looked dead and buried. But Strauss' departure, which poised Khan on a hat-trick, also swung the pendulum back India's way, before the match climaxed in a tie. It was for all intents and purposes a thrilling contest. England had made the seemingly unassailable reachable.

Zaheer Khan rescued India with a haul of three for 11 in his last three overs. But he, Patel and Chawla, though among the spoils, were a bit erratic.

In a day of high drama, India lost their last seven wickets for a paltry 33 runs. England surrendered their last six for 44.

Toss: India

Man of the Match: Andrew Strauss

India innings (50 overs maximum)		R	M	B	4s	6s	SR
V Sehwag	c †Prior b Bresnan	35	34	26	6	0	134.61
SR Tendulkar	c Yardy b Anderson	120	170	115	10	5	104.34
G Gambhir	b Swann	51	95	61	5	0	83.60
Yuvraj Singh	c Bell b Yardy	58	76	50	9	0	116.00
MS Dhoni*†	c sub (LJ Wright) b Bresnan	31	38	25	3	1	124.00
YK Pathan	c Swann b Bresnan	14	12	8	1	1	175.00
V Kohli	b Bresnan	8	12	5	1	0	160.00
Harbhajan Singh	lbw b Bresnan	0	4	1	0	0	0.00
Z Khan	run out (Bresnan/†Prior)	4	10	5	0	0	80.00
PP Chawla	run out (Anderson)	2	5	4	0	0	50.00
MM Patel	not out	0	1	0	0	0	-

Extras: (lb 3, w 7, nb 5) 15

Total: (all out; 49.5 overs; 233 mins) 338 (6.78 runs per over)

FoW: 1-46 (Sehwag, 7.5 ov), 2-180 (Gambhir, 29.4 ov), 3-236 (Tendulkar, 38.2 ov), 4-305 (Yuvraj Singh, 45.6 ov), 5-305 (Dhoni, 46.1 ov), 6-327 (Pathan, 48.1 ov), 7-327 (Kohli, 48.2 ov), 8-328 (Harbhajan Singh, 48.4 ov), 9-338 (Chawla, 49.4 ov), 10-338 (Khan, 49.5 ov)

Bowling	O	M	R	W	Econ	0s	4s	6s	
JM Anderson	9.5	0	91	1	9.25	21	13	1	(1nb, 1w)
A Shahzad	8	0	53	0	6.62	25	8	0	(2w)
TT Bresnan	10	1	48	5	4.80	31	5	0	
GP Swann	9	1	59	1	6.55	28	5	3	(2w)
PD Collingwood	3	0	20	0	6.66	8	0	2	
MH Yardy	10	0	64	1	6.40	19	4	1	(2w)

England innings (target: 339 runs from 50 overs)		R	M	B	4s	6s	SR
AJ Strauss*	lbw b Khan	158	188	145	18	1	108.96
KP Pietersen	c & b Patel	31	45	22	5	0	140.90
IJL Trott	lbw b Chawla	16	30	19	1	0	84.21
IR Bell	c Kohli b Khan	69	108	71	4	1	97.18
PD Collingwood	b Khan	1	12	5	0	0	20.00

MJ Prior†	c sub (SK Raina) b Harbhajan Singh	4	15	8	0	0	50.00
MH Yardy	c Sehwag b Patel	13	17	10	1	0	130.00
TT Bresnan	b Chawla	14	18	9	0	1	155.55
GP Swann	not out	15	12	9	0	1	166.66
A Shahzad	not out	6	5	2	0	1	300.00

Extras: (b 1, lb 7, w 3) 11

Total: (8 wickets; 50 overs; 229 mins) 338 (6.76 runs per over)

DNB: JM Anderson

FoW: 1-68 (Pietersen, 9.3 ov), 2-111 (Trott, 16.4 ov), 3-281 (Bell, 42.4 ov), 4-281 (Strauss, 42.5 ov), 5-285 (Collingwood, 44.3 ov), 6-289 (Prior, 45.2 ov), 7-307 (Yardy, 47.3 ov), 8-325 (Bresnan, 48.6 ov)

Bowling	**O**	**M**	**R**	**W**	**Econ**	**0s**	**4s**	**6s**	
Z Khan	10	0	64	3	6.40	27	8	0	(1w)
MM Patel	10	0	70	2	7.00	20	5	1	(1w)
PP Chawla	10	0	71	2	7.10	22	5	3	(1w)
Harbhajan Singh	10	0	58	1	5.80	18	4	0	
Yuvraj Singh	7	0	46	0	6.57	15	4	1	
YK Pathan	3	0	21	0	7.00	7	3	0	

6 March: Bangalore

Khan bowled a tidy opening spell to have Ireland tottering on nine for two after Mahendra Dhoni asked them to take first strike. However, a 113-run third wicket stand between William Porterfield and Niall O'Brien, thereafter, advanced Ireland to a respectable 122 for two.

At this juncture, though, O'Brien was run out; and the Irish lost their way. Where India's specialist spinners had proved to be ineffective, the supporting left-arm spinner Yuvraj wrought havoc. The Punjab all-rounder doesn't exhibit turn and bounce; but he does emit a clever variation. Batsmen make the mistake of underestimating him.

Flatteringly, he grabbed career-best five wickets—three of them via catches and another two with arm balls that kept low to win lbw shouts. In 17 overs, Ireland lost six wickets; their last eight wickets going down for 85 runs.

But Ireland were not in a mood to go down without a fight. They bowled a restrictive line and length, which resulted in India losing wickets at regular intervals. 24 for two became 100 for four and then 167 for five, when Yusuf Pathan joined Yuvraj; and the former blasted 30 runs off 24 balls, while the other coasted to a half-century. India romped home by five wickets.

Toss: India

Man of the Match: Yuvraj Singh

Ireland innings (50 overs maximum)		R	M	B	4s	6s	SR
WTS Porterfield*	c Harbhajan Singh b Yuvraj Singh	75	146	104	6	1	72.11
PR Stirling	b Khan	0	2	1	0	0	0.00
EC Joyce	c †Dhoni b Khan	4	8	5	1	0	80.00
NJ O'Brien†	run out (Kohli/ †Dhoni)	46	93	78	3	0	58.97
AR White	c †Dhoni b Yuvraj Singh	5	8	10	0	0	50.00
KJ O'Brien	c & b Yuvraj Singh	9	14	13	1	0	69.23
AR Cusack	lbw b Yuvraj Singh	24	49	30	3	0	80.00
JF Mooney	lbw b Yuvraj Singh	5	19	17	0	0	29.41
DT Johnston	lbw b Patel	17	38	20	2	0	85.00
GH Dockrell	c †Dhoni b Khan	3	19	10	0	0	30.00
WB Rankin	not out	1	5	1	0	0	100.00

Extras: (lb 4, w 8, nb 6) 18

Total: (all out; 47.5 overs; 205 mins) 207 (4.32 runs per over)

FoW: 1-1 (Stirling, 0.4 ov), 2-9 (Joyce, 2.3 ov), 3-122 (NJ O'Brien, 26.5 ov), 4-129 (White, 29.1 ov), 5-147 (KJ O'Brien, 33.4 ov), 6-160 (Porterfield, 37.1 ov), 7-178 (Mooney, 41.5 ov), 8-184 (Cusack, 43.4 ov), 9-201 (Dockrell, 46.6 ov), 10-207 (Johnston, 47.5 ov)

Bowling	O	M	R	W	Econ	0s	4s	6s	
Z Khan	9	1	30	3	3.33	38	4	0	(1w)
MM Patel	4.5	0	25	1	5.17	16	3	0	(1w)
YK Pathan	7	1	32	0	4.57	22	3	0	
Harbhajan Singh	9	1	29	0	3.22	32	1	0	(1w)
PP Chawla	8	0	56	0	7.00	20	3	1	(2nb, 3w)
Yuvraj Singh	10	0	31	5	3.10	38	2	0	(1w)

India innings (target: 208 runs from 50 overs)		R	M	B	4s	6s	SR
V Sehwag	c & b Johnston	5	5	3	1	0	166.66
SR Tendulkar	lbw b Dockrell	38	91	56	4	0	67.85
G Gambhir	c Cusack b Johnston	10	18	15	2	0	66.66
V Kohli	run out (Dockrell/ KJ O'Brien)	34	82	53	3	0	64.15
Yuvraj Singh	not out	50	108	75	3	0	66.66
MS Dhoni*†	lbw b Dockrell	34	68	50	2	0	68.00
YK Pathan	not out	30	23	24	2	3	125.00

Extras: (lb 4, w 5) 9

Total: (5 wickets; 46 overs; 200 mins) 210 (4.56 runs per over)

DNB: Harbhajan Singh, PP Chawla, Z Khan, MM Patel

FoW: 1-9 (Sehwag, 1.1 ov), 2-24 (Gambhir, 5.2 ov), 3-87 (Tendulkar, 20.1 ov), 4-100 (Kohli, 23.4 ov), 5-167 (Dhoni, 40.1 ov)

Bowling	O	M	R	W	Econ	0s	4s	6s	
WB Rankin	10	1	34	0	3.40	38	3	0	(2w)
DT Johnston	5	1	16	2	3.20	21	2	0	(1w)
GH Dockrell	10	0	49	2	4.90	32	3	2	
JF Mooney	2	0	18	0	9.00	3	3	0	
PR Stirling	10	0	45	0	4.50	31	2	1	(2w)
AR White	5	0	23	0	4.60	13	2	0	
KJ O'Brien	1	0	3	0	3.00	3	0	0	
AR Cusack	3	0	18	0	6.00	7	2	0	

9 March: Delhi

Opting to bat, Netherlands started steadily with an opening partnership of 56, which equalled their best in the World Cup. But this became 108 for six as the middle order fragmented in the face of seamers and spinners alike. There were also two run outs as the Dutch caved in for 189.

Piyush Chawla began the rot with a trademark googly. Much depended on Ryan ten Doeschate and to a certain extent Tom Cooper, but neither quite ignited. From 99 for three, the Dutch collapsed to 127 for eight.

Netherlands skipper Peter Borren, batting at number eight, chanced his arm to post 38 in 36 balls. But it wasn't good enough; and he was mopped up by a persevering Khan, whose reverse swing was again a factor to be reckoned with.

India's first four batsmen achieved a strike rate of a run a ball or better, with Sehwag the most rapid with 39 runs off 26 balls. At one stage India were 69 for no loss in the eighth over, with the Delhiite and Tendulkar going great guns. But soon India were struggling at 99 for four, after left-arm spinner Pieter Seelaar struck thrice in quick succession.

Yuvraj, though, completed another fine, all round performance to avert embarrassment. It was also his third half-century in successive matches. India prevailed with more than 13 overs to spare.

Tougher opposition awaited the Indians. But at this point, they topped the Group B table.

Toss: Netherlands

Man of the Match: Yuvraj Singh

Netherlands innings (50 overs maximum)		R	M	B	4s	6s	SR
ES Szwarczynski	b Chawla	28	59	42	4	0	66.66
W Barresi†	lbw b Yuvraj Singh	26	67	58	2	0	44.82
TLW Cooper	c †Dhoni b Nehra	29	52	47	2	0	61.70
RN ten Doeschate	c Khan b Yuvraj Singh	11	29	28	1	0	39.28
AN Kervezee	c Harbhajan Singh b Chawla	11	45	23	1	0	47.82
B Zuiderent	lbw b Khan	0	10	6	0	0	0.00
TN de Grooth	run out (Chawla/ †Dhoni)	5	14	11	0	0	45.45
PW Borren*	c Nehra b Khan	38	46	36	3	2	105.55
BP Kruger	run out (Kohli/ †Dhoni)	8	16	12	1	0	66.66
Mudassar Bukhari	b Khan	21	20	18	1	2	116.66
PM Seelaar	not out	0	2	0	0	0	-

Extras: (b 6, lb 3, w 2, nb 1) 12

Total: (all out; 46.4 overs; 191 mins) 189 (4.05 runs per over)

FoW: 1-56 (Szwarczynski, 15.2 ov), 2-64 (Barresi, 18.6 ov), 3-99 (ten Doeschate, 28.2 ov), 4-100 (Cooper, 29.1 ov), 5-101 (Zuiderent, 30.6 ov), 6-108 (de Grooth, 34.2 ov), 7-127 (Kervezee, 38.1 ov), 8-151 (Kruger, 42.2 ov), 9-189 (Borren, 46.1 ov), 10-189 (Mudassar Bukhari, 46.4 ov)

Bowling	O	M	R	W	Econ	0s	4s	6s	
Z Khan	6.4	0	20	3	3.00	30	3	0	
A Nehra	5	1	22	1	4.40	21	2	1	
YK Pathan	6	1	17	0	2.83	25	2	0	
Harbhajan Singh	10	0	31	0	3.10	39	0	1	(2w)
PP Chawla	10	0	47	2	4.70	34	3	2	(1nb)
Yuvraj Singh	9	1	43	2	4.77	29	5	0	

India innings (target: 190 runs from 50 overs)		R	M	B	4s	6s	SR
V Sehwag	c Kervezee b Seelaar	39	36	26	5	2	150.00
SR Tendulkar	c Kruger b Seelaar	27	45	22	6	0	122.72
YK Pathan	c & b Seelaar	11	12	10	1	1	110.00
G Gambhir	b Mudassar Bukhari	28	57	28	3	0	100.00
V Kohli	b Borren	12	16	20	2	0	60.00
Yuvraj Singh	not out	51	93	73	7	0	69.86
MS Dhoni*†	not out	19	56	40	2	0	47.50

Extras: (w 4) 4

Total: (5 wickets; 36.3 overs; 160 mins) 191 (5.23 runs per over)

DNB: Harbhajan Singh, PP Chawla, Z Khan, A Nehra

FoW: 1-69 (Sehwag, 7.3 ov), 2-80 (Tendulkar, 9.1 ov), 3-82 (Pathan, 9.5 ov), 4-99 (Kohli, 14.3 ov), 5-139 (Gambhir, 23.1 ov)

Bowling	O	M	R	W	Econ	0s	4s	6s	
Mudassar Bukhari	6	1	33	1	5.50	24	4	1	(2w)
RN ten Doeschate	7	0	38	0	5.42	25	6	0	(2w)
PM Seelaar	10	1	53	3	5.30	35	7	1	
PW Borren	8	0	33	1	4.12	30	3	1	
TLW Cooper	2	0	11	0	5.50	7	2	0	
BP Kruger	3.3	0	23	0	6.57	10	4	0	

12 March: Nagpur

From the commanding heights of 268 for one, India crumbled to 296 all out. The first pair of Sehwag and Tendulkar put on 142. The former recorded 73 off 66 balls; and the little master 111 in 101 deliveries—his second hundred of the tournament. Gambhir, too, contributed a sprightly 75-ball 69. Thereafter, it was a spectacular slide.

Nonetheless, a total of 296 wasn't uncompetitive. Hashim Amla and Jacques Kallis laid the foundation of a chase with respective half-centuries. Following this A B de Villiers pinned a 39-ball 52, which took the South Africans closer, before Faf du Plessis and Robin Peterson held their nerve to finish the job.

13 runs were needed off the last over. Dhoni entrusted the ball to the experienced Ashish Nehra. Peterson fortuitously got a four to fine leg off the first ball, but banged the next over long on for a decisive six. Two more runs ensued off the third ball, before a cover drive to the fence settled the issue.

Dhoni, who remained unbeaten on 12 in India's incredible capitulation with the bat, angrily and publicly remarked: "You don't play for the crowd, you play for the country."

Harbhajan was the pick of the Indian bowlers. He made the occasional one worryingly cock up. However, with Kallis run out, South Africa still had to score 124 runs at nearly nine an over. The powerplay made a difference, as de Villiers, in particularly, took advantage of this. But Harbhajan wrenched it back for India when the South African, in full cry, slog swept the off-spinner down midwicket's throat.

The asking rate was still close to eight an over. But the South Africans crossed the line much to the disappointment of a partisan crowd; the margin being three wickets.

Toss: India

Man of the Match: Dale Steyn

India innings (50 overs maximum)		R	M	B	4s	6s	SR
V Sehwag	b du Plessis	73	87	66	12	0	110.60
SR Tendulkar	c Duminy b Morkel	111	184	101	8	3	109.90
G Gambhir	c Kallis b Steyn	69	98	75	7	0	92.00
YK Pathan	c Smith b Steyn	0	4	2	0	0	0.00
Yuvraj Singh	c Botha b Kallis	12	15	9	0	1	133.33
MS Dhoni*†	not out	12	37	21	0	0	57.14
V Kohli	c & b Peterson	1	2	3	0	0	33.33
Harbhajan Singh	b Steyn	3	8	9	0	0	33.33
Z Khan	c Morkel b Peterson	0	3	3	0	0	0.00
A Nehra	c Smith b Steyn	0	2	3	0	0	0.00
MM Patel	b Steyn	0	1	1	0	0	0.00

Extras: (lb 2, w 12, nb 1) 15

Total: (all out; 48.4 overs; 229 mins) 296 (6.08 runs per over)

FoW: 1-142 (Sehwag, 17.4 ov), 2-267 (Tendulkar, 39.4 ov), 3-268 (Gambhir, 40.1 ov), 4-268 (Pathan, 40.3 ov), 5-283 (Yuvraj Singh, 42.6 ov), 6-286 (Kohli, 43.6 ov), 7-293 (Harbhajan Singh, 46.5 ov), 8-294 (Khan, 47.4 ov), 9-296 (Nehra, 48.3 ov), 10-296 (Patel, 48.4 ov)

Bowling	O	M	R	W	Econ	0s	4s	6s	
DW Steyn	9.4	0	50	5	5.17	35	3	1	(2w)
M Morkel	7	0	59	1	8.42	18	10	0	(1nb)
JH Kallis	8	0	43	1	5.37	22	4	0	(1w)
RJ Peterson	9	0	52	2	5.77	20	3	1	(2w)
JP Duminy	3	0	29	0	9.66	4	3	1	
J Botha	9	0	39	0	4.33	30	2	1	(2w)
F du Plessis	3	0	22	1	7.33	4	2	0	(1w)

South Africa innings (target: 297 runs from 50 overs)		R	M	B	4s	6s	SR
HM Amla	c †Dhoni b Harbhajan Singh	61	114	72	5	0	84.72
GC Smith*	c Tendulkar b Khan	16	39	29	2	0	55.17
JH Kallis	run out (†Dhoni/) Harbhajan Singh	69	120	88	4	0	78.40
AB de Villiers	c Kohli b Harbhajan Singh	52	67	39	6	1	133.33
JP Duminy	st †Dhoni b Harbhajan Singh	23	40	20	2	1	115.00
F du Plessis	not out	25	52	23	0	1	108.69
MN van Wyk†	lbw b Patel	5	7	5	1	0	100.00
J Botha	c sub (SK Raina) b Patel	23	15	15	2	1	153.33
RJ Peterson	not out	18	15	7	2	1	257.14

Extras: (lb 7, w 1) 8

Total: (7 wickets; 49.4 overs; 236 mins) 300 (6.04 runs per over)

DNB: M Morkel, DW Steyn

FoW: 1-41 (Smith, 8.3 ov), 2-127 (Amla, 27.2 ov), 3-173 (Kallis, 35.4 ov), 4-223 (de Villiers, 40.3 ov), 5-238 (Duminy, 42.3 ov), 6-247 (van Wyk, 43.6 ov), 7-279 (Botha, 47.5 ov)

Bowling	O	M	R	W	Econ	0s	4s	6s
Z Khan	10	0	43	1	4.30	35	4	1
A Nehra	8.4	0	65	0	7.50	24	9	1
MM Patel	10	0	65	2	6.50	21	6	1
YK Pathan	4	0	20	0	5.00	6	0	0
Yuvraj Singh	8	0	47	0	5.87	18	2	1
Harbhajan Singh	9	0	53	3	5.88	19	3	1 (1w)

20 March: Chennai

India preferred first use of the willow.

There was a bit of bounce in the pitch; and fast medium Ravi Rampaul, making his debut in a World Cup, celebrated this by capturing five wickets. Premeditatedly, the West Indies opened the bowling with the burly left-arm spinner Sulieman Benn—and he claimed the prized wicket of Tendulkar. But short-pitched stuff thereafter, paid dividends. Only Yuvraj stood his ground, despite being sick on the field, to notch up a maiden World Cup century.

Yuvraj was fortunate in that the West Indian skipper Darren Sammy dropped two difficult chances off him early in his innings. With Kohli, who had preceded him in the batting order at number three, he added 122 runs for the third wicket, before the right-hander was cleaned up by Rampaul for a responsible knock of 59.

Unsurprisingly, the West Indian quicks peppered Yuvraj with bouncers. But in between, he contrived a decent though not exceptional run rate. Anything not above waist height, he flayed with characteristic elegance and timing. Leg-spinner Devendra Bishoo and Sammy suffered as a result.

When it came to the West Indies' turn to bat, opener Devon Smith motored his side to 146 for two, before a slower ball from Khan brought his 97 ball 81 to a close. Ramnaresh Sarwan's 39 was the only other notable contribution as the West Indies surrendered their last eight wickets for a meagre 34 runs. Darren Bravo—a poor man's Brian Lara—flattered to deceive.

It was a tale of two collapses. India fragmented from 218 for three to 268 all down; the West Indies from 154 for two to 188 all out.

The outcome meant India would confront defending champions Australia in the quarter-finals; and the West Indies would meet Pakistan at the same stage.

Toss: India

Man of the Match: Yuvraj Singh

India innings (50 overs maximum)		R	M	B	4s	6s	SR
G Gambhir	c Russell b Rampaul	22	34	26	4	0	84.61
SR Tendulkar	c †Thomas b Rampaul	2	4	4	0	0	50.00
V Kohli	b Rampaul	59	128	76	5	0	77.63
Yuvraj Singh	c & b Pollard	113	163	123	10	2	91.86
MS Dhoni*†	st †Thomas b Bishoo	22	41	30	1	0	73.33
SK Raina	c Rampaul b Sammy	4	14	8	0	0	50.00
YK Pathan	b Rampaul	11	16	10	1	0	110.00
Harbhajan Singh	c Pollard b Russell	3	16	6	0	0	50.00
R Ashwin	not out	10	14	7	1	0	142.85
Z Khan	b Rampaul	5	4	3	1	0	166.66
MM Patel	b Russell	1	1	2	0	0	50.00

Extras: (b 5, lb 2, w 9) 16

Total: (all out; 49.1 overs; 222 mins) 268 (5.45 runs per over)

FoW: 1-8 (Tendulkar, 0.6 ov), 2-51 (Gambhir, 8.3 ov), 3-173 (Kohli, 32.2 ov), 4-218 (Dhoni, 41.4 ov), 5-232 (Raina, 43.5 ov), 6-240 (Yuvraj Singh, 44.6 ov), 7-251 (Pathan, 46.4 ov), 8-259 (Harbhajan Singh, 47.5 ov), 9-267 (Khan, 48.5 ov), 10-268 (Patel, 49.1 ov)

Bowling	O	M	R	W	Econ	0s	4s	6s	
R Rampaul	10	0	51	5	5.10	29	4	0	(1w)
SJ Benn	4	0	32	0	8.00	10	6	0	
AD Russell	9.1	1	46	2	5.01	23	3	0	(2w)
DJG Sammy	6	0	35	1	5.83	17	1	2	(1w)
D Bishoo	10	0	48	1	4.80	29	5	0	
KA Pollard	10	0	49	1	4.90	29	4	0	(1w)

West Indies innings (target: 269 runs from 50 overs)		R	M	B	4s	6s	SR
DS Smith	b Khan	81	117	97	7	1	83.50
KA Edwards	lbw b Ashwin	17	26	17	1	1	100.00
DM Bravo	c Harbhajan Singh b Raina	22	35	29	1	1	75.86
RR Sarwan	c Ashwin b Khan	39	111	68	3	0	57.35
KA Pollard	c Pathan b Harbhajan Singh	1	6	3	0	0	33.33

DC Thomas†	st †Dhoni b Yuvraj Singh	2	12	8	0	0	25.00
DJG Sammy*	run out (Raina/Patel)	2	7	4	0	0	50.00
AD Russell	c Pathan b Yuvraj Singh	0	5	5	0	0	0.00
SJ Benn	c Patel b Khan	3	15	12	0	0	25.00
D Bishoo	not out	6	13	11	1	0	54.54
R Rampaul	b Ashwin	1	7	4	0	0	25.00

Extras: (lb 8, w 6) 14

Total: (all out; 43 overs; 181 mins) 188 (4.37 runs per over)

FoW: 1-34 (Edwards, 6.2 ov), 2-91 (Bravo, 16.6 ov), 3-154 (Smith, 30.3 ov), 4-157 (Pollard, 31.5 ov), 5-160 (Thomas, 34.2 ov), 6-162 (Sammy, 35.3 ov), 7-165 (Russell, 36.6 ov), 8-179 (Benn, 39.6 ov), 9-182 (Sarwan, 41.1 ov), 10-188 (Rampaul, 42.6 ov)

Bowling	**O**	**M**	**R**	**W**	**Econ**	**0s**	**4s**	**6s**	
R Ashwin	10	0	41	2	4.10	32	2	1	(1w)
Z Khan	6	0	26	3	4.33	22	3	0	(2w)
Harbhajan Singh	9	1	35	1	3.88	36	3	1	(1w)
YK Pathan	7	0	28	0	4.00	21	2	0	
SK Raina	2	0	12	1	6.00	4	1	0	
Yuvraj Singh	4	0	18	2	4.50	15	1	1	
MM Patel	5	0	20	0	4.00	16	1	0	(1w)

Quarter-final, 24 March: Ahmedabad

This was clearly the biggest match of the championship for India; a clash against the champions in the last three World Cups, unmatched four times winners of the trophy since its inception and whether at their best or not or at home in the sub-continental playing conditions or not, mentally the strongest side. In short, the greatest cricketing force of all time—Australia! If India won this contest, they would most likely win the tournament.

"Playing against Australia is always a high-pressure contest and a knockout game even more so," is Tendulkar's view.

Australian captain Ricky Ponting had proved to be one of the great batsmen of his generation. Presently, he produced a 118-ball 104 on a slow turner after electing to bat first. He was playing his last World Cup; he made it count. However, there was little support from his fellow batters, other than from opener Brad Haddin and to a certain extent David Hussey.

Haddin, promoted to open the innings, chipped in with a half-century and realised 70 runs for the second wicket with Ponting. Hussey, batting as low as number seven, conjured a late flurry—38 not out in 26 balls.

The stakes were high and Ponting was not in the greatest of touch. He nevertheless prevailed, thus demonstrating what application can accomplish even if you are not at your best.

The Indian bowling was once more ordinary, with the exception of an inspired Yuvraj. The abrasive surface facilitated Khan's reverse swing. Ravi Ashwin, handed the new ball, revealed his bag of tricks, including a carom ball. He eventually ensnared Ponting's prized scalp. Harbhajan varied the angle of his deliveries. But none was quite economical.

Indeed, it was Yuvraj's unpretentious left-arm spin that reined in the potentially rampant Aussies. He cut short Haddin's charge and removed the dangerous Michael Clarke.

Australia looked shaky at 140 for four. But the batting powerplay yielded 44 runs without the loss of a wicket to boost them to a competitive total. The pressure of a knockout situation, then, confronted India. "We knew it wouldn't be easy to chase down that total under lights," admits Tendulkar.

Tendulkar hadn't slept well the previous night, but he eased the pressure with a splendid fifty before he was caught behind. He stitched 50 runs for the second wicket with Gambhir, who, too, got a half-century till he was run out. But was a 74-run sixth wicket stand between left-handers Yuvraj and Suresh Raina that really decided the contest.

The psychological burden mounted and India slid from 143 for two to 187 for five, which included the exit of the otherwise excellent finisher Dhoni. But Yuvraj now gave glimpses of his majestic possibilities. On a pensive track, he was unperturbed by the Australians' extra pace as he pierced both sides of the field. Raina pulled anything even fractionally short to the onside fence.

India breasted the tape with 14 balls and five wickets to spare. It was the Indians' first victory over Australia in the World Cup since defeating them in a league match at the Feroz Shah Kotla in 1987.

"When Yuvi hit the final boundary, the Indian dressing room went mad," Tendulkar remembers. "It was an unforgettable match."

Toss: Australia

Man of the Match: Yuvraj Singh

Australia innings (50 overs maximum)		R	M	B	4s	6s	SR
SR Watson	b Ashwin	25	39	38	5	0	65.78
BJ Haddin†	c Raina b Yuvraj Singh	53	95	62	6	1	85.48
RT Ponting*	c Khan b Ashwin	104	172	118	7	1	88.13
MJ Clarke	c Khan b Yuvraj Singh	8	30	19	0	0	42.10
MEK Hussey	b Khan	3	15	9	0	0	33.33
CL White	c & b Khan	12	36	22	0	0	54.54
DJ Hussey	not out	38	44	26	3	1	146.15
MG Johnson	not out	6	7	6	0	0	100.00

Extras: (lb 2, w 9) 11

Total: (6 wickets; 50 overs; 220 mins) 260 (5.20 runs per over)

DNB: B Lee, JJ Krejza, SW Tait

FoW: 1-40 (Watson, 9.6 ov), 2-110 (Haddin, 22.5 ov), 3-140 (Clarke, 30.4 ov), 4-150 (MEK Hussey, 33.3 ov), 5-190 (White, 41.2 ov), 6-245 (Ponting, 48.3 ov)

Bowling	O	M	R	W	Econ	0s	4s	6s	
R Ashwin	10	0	52	2	5.20	30	3	2	(1w)
Z Khan	10	0	53	2	5.30	27	6	0	
Harbhajan Singh	10	0	50	0	5.00	30	2	0	(4w)
MM Patel	7	0	44	0	6.28	22	7	0	
Yuvraj Singh	10	0	44	2	4.40	34	3	1	
SR Tendulkar	2	0	9	0	4.50	5	0	0	
V Kohli	1	0	6	0	6.00	1	0	0	

India innings (target: 261 runs from 50 overs)		R	M	B	4s	6s	SR
V Sehwag	c MEK Hussey b Watson	15	46	22	2	0	68.18
SR Tendulkar	c †Haddin b Tait	53	93	68	7	0	77.94
G Gambhir	run out (White/ DJ Hussey)	50	116	64	2	0	78.12
V Kohli	c Clarke b DJ Hussey	24	38	33	1	0	72.72
Yuvraj Singh	not out	57	90	65	8	0	87.69
MS Dhoni*†	c Clarke b Lee	7	19	8	1	0	87.50
SK Raina	not out	34	48	28	2	1	121.42

Extras: (lb 3, w 16, nb 2) 21

Total: (5 wickets; 47.4 overs; 232 mins) 261 (5.47 runs per over)
DNB: R Ashwin, Harbhajan Singh, Z Khan, MM Patel
FoW: 1-44 (Sehwag, 8.1 ov), 2-94 (Tendulkar, 18.1 ov), 3-143 (Kohli, 28.3 ov), 4-168 (Gambhir, 33.2 ov), 5-187 (Dhoni, 37.3 ov)

Bowling	O	M	R	W	Econ	0s	4s	6s	
B Lee	8.4	1	45	1	5.19	31	5	1	(3w)
SW Tait	7	0	52	1	7.42	19	4	0	(2nb, 6w)
MG Johnson	8	0	41	0	5.12	30	5	0	(2w)
SR Watson	7	0	37	1	5.28	20	4	0	(1w)
JJ Krejza	9	0	45	0	5.00	20	2	0	
MJ Clarke	3	0	19	0	6.33	3	1	0	
DJ Hussey	5	0	19	1	3.80	17	2	0	

Semifinal, 29 March: Colombo

After opting to bat first, a number of New Zealand batsmen got set and then got out. Martin Guptill and Ross Taylor were the main culprits. The former a victim of a Lasith Malinga yorker in his second spell; the other seduced by a short pitched ball from Ajantha Mendis to perish at deep midwicket. Brendon Mcullum, too, got carried away against the underrated Rangana Herath after sweeping the same bowler for six.

It was, therefore, left to the veteran Scott Styris to shepherd the Kiwi innings with a 77-ball 57, before he was trapped lbw by Muttiah Muralitharan. His 77 run partnership for the fourth wicket with Taylor was the most progressive of the venture. But this was undone, as New Zealand sank from 192 for four to 217 all out, which included four wickets going down in the space of four runs and 12 balls.

To chase it down, Upul Tharanga appeared in an uncharacteristic incarnation, racing to a run a ball 30 until a brilliant catch by Jesse Ryder put paid to his ambitions. Tillakaratne Dilshan and Kumar Sangakkara, thereafter, put on 120 for the second wicket to catapult Sri Lanka to 160 for 1 in the 33rd over. The right-hander, though, became Tim Southee's second of three wickets, as he attempted a cut without quite applying himself to be caught at point.

The next over, Daniel Vettori had Mahela Jayawardene plumb in front. Soon after, the sublime Sangakkara tried to scoop a delivery over the 'keeper only to spoon a catch to thirdman. New Zealand had suddenly picked up three wickets for eight runs off 22 balls.

Jolted by the procession, the Sri Lankans momentarily closed shutters; but it was inevitable they would reach their destination, given the fact that New Zealand had too modest a score to defend. Thilan Samaraweera duly steered them home, with five wickets to spare.

It was Vettori's last match as captain. In reaching the semifinals six times in 10 campaigns New Zealand gave him a fitting farewell.

And India's southern neighbours reached a second successive World Cup final, having otherwise triumphed in 1996.

Toss: New Zealand
Man of the Match: Kumar Sangakkara

New Zealand innings (50 overs maximum)		R	M	B	4s	6s	SR
MJ Guptill	b Malinga	39	91	65	3	0	60.00
BB McCullum†	b Herath	13	27	21	1	1	61.90
JD Ryder	c †Sangakkara b Muralitharan	19	48	34	2	0	55.88
LRPL Taylor	c Tharanga b Mendis	36	90	55	1	0	65.45
SB Styris	lbw b Muralitharan	57	119	77	5	0	74.02
KS Williamson	lbw b Malinga	22	23	16	3	0	137.50
NL McCullum	c †Sangakkara b Malinga	9	9	9	0	1	100.00
JDP Oram	c Jayawardene b Dilshan	7	14	9	1	0	77.77
DL Vettori*	not out	3	10	3	0	0	100.00
TG Southee	c †Sangakkara b Mendis	0	3	3	0	0	0.00
AJ McKay	b Mendis	0	1	2	0	0	0.00

Extras: (lb 5, w 6, nb 1) 12
Total: (all out; 48.5 overs; 222 mins) 217 (4.44 runs per over)
FoW: 1-32 (BB McCullum, 7.1 ov), 2-69 (Ryder, 18.3 ov), 3-84 (Guptill, 21.3 ov), 4-161 (Taylor, 39.1 ov), 5-192 (Williamson, 43.3 ov), 6-204 (NL McCullum, 45.1 ov), 7-213 (Styris, 46.6 ov), 8-215 (Oram, 47.4 ov), 9-217 (Southee, 48.3 ov), 10-217 (McKay, 48.5 ov)

Bowling	O	M	R	W	Econ	0s	4s	6s	
SL Malinga	9	0	55	3	6.11	30	8	0	(1nb)
HMRKB Herath	9	1	31	1	3.44	33	1	1	(1w)
AD Mathews	6	0	27	0	4.50	21	3	0	
BAW Mendis	9.5	0	35	3	3.55	35	2	0	
M Muralitharan	10	1	42	2	4.20	36	2	1	(2w)
TM Dilshan	5	0	22	1	4.40	12	0	0	(1w)

Sri Lanka innings (target: 218 runs from 50 overs)		R	M	B	4s	6s	SR
WU Tharanga	c Ryder b Southee	30	29	31	4	1	96.77
TM Dilshan	c Ryder b Southee	73	142	93	10	1	78.49
KC Sangakkara*†	c Styris b McKay	54	132	79	7	1	68.35
DPMD Jayawardene	lbw b Vettori	1	3	3	0	0	33.33
TT Samaraweera	not out	23	77	38	2	0	60.52
LPC Silva	b Southee	13	29	25	2	0	52.00
AD Mathews	not out	14	31	18	1	1	77.77

Extras: (lb 2, w 10) 12

Total: (5 wickets; 47.5 overs; 223 mins) 220 (4.59 runs per over)

DNB: SL Malinga, HMRKB Herath, BAW Mendis, M Muralitharan

FoW: 1-40 (Tharanga, 7.2 ov), 2-160 (Dilshan, 32.4 ov), 3-161 (Jayawardene, 33.1 ov), 4-169 (Sangakkara, 36.2 ov), 5-185 (Silva, 42.2 ov)

Bowling	O	M	R	W	Econ	0s	4s	6s	
NL McCullum	6	0	33	0	5.50	23	3	2	(1w)
TG Southee	10	2	57	3	5.70	40	8	1	(1w)
DL Vettori	10	0	36	1	3.60	37	3	0	
JDP Oram	8	1	29	0	3.62	37	4	1	
AJ McKay	9.5	1	37	1	3.76	40	4	0	(2w)
SB Styris	2	0	12	0	6.00	3	1	0	
JD Ryder	2	0	14	0	7.00	7	3	0	

Semifinal, 30 March: Mohali

"Playing Pakistan in a World Cup semifinal on Indian soil—it just couldn't get any bigger," pens Tendulkar. The Indian prime minister Manmohan Singh and his Pakistani counterpart Yousaf Raza Gilani, both Punjabis, witnessed the face-off in the outskirts of the capital of Indian Punjab.

India plumped for first use of the willow. There was a buzz in the ground with Tendulkar being on the brink of 100 international centuries. But rarely if ever has Tendulkar been so fortuitous in course of an innings. He was dropped four times, making people wonder what was going on! The easiest of the chances went to Younis Khan at cover off Shahid Afridi. Umar's spill at wide midon—Mohammad Hafeez was the sufferer—was not expected of an international cricketer. Tendulkar got the benefit of the doubt in two vociferous calls for lbw, as well.

If the Indo-Pak factor was at play, this didn't affect Sehwag, who rollicked to 38 in 25 balls, helping himself to 21 runs in an over from Umar Gul. He was, though, stopped in his tracks by a successful leg before wicket shout from Wahab Riaz, left-arm, genuinely fast and the standout Pakistani bowlers with a return of five for 46.

Tendulkar finally departed on 85, which consumed 115 deliveries. The respected off-spinner Saeed Ajmal, censured by the ICC in 2014 for an illegal bowling action, had him caught at cover. It was an effort Tendulkar would probably like to forget; yet his was the highest number of runs from an individual in the match. Besides, his 68-run association for the second wicket with Gambhir was the best in the game.

Dhoni, too, could have been caught behind early, but didn't cash in. But once more, Raina, entering the scene at number seven, produced a strokeful finale to forge India to a defendable total. Tendulkar's assessment being: "It was a good total but not a clear winning score on a decent pitch."

Pakistan never constructed a substantial partnership; and the Indians fielded out of their socks. Hafeez promised much, but couldn't materially capitalise. Patel strangled him with an uninterrupted series of eight dot balls. Misbah-ul-Haq top scored with a half-century, but was not dominant enough.

Umar Akmal provided hope to Pakistan with two sixes off Yuvraj, who in this match recorded a rare failure with the bat in the tournament. But Harbhajan—who with the generally unfailing Patel and Ashish Nehra comprised the trio that trumped their South Asian rivals—deceived him with a straighter ball from around the wicket.

Afridi, too, albeit briefly, threatened to turn the tables. But he mistimed a Harbhajan full toss to pay the penalty. Tendulkar sizes up: "Pakistan still had a chance while Afridi and Misbah were batting...It was one of those days when things seemed destined to go our way."

Earlier, Asad Shafiq valiantly, but sedately kept Pakistan in the hunt. But he ill-advisedly ventured to cut a ball not short enough for the stroke.

So India overcame by 29 runs, maintaining their hundred percent success against Pakistan in the World Cup; and with it qualified for the final for the second time in the last three World Cups. "It was a night that India could never forget and we, having played a part in it, will never want to forget," concludes Tendulkar.

Toss: India

Man of the Match: Sachin Tendulkar

India innings (50 overs maximum)		R	M	B	4s	6s	SR
V Sehwag	lbw b Wahab Riaz	38	32	25	9	0	152.00
SR Tendulkar	c Shahid Afridi b Saeed Ajmal	85	160	115	11	0	73.91
G Gambhir	st †Kamran Akmal b Mohammad Hafeez	27	55	32	2	0	84.37
V Kohli	c Umar Akmal b Wahab Riaz	9	20	21	0	0	42.85
Yuvraj Singh	b Wahab Riaz	0	1	1	0	0	0.00
MS Dhoni*†	lbw b Wahab Riaz	25	64	42	2	0	59.52
SK Raina	not out	36	69	39	3	0	92.30
Harbhajan Singh	st †Kamran Akmal b Saeed Ajmal	12	28	15	2	0	80.00
Z Khan	c †Kamran Akmal b Wahab Riaz	9	14	10	1	0	90.00
A Nehra	run out (Wahab Riaz/ †Kamran Akmal)	1	1	2	0	0	50.00
MM Patel	not out	0	1	0	0	0	-

Extras: (lb 8, w 8, nb 2) 18

Total: (9 wickets; 50 overs; 231 mins) 260 (5.20 runs per over)

FoW: 1-48 (Sehwag, 5.5 ov), 2-116 (Gambhir, 18.5 ov), 3-141 (Kohli, 25.2

ov), 4-141 (Yuvraj Singh, 25.3 ov), 5-187 (Tendulkar, 36.6 ov), 6-205 (Dhoni, 41.4 ov), 7-236 (Harbhajan Singh, 46.4 ov), 8-256 (Khan, 49.2 ov), 9-258 (Nehra, 49.5 ov)

Bowling	O	M	R	W	Econ	0s	4s	6s	
Umar Gul	8	0	69	0	8.62	26	13	0	(2nb, 1w)
Abdul Razzaq	2	0	14	0	7.00	6	2	0	
Wahab Riaz	10	0	46	5	4.60	38	5	0	(4w)
Saeed Ajmal	10	0	44	2	4.40	33	4	0	(2w)
Shahid Afridi	10	0	45	0	4.50	30	4	0	
Mohammad Hafeez	10	0	34	1	3.40	35	2	0	

Pakistan innings (target: 261 runs from 50 overs)		R	M	B	4s	6s	SR
Kamran Akmal†	c Yuvraj Singh b Khan	19	40	21	3	0	90.47
Mohammad Hafeez	c †Dhoni b Patel	43	66	59	7	0	72.88
Asad Shafiq	b Yuvraj Singh	30	61	39	2	0	76.92
Younis Khan	c Raina b Yuvraj Singh	13	44	32	0	0	40.62
Misbah-ul-Haq	c Kohli b Khan	56	134	76	5	1	73.68
Umar Akmal	b Harbhajan Singh	29	35	24	1	2	120.83
Abdul Razzaq	b Patel	3	12	9	0	0	33.33
Shahid Afridi*	c Sehwag b Harbhajan Singh	19	25	17	1	0	111.76
Wahab Riaz	c Tendulkar b Nehra	8	16	14	1	0	57.14
Umar Gul	lbw b Nehra	2	9	3	0	0	66.66
Saeed Ajmal	not out	1	18	5	0	0	20.00

Extras: (w 8) 8

Total: (all out; 49.5 overs; 239 mins) 231 (4.63 runs per over)

FoW: 1-44 (Kamran Akmal, 8.6 ov), 2-70 (Mohammad Hafeez, 15.3 ov), 3-103 (Asad Shafiq, 23.5 ov), 4-106 (Younis Khan, 25.4 ov), 5-142 (Umar Akmal, 33.1 ov), 6-150 (Abdul Razzaq, 36.2 ov), 7-184 (Shahid Afridi, 41.5 ov), 8-199 (Wahab Riaz, 44.5 ov), 9-208 (Umar Gul, 46.1 ov), 10-231 (Misbah-ul-Haq, 49.5 ov)

Bowling	O	M	R	W	Econ	0s	4s	6s
Z Khan	9.5	0	58	2	5.89	31	6	0 (2w)
A Nehra	10	0	33	2	3.30	39	3	0 (1w)
MM Patel	10	1	40	2	4.00	43	5	1 (1w)
Harbhajan Singh	10	0	43	2	4.30	28	3	0
Yuvraj Singh	10	1	57	2	5.70	27	3	2

Final, 2 April: Mumbai

In the din of a jam-packed Wankhede Stadium, there was some confusion about the toss. It was, however, decreed Sri Lanka had won it.

Then, on a day of ebb and flow, much like the waters of the Arabian Sea lapping the beaches of Mumbai, local hero Zaheer Khan produced a remarkable opening spell of five overs. Three of these were maidens, he conceded just six runs and had Tharanga caught at slip.

But from this juncture, Jayawardene etched a typically delicate yet devastating innings. His 103 not out off 88 balls began carefully, but ended in a flourish. It was embellished with 13 high quality fours.

Sri Lanka could only muster 31 for one in the first 10 overs of the bowling powerplay; but pummelled 63 runs in the batting powerplay to stun the overwhelmingly pro-India crowd into stupefied silence.

As Jayawardene unfolded his essay, Dilshan and skipper Sangakkara were steady rather than speedy at the other end. Kulasekara, with 32 off 30, and Perera, with 22 off nine, did, of course, inject momentum towards the close, with the previously immaculate Khan being despatched for 35 runs in his last two overs. With Kapugedera's wicket he drew level with Afridi as the competition's highest wicket-taker.

Tendulkar writes: "It (the target) was not insurmountable, but it was important for us to forge partnerships in the early overs, because the wicket was expected to become slightly easier as the match progressed." He goes on to inscribe: "The outfield was dewy and I thought it was important for us to try to get the ball outside the thirty-yard circle to make it wet. That would mean the ball would stop swinging."

India were zero for one and then 32 for two in the seventh over, as Malinga's skimming, round-arm deliveries removed Sehwag lbw and Tendulkar, who looked in good nick, caught behind.

On paper, it was a crisis. But in practice, there was too much depth in the Indian batting and correspondingly limited bowling resources in the Sri Lankan camp—with Muralitharan half fit—for it to be deemed to be one.

Young Kohli joined hands with his seasoned fellow Delhiite Gambhir. They put on 83 for the third wicket as the latter responsibly adopted a sheet-anchor role. This was followed by a defining and decisive collaboration of 109 runs for the fourth wicket between the left-hander and Dhoni, who dramatically promoted himself to number five and with power and precision inexorably took the match away from the Sri Lankans. The stand was the best for India in three World Cup finals.

Dhoni's short-arm cover drives for four—mainly at the expense of off-spinner Murali—frustrated the Sri Lankans. He finished with a thunderous six to cap a 79-ball 91. His statuesque pose after completing the shot not merely represented his personal and team's relief at meeting the extraordinary expectations of a country of 1.2 billion, but respite for a nation whose dream of crowning glory in one-day cricket became boundless after the *coup de tat* in England in 1983. Such hopes were dashed at home in 1987 and 1996. The dream was fulfilled after a 28-year wait.

It was the highest successful run chase in a World Cup final. Jayawardene's epic effort was to go in vain.

Gambhir's investment was immense. 97 off 122 balls with nine boundaries was a rock-like effort that shouldered India from tricky straits to a singular triumph. Misjudgement caused by tiredness in the energy extracting Mumbai heat eventually resulted in his fall.

Tendulkar had as always played his part. His aggregate of 482 runs was the highest for India and the second highest in the tournament. He averaged a splendid 54 with two centuries.

The final, though, was not quite his day. Nevertheless, in their lap of honour around the stadium, the Indians hoisted Tendulkar—who was walking into the sunset after six World Cups appearances—on their shoulders. An excited 22-year-old Kohli, for whom Tendulkar was an idol since childhood, remarked: "He's carried the burden of our nation for 21 years; it was time to carry him on our shoulders today."

Tendulkar discloses he and Sehwag (at the former's insistence) were praying in the interior of the dressing room and not watching the match when Dhoni exploded with the match-winning over boundary. The victory was "one of those life-changing moments" to the most prolific run-getter in ODI history. "It was liberation. I had finally scaled cricket's Everest..."

Toss: Sri Lanka

Man of the Match: Mahendra Dhoni

Sri Lanka innings (50 overs maximum)		R	M	B	4s	6s	SR
WU Tharanga	c Sehwag b Khan	2	30	20	0	0	10.00
TM Dilshan	b Harbhajan Singh	33	87	49	3	0	67.34
KC Sangakkara*†	c †Dhoni b Yuvraj Singh	48	102	67	5	0	71.64
DPMD Jayawardene	not out	103	159	88	13	0	117.04
TT Samaraweera	lbw b Yuvraj Singh	21	53	34	2	0	61.76
CK Kapugedera	c Raina b Khan	1	6	5	0	0	20.00
KMDN Kulasekara	run out (†Dhoni)	32	41	30	1	1	106.66
NLTC Perera	not out	22	10	9	3	1	244.44

Extras: (b 1, lb 3, w 6, nb 2) 12

Total: (6 wickets; 50 overs; 246 mins) 274 (5.48 runs per over)

DNB: SL Malinga, S Randiv, M Muralitharan

FoW: 1-17 (Tharanga, 6.1 ov), 2-60 (Dilshan, 16.3 ov), 3-122 (Sangakkara, 27.5 ov), 4-179 (Samaraweera, 38.1 ov), 5-182 (Kapugedera, 39.5 ov), 6-248 (Kulasekara, 47.6 ov)

Bowling	O	M	R	W	Econ	0s	4s	6s	
Z Khan	10	3	60	2	6.00	32	6	2	(1w)
S Sreesanth	8	0	52	0	6.50	26	8	0	(2nb)
MM Patel	9	0	41	0	4.55	31	4	0	(1w)
Harbhajan Singh	10	0	50	1	5.00	24	3	0	(1w)
Yuvraj Singh	10	0	49	2	4.90	28	5	0	
SR Tendulkar	2	0	12	0	6.00	4	0	0	(3w)
V Kohli	1	0	6	0	6.00	3	1	0	

India innings (target: 275 runs from 50 overs)		R	M	B	4s	6s	SR
V Sehwag	lbw b Malinga	0	2	2	0	0	0.00
SR Tendulkar	c †Sangakkara b Malinga	18	21	14	2	0	128.57
G Gambhir	b Perera	97	187	122	9	0	79.50
V Kohli	c & b Dilshan	35	69	49	4	0	71.42
MS Dhoni*†	not out	91	128	79	8	2	115.18
Yuvraj Singh	not out	21	39	24	2	0	87.50

Extras: (b 1, lb 6, w 8) 15

Total: (4 wickets; 48.2 overs; 230 mins) 277 (5.73 runs per over)

DNB: SK Raina, Harbhajan Singh, Z Khan, MM Patel, S Sreesanth

FoW: 1-0 (Sehwag, 0.2 ov), 2-31 (Tendulkar, 6.1 ov), 3-114 (Kohli, 21.4 ov), 4-223 (Gambhir, 41.2 ov)

Bowling	O	M	R	W	Econ	0s	4s	6s	
SL Malinga	9	0	42	2	4.66	31	4	0	(2w)
KMDN Kulasekara	8.2	0	64	0	7.68	20	8	1	
NLTC Perera	9	0	55	1	6.11	27	5	1	(2w)
S Randiv	9	0	43	0	4.77	24	3	0	
TM Dilshan	5	0	27	1	5.40	14	2	0	(1w)
M Muralitharan	8	0	39	0	4.87	23	3	0	(1w)

CHAPTER EIGHT

2015
Up to Expectation

While cricket is undoubtedly a game of delightful unpredictability—the shorter formats more so—since 1999 it has not been too difficult to identify the winners of a World Cup.

Before the 2015 event I wrote, "All aspects considered, there is an advantage of playing at home. This assumes greater significance if the hosts are also the number one ranked unit, as is the case with Australia. Admittedly, only once in World Cup history—in the immediately preceding edition—has a side triumphed on home soil. In 1992, the last time the event was held in Australasia, Australia did not even qualify for the semifinals. That said, the Australian team of 2015 are unrecognisable from that of 1992, regardless of the fact that they are not the same all-conquering a force they were in 2003 and 2007. In short, if Michael Clarke recovers from surgery to cure a hamstring injury, the Aussies placed as they are at the pinnacle of the one-day pyramid and turning out at home, would start the championship as favourites." Clarke recovered and Australia duly emerged as champions.

Prior to the competition, I also penned, "On the grounds of home advantage, New Zealand cannot be taken lightly, either. They have more often than not punched above their weight in the World Cup, including reaching the semifinals in 1992. Presently, with batsmen like Brendon McCullum, who will lead the New Zealanders, Ross Taylor, Kane Williamson and Martin Guptill in their ranks and decent bowlers to boot, such as Kyle Mills, Tim Southee, both fast-medium, and left-arm spinner Daniel Vettori, not to mention the all-round abilities of James Franklin, they will be no push-over." As it transpired, the Kiwis finished as runners-up, having beaten Australia in Auckland at the group level.

Australasia is a wonderful setting for a Cricket World Cup. In particular, the facilities in Australia for both the players and the public are grand and outstanding. Cricket is the country's number one sport and it showcases this beautifully, with magnificently maintained historic grounds and world-class infrastructure. It also boasts of the world's largest and one of the most iconic cricket stadiums—the Melbourne Cricket Ground—where the final was hosted.

Even in New Zealand, where, except in Auckland, the set-up is relatively modest, the player and spectator experience is of high standard. And there is no dearth of overseas Indians in either country to root for their team and pamper them with the diet and hospitality they are accustomed to at home.

The only lacunae were the long flights criss-crossing a continent. Perth to Hamilton—a journey the Indian side undertook between matches—was a seven-hour flight, not taking into account the connection at Auckland. Besides, there's a five-hour time difference between the two places, making it a challenge to adjust one's body clock, which the players had to accomplish in less than three days!

An Oceania World Cup can also be unfriendly to television audiences in other parts of the world; but a plethora of day/night fixtures eased this issue. Majority of the viewership was, as usual, from the Indian subcontinent, England and South Africa. Notwithstanding the slightly inconvenient timings in some regions and the awkwardness of daytime games on weekdays—not that either mattered in cricket-mad South Asia—the following on TV was reportedly at a record level.

The structure of the 2015 World Cup was the same as in 2011. The number of teams partaking was 14–10 full members of the International Cricket Council (ICC) gained automatic entries, with four associate members qualifying into the draw. They were then divided into two pools of seven teams each. Pool A had Afghanistan, hosts Australia, Bangladesh, England, co-hosts New Zealand, Scotland and Sri Lanka. Pool B had holders India, Ireland, Pakistan, South Africa, the United Arab Emirates, the West

Indies and Zimbabwe. The top four teams on the basis of points obtained at the league stage proceeded to the quarter-finals or the knockout phase of the championship.

The six-week spectacle got underway on a Saturday, 14 February—the opening matches were New Zealand versus Sri Lanka at Christchurch, a day match and Australia versus England at Melbourne, a day/nighter. On the following day, India were pitted against Pakistan at Adelaide in a day/night affair. The Australia-England encounter—because of their ancient Ashes rivalry—and the India-Pakistan clash, given the passion such a pairing inflames in the peoples of the two countries, were ideally scheduled to trigger the tournament to a flying start.

In 1992, India's display was unimpressive, but this was no longer a yardstick of their aptitude and potential in 2015. The Indians on this occasion were a far more organised ensemble, instilled with calibre and confidence. They were also mentored by the motivating personal example of Mahendra Singh Dhoni, as testified by him in the final at Wankhede Stadium four years earlier, when he took the bull by the horns to deliver an emphatic *coup de grace*.

The limited overs versions of cricket generally do not demand an exceptional strategic brain, for there is virtually a preconceived formula for captaincy on the field, but out-of-the-box tactics, such as entrusting the new ball to a spinner, can sometimes be a bonus. In the run-up to the tourney, there was gossip in Indian cricket circles that Dhoni might get implicated in the Twenty20 Indian Premier League (IPL) betting scandal. This was succeeded by further speculation following his sudden retirement from tests without completing the winter's India-Australia series.

It could be said the Indian players, having spent 11 weeks in Australia immediately before the tournament, were well acclimatised to Australian surfaces. But historically this had not been an advantage. In the 1985 World Championship of Cricket hosted in Australia and the 1992 World Cup, the West Indies and India respectively looked exhausted and performed below par after their extended tours of Australia. The situation was almost identical, as India were coming off the back of a two-and-a-half month tour of Down Under, which involved, as usual, covering vast distances and engaging in enfeebling cricket just before the World Cup. A majority of players who had rendered duty in the test XI in Australia were featuring in the Indian XV for the World Cup. Yet, the Indians to their credit did not show up devitalised. The support staff did a splendid job of eradicating both mental and physical fatigue. The Indians have, in fact, become quite adept at managing demands wherein they are called upon to play cricket for 9–10 months a year.

Virat Kohli, the most complete batsman in the world today, was in 2015 already the mainstay of the Indian batting and much was expected of him. Claiming a batting average of 52.61 in ODIs—which was superior to Sachin Tendulkar's —he was capable of winning matches on his own. Indeed, India's asset was the versatility of their batsmen. Rohit Sharma and Ajinkya Rahane could open or bat lower down. Suresh Raina had the ability to keep the score ticking even in a crisis, while Dhoni had the ability to intervene decisively up the order, as and when the need arose. In the end, though, Kohli did not fulfil expectations and failed in the vital semifinal versus Australia.

The question was, how would the Indian quicks fare with the white Kookaburra, which has a less pronounced seam as compared to the balls in England and India and deviates comparatively little in the air or off the wicket. The question was would their spinners prove to be expensive since the ball was unlikely to turn the way it does in the subcontinent? India's steamrolling of sides on dry, flat Indian wickets—for instance, the trouncing of Sri Lanka in November 2014—did not count for much, as both Australia and New Zealand presented bouncier squares and a changeable climate. Indeed, other than winning series in Australia in 2008 and New Zealand in 2009, India's one-day exhibition in Australasia over the years was lacklustre. At the same time of late when it came to a pinch, India had acquitted themselves admirably in alien conditions, including securing the Champions Trophy in England in 2013.

Given the colossal amount of money and man-hours the Board of Control for Cricket in India (BCCI) sink into limited overs cricket, anything short of the Indians qualifying for the semifinals would not have been commensurate with such investment. The outcome, therefore, perhaps broke even with the resources expended. Besides, in an India-centred cricket economy, a premature Indian exit would have been unhelpful for both the game's finances and Australia's turnover. Their extended stay in the championship turned out to be a bonanza for Australian tourism.

15 February: Adelaide (Day/Night)

The South Australian capital is a much smaller city as compared to Melbourne or Sydney. But the Adelaide Oval, tastefully modernised, is no less distinguished a cricketing venue than the MCG or the SCG. On this occasion, it was packed to the rafters with more Indian supporters and sizeable Pakistani fans as well present to witness an inevitably tense encounter. Dhoni, who wears the triple crown in limited overs cricket, having won the World Twenty20, the Champions Trophy and the World Cup, opted for first strike on an encouraging batting track and Kohli duly capitalised with a 22nd ODI hundred. Surprisingly, while India have invariably vanquished their arch-rivals in the World Cup—including beating them in the championship Pakistan won in Australia in 1992 under Imran Khan, now the country's prime minister—this was the first three-figure knock by an Indian against their western neighbours in the competition. He posted century partnerships with his Delhi teammate and opener Shikhar Dhawan—before the latter was run out—and Raina. Both being left-handers, it rather reinforced how a left-right pair of batsmen can throw bowlers off their line. Kohli, after his 126-ball essay, was finally caught behind off the fast-medium Sohail Khan, who finished with a bag of five wickets. Wahab Riaz, left-arm fast bowled with fire but was less fortunate. The Indian total was perhaps 20 runs below what was gettable; yet, it was still beyond the Pakistani batsmen's capabilities. Once the chase collapsed from 102 for two to 103 for five, it was left to captain Misbah-ul-Haq to play for pride in a lost cause. Eventually, he became one of Mohammed Shami's four victims—the Bengal quick being the pick of the Indian bowlers. India coasted home by 76 runs.

Man of the Match: Virat Kohli

India 300/7 in 50 overs (Virat Kohli 107, Suresh Raina 74, Shikhar Dhawan 73, Sohail Khan 5/55). **Pakistan** 224 all out in 47 overs (Misbah-ul-Haq 76, Ahmed Shehzad 47, Mohammed Shami 4/35, Mohit Sharma 2/35).

22 February: Melbourne (Day/Night)

India again won the toss and went about their task against South Africa in a meticulous manner. They were cautious against the new ball, but made amends, with Dhawan powering his way to a career-best ODI 100 in 146 balls. He was lucky to be let-off by Hashim Amla off Wayne Parnell when just past his half-century. The bowler otherwise conceded a profligate 85 runs in his nine overs. But Dhawan in tandem with Kohli and then Rahane produced exhilarating 127 and 125 run stands respectively. Rahane's was, in fact, a brilliant innings off just 60 balls as the defending champions walloped a South African attack handicapped by Vernon Philander leaving the field with a hamstring pull after bowling only four overs. The Proteas responded with skipper Abraham de Villiers looking promising as he sped to 30 off 38 balls. His run out, though, effectively snuffed out the chase. With Ravichandran Ashwin keeping batsmen guessing with his varied off-spin, only Faf du Plessis stood in the way with a solitary 50, before he misjudged the length of a shorter delivery to hole out at mid-off off Mohit Sharma, who and Shami were once more impressive. India won by 130 runs.

Man of the Match: Shikhar Dhawan
India 307/7 in 50 overs (Shikhar Dhawan 137, Ajinkya Rahane 79, Virat Kohli 46, Morne Morkel 2/59). **South Africa** 177 all out in 40.2 overs (Faf du Plessis 55, Ravichandran Ashwin 3/41, Mohammed Shami 2/30, Mohit Sharma 2/31).

28 February: Perth (Day/Night)

The spin of the coin favoured the United Arab Emirates, but that's where predictably their purple patch ended. Umesh Yadav was far too menacing for the minnows, while Ashwin mesmerised them with his best figures in a one-day international. Only Shaiman Anwar resisted for a while before Yadav disfigured his stumps. India triumphed by nine wickets, with Rohit Sharma, hitherto short of runs, not missing out against a modest set of bowlers.

Man of the Match: Ravichandran Ashwin
The United Arab Emirates 102 all out in 31.2 overs (Shaiman Anwar 35,

Ravichandran Ashwin 4/25, Umesh Yadav 2/15, Ravindra Jadeja 2/23). **India** 104/1 in 18.5 overs (Rohit Sharma 57 not out).

6 March: Perth (Day/Night)

Long gone are the days when a team would tremble at the thought of facing the West Indies, that too, at the WACA—once a paradise for fast bowlers. After calling correctly, the West Indian top order lacked intent against the steady Indian bowlers, particularly the consistent Shami. Only captain Jason Holder lower down the order displayed a business-like approach as he flayed the ball valiantly for the only half-century of the match, before Ravindra Jadeja made him miscue to long off. The West Indian pacemen spearheaded by the Jamaican Jerome Taylor thereafter reduced India to 134 for six. But the characteristic calmness of Dhoni ensured there would be no further hiccups. India reached their target with four wickets to spare.

Man of the Match: Mohammed Shami
West Indies 182 all out in 44.2 overs (Jason Holder 57, Mohammed Shami 3/35, Ravindra Jadeja 2/27, Umesh Yadav 2/42). **India** 185/7 in 39.1 overs (Mahendra Dhoni 45 not out, Jerome Taylor 2/33, Andre Russell 2/43).

10 March: Hamilton (Day/Night)

Without underrating Ireland's plucky performance, the game for the Indians was a matter of recovering from a flight across the breadth of Australasia as well as an intercontinental time difference in a little over 60 hours. The Irish, having chosen to bat first, notched up 60 runs in the first 10 overs. This was the most expensive power play the Indian bowlers had experienced in the tourney so far, with William Porterfield proceeding to record a score of 67. Hereafter, the spinners applied the brakes and the pressure resulted in Ireland surrendering their last seven wickets for a mere 53 runs. Niall O'Brien top-scored with a run-a-ball innings before clipping Shami to square leg. The Irish total was the highest against India in the tournament up to this point. Undaunted, Dhawan, unleashing five sixes, pulverised the Irish bowlers with an 85-ball 100, albeit after escaping twice to butterfingers. His 174-run opening gambit with Rohit Sharma, who, too, was brisk with an almost 100 per cent strike rate, was India's best ever in a World Cup and laid the foundation of a facile victory by eight wickets.

Man of the Match: Shikhar Dhawan
Ireland 259 all out in 49 overs (Niall O'Brien 75, William Porterfield 67, Mohammed Shami 3/41, Ravichandran Ashwin 2/38). **India** 260/2 in 36.5 overs (Shikhar Dhawan 100, Rohit Sharma 64, Virat Kohli 44 not out, Stuart Thompson 2/45).

14 March: Auckland (Day/Night)

Zimbabwe's was an impressive show of resistance. They were in trouble at 33 for three after being invited to bat first. But their helmsman Brendan Taylor piloted a rearguard action followed by a counter-attack; he himself registering a second century in successive matches in a World Cup. He added 93 runs with Sean Williams—who nailed a half-century off 57 balls—and another 109 with Craig Ervine for the 4th and 5th wickets respectively. Taylor's three figures, studded with five sixes, came off 101 balls before he accelerated further to an eventual strike rate of 125.45. Zimbabwe, thereby, veritably threw the gauntlet, asking India to chase down the biggest total they had confronted in the championship so far. Indeed, the reply was shaky. Two wickets went down for 21 and four for 92. But Raina and Dhoni remained unseparated in a stand of 196 to extinguish the Zimbabwean ambition. The former, let-off at 47, motored to a timely century at a strike rate of 105.76. The skipper's stats were 111.84. The six-wicket margin reflected India's sixth straight win in the competition. In effect, India qualified for the quarter-finals or the knockout stage with a clean slate.

Man of the Match: Suresh Raina
Zimbabwe 287 all out in 48.5 overs (Brendan Taylor 138, Sean Williams 50, Umesh Yadav 3/43, Mohit Sharma 3/48, Mohammed Shami 3/48). **India** 288/4 in 48.4 overs (Suresh Raina 110 not out, Mahendra Dhoni 85 not out, Tinashe Panyangara 2/53).

Quarter-final, 19 March: Melbourne (Day/Night)

India preferred first use of the wicket but did not really consolidate until Raina joined Rohit Sharma to realise 122 runs for the 4th wicket. The latter conjured the kind of long innings that typifies him, culminating in a slightly better than a run-a-ball three-figure essay. His left-handed ally produced an even superior strike rate for his half-century before being stumped off the Bangladeshi skipper and medium pacer Mashrafe Mortaza. Bangladesh on the other hand never came to terms with the target. They found Yadav too hot to handle. Their wickets fell at regular intervals, with the last four tumbling in a space of 13 runs. The highest individual contribution was a lower order 35. In the run-up to the match, Bangladeshi supporters had reminded their Indian counterparts of the Ides of March or when they upset their more fancied rivals at Port of Spain in the 2007 World Cup. This was not to be. They lost by a not insignificant 109 runs. However, Sharma was on 90 when he was caught at midwicket off Rubel Hossain. Umpire Aleem Dar, though, called it an above-the-waist no-ball. It was a borderline case; and led to an unbecoming charge of a conspiracy in favour of India by Mustafa Kamal, the Bangladeshi president of the ICC. Sharma was finally fifth out, bowled by a persevering, but costly Taskin Ahmed. It was clearly a standout showing.

Man of the Match: Rohit Sharma
India 302/6 in 50 overs (Rohit Sharma 137, Suresh Raina 65, Taskin Ahmed 3/69). **Bangladesh** 193 all out in 45 overs (Nasir Hossain 35, Umesh Yadav 4/31, Mohammed Shami 2/37, Ravindra Jadeja 2/42).

Semifinal, 24 March: Auckland (Day/Night)

South Africa batted first after winning the toss; and skipper de Villiers starred with a strike rate of 144.44, although the top score of the innings emanated from du Plessis. Indeed, a determined middle order effort represented a run rate of 6.53 in a venture restricted to 43 overs because of rain. After Trent Boult, bowling with an aggressive field, had pinned the visitors to the backfoot, du Plessis with Rilee Rossouw realised 103 runs for the 4th wicket, while de Villiers combining with David Miller put on 55 for the 5th wicket in just four overs. The latter in rattling his runs in 18 balls pegged a strike rate of 272.22. Both du Plessis and Miller were stumped off the medium pace of Corey Anderson, who was of course in general rather expensive. The target for New Zealand became stiffer as it was reset to 298 under the Duckworth/Lewis method. Captain Brendon McCullum flagged off with a flaming innings at a strike rate of 226.92 before he rushed out to a ball from Morkel, not full enough for the purpose to hole out at mid-on. This was followed by a 50 from Anderson at better than a run a ball until he was caught pulling a rising delivery around off-stump from the same bowler. The final blow was delivered, though, by Johannesburg-born Grant Elliott with a substantial unbeaten half-century. In a dramatic final over, with the Kiwis still needing 12 runs for victory, Elliott smote the second last ball over long-on for six to a delirious reaction from the crowd. The home side achieved a run rate of 6.98 to prevail by four wickets. They were, thus, in the final of a Cricket World Cup for the first time.

Man of the Match: Grant Elliott
South Africa 281/5 in 43 overs (Faf du Plessis 82, Abraham de Villiers 65 not out, David Miller 49, Corey Anderson 3/72, Trent Boult 2/53). **New Zealand** 299/6 in 42.5 overs (Grant Elliott 84 not out, Brendon McCullum 59, Corey Anderson 58, Morne Morkel 3/59).

Semifinal, 26 March: Sydney (Day/Night)

In their respective passages to the last four, Australia had lost to New Zealand at the league stage, whereas India's progress had been without blemish. Presently, before a capacity crowd, with apparently nearly as many Indians as Australians in the galleries, the coin came down in Australia's favour. In the test series preceding the World Cup, Steve Smith had proved to be a thorn in India's flesh. He continued in this vein with a better than a run-a-ball three-figure knock, dominating a second wicket partnership of 182 with Aaron Finch. On a pensive pitch the Indian pacers were uniformly expensive and hitherto the most successful of them—Shami—went wicketless. Only Ashwin, obtaining a bit of turn, maintained a leash on the lavish stroke play; but he returned only a solitary scalp. Ultimately Yadav's extra velocity forced Finch to defend inadequately and the ball flew to midwicket, while a bouncer to Smith invited a top-edged hook to square leg. Subsequent pyrotechnics from Mitchell Johnson ensured India would have to attain a run rate in excess of 6.56 per over to win. India's opening stand of 76 in 12.5 overs laid a promising foundation. But star-man Kohli's early exit—top-edging a bouncer from the left-arm Johnson—fairly dashed their hopes;

and though the resilient Dhoni produced a run a ball half-century before he was run out—and Rahane realised 70 runs with him for the 5th wicket, the assignment was somewhat beyond India's grasp and they disintegrated tamely to lose by a margin of 95 runs. Mitchell Starc, also left-arm, speared down his deliveries with accuracy and pace, allowing few liberties to the batsmen. In contrast, when it came to the crunch the Indian pace trio had lacked penetration. More yorkers than short-pitched stuff would have been sensible. Overall in the tournament, India had given a fine account of themselves. But it was now the end of the road.

Man of the Match: Steve Smith
Australia 328/7 in 50 overs (Steve Smith 105, Aaron Finch 81, Umesh Yadav 4/72, Mohit Sharma 2/75). **India** 233 all out in 46.5 (Mahendra Dhoni 65, Shikhar Dhawan 45, Ajinkya Rahane 44, James Faulkner 3/59, Mitchell Starc 2/28, Mitchell Johnson 2/50).

Final, 29 March: Melbourne (Day/Night)

The world's most ample cricket stadium, which cavernously accommodates over 90,000 spectators, was jam-packed for the climax of the festival of one-day cricket which is the World Cup. New Zealand won the toss and elected to bat, but they were soon 39 for three, which included the departures of the dangerous McCullum, Guptill, who had been quite prolific in the tourney so far, and potentially their most durable batsman Williamson. Elliott—with a better than a run-a-ball innings—and Taylor in a stand of 111 for the 4th wicket rekindled faith across the Tasman Sea. But this was short-lived, as the pressure exerted by the Australian bowlers' economy, especially Starc's, caused the lower middle order to self-destruct after both Taylor and Elliott were caught behind off Faulkner. Indeed, the Kiwis from 150 for three lost their remaining wickets for a paltry 33 runs. Their total, though, was a duplicate of India's in the 1983 World Cup final—where they emerged on top against the invincible West Indies of that era. But Australia refused to be overwhelmed by the occasion. After David Warner had given the Aussies a bright start, Smith joined by Clarke in his farewell appearance in international cricket mercilessly finished the job. The latter's better than a run-a-ball top score for his side was, in fact, the *piece de resistance*. So, Australia comprehensively outplayed New Zealand to regain the crown and lift the trophy for a peerless fifth time.

Man of the Match: James Faulkner

New Zealand 183 all out in 45 overs (Grant Elliot 83, Ross Taylor 40, Mitchell Johnson 3/30, James Faulkner 3/36, Mitchell Starc 2/20). **Australia** 186/3 in 33.1 overs (Michael Clarke 74, Steve Smith 56, David Warner 45, Matthew Henry 2/46).

Of the total prize money of $10.23 million on offer, Australia pocketed $3.98 million, while New Zealand's share came to $1.75 million. Interestingly, Kamal, who should customarily have presented the trophy, was denied this privilege. Instead, the organisation's Indian chairman Narayanaswami Srinivasan appropriated for himself the honour. Kamal had done himself no favours with an unsporting outburst after the India-Bangladesh quarter-final. He threatened to expose the ICC but soon stepped down without a whimper.

Starc was fittingly upheld as the man of the tournament. It was anticipated that this tall, rugged fast bowler would generate high pace. He embellished this with late movement of the white ball to carve out a tally of 22 wickets at an average of 10. With Johnson and Faulkner, he formed an incisive trio of left-arm quicks, who angled the ball away from right-handed batsmen with beneficial results.

But the honour for the most torrid spell of the championship went to Pakistan's Wahab Riaz, who gave Shane Watson a working-over in the quarter-finals which the Australian batsman is unlikely to forget in a hurry. It was a rivetingly hostile spell by the left-armer from over the wicket and into the right-hander's ribs.

It was commendable that the ICC took a tough line against bowlers with questionable actions. Saeed Ajmal of Pakistan and Sunil Narine of the West Indies were thereby among those who were debarred from taking part in the tournament.

Batting-wise, Chris Gayle of the West Indies, with the assistance of 16 sixes, hit the fastest ODI double hundred in history at the expense of Zimbabwe. The West Indians were, in turn, tormented when Guptill struck 237 with 11 sixes and de Villiers etched a 66-ball 162 against them.

England, the founders of all formats of the sport, continued to not only be denied the World Cup mantle but also disappointed by failing to qualify for the last eight. The late appointment of Eoin Morgan as captain was one of the reasons for the Englishmen being unsettled.

South Africa reached the semifinals as they had done when they were first granted entry into the tournament in 1992 after apartheid was abolished in the country. In fact, they won a maiden match at the knockout stage; but by not climbing further, retained their reputation of being chokers at crucial times.

Other than Clarke, the elegant Sri Lankan left-hander Kumar Sangakkara, one of the great batsmen of his generation, played his last one-day match in the competition and in so doing helped himself to four centuries in successive matches—an all-time record. His teammate Mahela Jayawardene, Pakistanis Misbah-ul-Haq and Shahid Afridi and New Zealander Daniel Vettori, too, joined the ranks of the retired. Duncan Fletcher moved on after a four-year stint as India's coach.

CHAPTER NINE

2019 Disappointment

The fifth Cricket World Cup in England was expected to be a tale of two tournaments—favouring quicker bowlers in the first half, with spinners coming into their own in the second. In the event, it did not turn out to be quite so simple.

Fast or medium fast bowlers dominated in an electric final at Lord's, a decisive error by the umpires adding to the drama. England, inventors of this not merely a game but a way of life, lifted the cup for the first time, having thrice previously been the best man but not the groom, that is, finalists but not champions.

In the two semifinals too, seam and swing presided over the proceedings—with the exception of the England leg-spinner Adil Rashid—as New Zealand upset India at Old Trafford and the home side prevailed over arch-rivals Australia at Edgbaston.

Having said that, the fact that all fixtures were day matches rendered the meet an even playing field compared to a schedule sprinkled with day–night engagements.

Movement in the air or off the wicket or not, Rohit Sharma stamped his authority on the event with an aggregate of 648 runs (the most by a batsman in the tournament), an average of 81 and a strike rate of 98.33, not to forget his five centuries.

Jasprit Bumrah, making his debut in a World Cup, was, jointly with Mark Wood of England, the fourth highest wicket-taker with a bag of 18 victims. Mohammed Shami made only four appearances, yet he returned 14 scalps.

Indian leg-spinner Yuzvendra Chahal with 12 wickets was the most successful among slow bowlers. However, he ranked a mere 18th in the list of wicket-takers as a whole.

I had concluded in the 2019 edition of this book that 'it would transmit a tremor through the system if England and India failed to advance to the semifinals'. This was based as much on the commercial dampener their failure would cause as on the form and potential of the two sides. To that extent, I was right. Where I erred was in my confidence in the Indians thereafter. India duly topped the league but subsequently stumbled. In February 2019, India had registered an impressive 4–1 series success in New Zealand. But the Kiwis, perennially plucky performers on the world stage, turned the tables on India when it mattered.

The climax was by far the closest contest in the annals of the Cricket World Cup. Never in its 44-year history had totals been tied at the conclusion of the two innings in the finals, nor had there been a precedent of a super over play-off to decide the winner of the match. Even at the end of the pistols-at-dawn enactment of a super over the scores were level, both sides having posted 15 runs. It was edge-of-one's-seat stuff.

The cricketing cosmos was bewitched. Ironically, New Zealand-born Ben Stokes's heroics were largely instrumental in England, captained by the Irishman Eoin Morgan, crossing the line, albeit only on a technicality. Indeed, England's star Barbadian fast bowler, Jofra Archer, had only recently opted to represent England.

The gentleman New Zealand skipper Kane Williamson, for his performance as a batsman, stewardship of his squad and noticeable sportsmanship, was deservedly named Player of the Tournament.

The number of participants in the championship was trimmed to 10 from the 14 that had competed in Australia in 2015. Eight of them—Australia, Bangladesh, England, India, New Zealand, Pakistan, South Africa and Sri Lanka—were automatic entries by virtue of their International Cricket Council rankings. The other two—the West Indies and Afghanistan—earned the right to take part through an elimination process.

(What an upheaval in the sport that the Windies, invincible in the 1970s, were no longer default entrants!) All teams played each other in a round robin sequence, with the top four on points accumulated ascending to a knockout phase to determine the winners.

In the initial unfolding of the tourney, a captain winning the toss in greyish conditions usually put the opposition in to bat. But good fortune with the coin did not necessarily result in victory.

In a throwback to their old days, the West Indies began with a bang. They tamed Pakistan with bouncers in their first outing and had Australia reeling at 79 for five in the second. But akin to their latter day incarnation, they thereafter floundered and failed to breast the tape against the Aussies. The fuss over it being the Jamaican gladiator Chris Gayle's farewell World Cup was for them an unhelpful distraction.

Pakistan promised little, given their pre-tournament form, and disappointed commensurately. There were wishful comparisons with the 1992 squad's uninspiring initial run, before the talented men under Imran Khan dramatically metamorphosed to a memorable conquest. The accomplished batsman Babar Azam was consistent if not prolific, and the teenaged Shaheen Shah Afridi, left-arm fast, provided a glimpse of his promise.

Sri Lanka, the unexpected champions in the subcontinent in 1996 and finalists in 2007, were a mixed bag. Admittedly, they suffered from two of their matches being affected by rain. At the same time, their choice of Dimuth Karunaratne, who had not been selected for one-day internationals for the preceding four years, as captain hinted at a compromise compelled by non-sporting reasons.

South Africa have threatened to go all the way since their maiden appearance in the 1992 World Cup. But they have instead acquired a label of 'chokers'. Indeed, this turned out to be their most disappointing campaign. They only beat Afghanistan and Sri Lanka. Dale Steyn's shoulder injury and Lungi Ngidi's hamstring issue were extenuating reasons. But their batsmen largely failed to motor.

In contrast, Bangladesh, inspired by Shakib Al Hasan's brilliance at number three—which was emblazoned by two centuries and five half centuries—not to mention his economical left-arm orthodox bowling, were more competitive than their eighth place in the league suggests. They finished equal on points with South Africa and above the West Indies in the league table. The seasoned batsman Mushfiqur Rahim and left-arm seamer Mustafizur Rahman caught the eye. But skipper Mashrafe Mortaza, a member of Parliament of the ruling Awami League party in his country, playing his fifth World Cup, looked distinctly past his prime.

5 June: Ageas Bowl, Hampshire

The Ageas Bowl was yet to be built when the previous four World Cups were staged in England. But India's performance in three subsequent ODI appearances in Hampshire reflected merely a win over Kenya and two discouraging defeats to England.

Now, though, the incisive Jasprit Bumrah was extended first use of the wicket, and he duly had the Proteas two down for 24. They recovered somewhat with half-century partnerships for the third (between Faf du Plessis and Rassie van der Dussen) and the eighth (between Christopher Morris, who recorded a strike rate of 123, and Kagiso Rabada) wickets, but these were insufficient to post a challenging total.

One expected India to play three specialist quicks in conditions friendly to fast bowlers. But they chose to exploit the opposition's perceived inadequacy against wrist spin by including both Kuldeep Yadav (Chinaman) and Yuzvendra Chahal (leg-spin) in their eleven.

That paid dividends as Chahal twirled a web over his opponents. He struck twice in each of his two spells to break the backbone of the opposition's middle order. Indeed, his first two wickets—that of the quite settled van der Dussen and du Plessis—surfaced in the same over. South Africa were up against it after collapsing to 89 for five.

It's a moot point as to whether South Africa ought to have bowled first after winning the toss. Their express bowlers, Rabada and Morris, extracted disconcerting bounce off the pitch in their early overs, which could have been more rewarding in fresher morning conditions.

The hostile Rabada removed Shikhar Dhawan caught behind. But after initially discomfiting Rohit Sharma—who was dropped on one—Rabada paid the price for persisting in pitching short. The Indian vice-captain, having weathered the storm, cut loose with a hook and an upper cut for six and four respectively off consecutive balls in one over.

That Quinton de Kock was earlier caught at third slip was testimony to the aggressive field the Indian captain Virat Kohli could employ. On the other hand, du Plessis granted the same cordon to Rabada only too briefly. So it was Andile Phehlukwayo who captured the prized scalp of Kohli—caught behind off a rising delivery.

Sharma blended caution with characteristic aggression—a six to midwicket at Tabraiz Shamsi's expense being an example. He survived an appeal for leg before wicket when 22, but thereafter amplified in authority to record a hundred and in so doing comfortably ensured two points for India.

It should, however, be said that South Africa were handicapped by the unavailability of quicker bowlers Dale Steyn and Lungi Ngidi because of injuries.

Toss: South Africa
Man of the Match: Rohit Sharma
South Africa 227/9 in 50 overs (Chris Morris 42, Yuzvendra Chahal 4/51, Jasprit Bumrah 2/35, Bhuvneshwar Kumar 2/44). **India** 230/4 in 47.3 overs (Rohit Sharma 122*, Kagiso Rabada 2/39).

9 June: The Oval, London

India had played twice before at The Oval in World Cup fixtures. They lost on both occasions—to the West Indies in the group phase in 1983 and to Australia at the Super Six stage in 1999.

This time, if there was a striking difference to start with, it was the overwhelming presence in the galleries of Indian supporters sporting blue India limited overs shirts; their Australian counterparts were barely visible. Accompanying the multitude of Indian flags being waved in the stands were *dholaks* (subcontinental drums), converting a cricketing contest into a South Asian cultural festival.

India, on a traditionally batting-friendly wicket, predictably decided to take first strike. They had neither won the toss nor enjoyed batting first in their two previous World Cup outings at this fabled venue.

Apart from Rohit Sharma being dropped at square leg by Nathan Coulter-Nile off Mitchell Starc when he was on two, sharp Australian ground fielding curtailed the overall Indian total by at least 30 runs. Notwithstanding this, the combination of Sharma and left-handed Shikhar Dhawan lived up to their reputation, realising 127 runs for the opening wicket. Dhawan then put on another 93 for the second wicket with Virat Kohli to record a third World Cup century before holing out at deep square leg. Captain Kohli nailed a run-a-ball-plus half-century.

Dhawan, too, scored at better than a run a ball. To his credit, he valiantly batted through the agony of what was later diagnosed as a broken left thumb—having been hit by a short ball from Pat Cummins. This rendered him *hors de combat* for the rest of the tournament.

Sharma was caught behind attempting to steer Coulter-Nile to third man. Kohli failed to clear deep extra cover in a bid to loft one wide of him but not before he had rapidly added 81 for the third wicket with Hardik Pandya. Pandya's swashbuckling 48 off just 27 balls included three towering sixes and justified his promotion to number four.

Dhoni, too, registered a quicksilver cameo off merely 14 balls. The Indian innings judiciously gathered pace to finally achieve a stately run rate of seven an over.

In reply, Australia were never really ahead of the curve. With the sun playing hide-and-seek, the southpaw David Warner's effort was not brisk enough for purpose. Swing merchant Bhuvneshwar Kumar kept him honest. The opener pegged more dot balls than deliveries scored off.

Glenn Maxwell raised a flicker of hope for the Aussies with a flashing blade and a strike rate of 200. But once the mainstay Steve Smith departed following a half-century—adjudged leg before wicket to Kumar on referral—it was effectively curtains for the chase.

Alex Carey, having demonstrated acrobatics with the gloves, now impressed with the bat but to no avail as the tail caved in without a fight. Kumar and Jasprit Bumrah were predictably among the spoils. In summary, another couple of valuable points for the thus far impressive Indians.

Toss: India

Man of the Match: Shikhar Dhawan

India 352/5 in 50 overs (Shikhar Dhawan 117, Virat Kohli 82, Rohit Sharma 57, Marcus Stoinis 2/62). **Australia** 316 all out in 50 overs (Steve Smith 69, David Warner 56, Alex Carey 55*, Bhuvneshwar Kumar 3/50, Jasprit Bumrah 3/61, Yuzvendra Chahal 2/62).

13 June: Trent Bridge, Nottingham

Both India and New Zealand were unbeaten coming into this match. But due to incessant rain even the toss didn't take place. The teams thereby secured one point each.

'[It was a] sensible decision not to play, given the outfield wasn't fully fit,' commented Indian skipper Virat Kohli. His opposite number, Kane Williamson, remarked, '[It's] been about four days and we haven't seen the sun, so this doesn't surprise us.'

16 June: Old Trafford, Manchester

Located in the north-west of the country, England's second oldest international venue—which hosted an Ashes test match way back in 1884—was almost unrecognizable from 20 years earlier, which was the last time India and Pakistan clashed at this venue in a World Cup fixture. Other than the original distinctive rusty brick facade of the pavilion—which too was expanded upwards by two stories with a 21st-century glass fronted structure—virtually everything had changed.

The pitch had been realigned by a full 90 degrees to provide a straight view from the new pavilion, as opposed to the side-on perspective from the old. A gleaming, futuristic red construction opposite the ancient pavilion now housed the changing rooms and an enhanced media centre.

The catchment area of this Lancashire city houses more people of Pakistani descent than of Indian extraction. But ticket purchase having occurred online, Indian supporters cornered far more tickets. The galleries were full; even the 8,500 extra seats created by a temporary stand were gobbled up. *Wisden* reported 800,000 'had apparently applied for tickets' for this fixture.

Given the spell of atrocious weather that had afflicted the tournament in the run-up to this game, there was considerable speculation on whether rain would permit play, and if so, to what extent. An India–Pakistan encounter is generally the most watched cricketing tamasha in the world.

It was overcast when the toss took place, which probably prompted Pakistan's captain Sarfaraz Ahmed to field first. But the makeshift (because of Shikhar Dhawan's injury), but still robust, Indian opening pair of Rohit Sharma and Kannaur Lokesh Rahul not only saw out the new ball fairly comfortably but, as the sun made a welcome appearance, tore into the unpenetrative Pakistani bowling. Indeed, the duo celebrated a partnership of 136 runs in their maiden association as openers in a World Cup outing. Sharma went on to inscribe a second hundred on his third visit to the crease in the competition.

However, both exited softly—Rahul, after grabbing his opportunity with a half-century, spooned a catch to short extra cover off a slower ball and Sharma tucked one into the hands of short fine leg, perhaps forgetting a man had been stationed there. Virat Kohli then feasted on the Pakistani bowling for his second run-a-ball 50 of the tournament.

The left-arm fast-medium Mohammad Amir, once banned for five years for spot-fixing, was the pick of the Pakistani bowlers, scalping Kohli, Hardik Pandya and Mahendra Dhoni in a space of 29 runs.

When it came to Pakistan's turn with the willow, medium pacer Vijay Shankar, who was handed the ball after Bhuvneshwar Kumar left the field with a hamstring injury, dismissed the bespectacled Imam-ul-Haq early. Thereafter, Fakhar Zaman and Babar Azam posted a promising three-figure partnership for the second wicket. But Kuldeep Yadav, with his left-arm wrist spin, removed both in a span of eight balls and Pakistan thereupon somewhat lost their way to descend to 165 for six.

Eventually, though, the contest was decided by the Duckworth–Lewis method, after Pakistan were set a revised target of 302 in 40 overs. Imad Wasim's lower order flourish was too little, too late for Pakistan. In effect, Pakistan's lack of success against India in the World Cup—even after seven meetings—continued unchanged.

Toss: Pakistan

Man of the Match: Rohit Sharma

India 336/5 in 50 overs (Rohit Sharma 140, Virat Kohli 77, KL Rahul 57, Mohammad Amir 3/47). **Pakistan** 212/6 in 40 overs (Fakhar Zaman 62, Babar Azam 48, Imad Wasim 46*, Vijay Shankar 2/22, Kuldeep Yadav 2/32, Hardik Pandya 2/44).

India won by 89 runs (D/L method).

22 June: Ageas Bowl, Hampshire

Afghanistan restricted India to their lowest total in the tournament up to this point on a pitch that behaved contrastingly between the two ends. In fact, but for a third 50 on the trot from Virat Kohli and a first from Kedar Jadhav, who had been promoted to number four, it could have been an embarrassment equal to losing to the then non-test-playing Sri Lanka at Old Trafford in 1979.

Kohli was the fourth to depart, cutting to short point off Mohammad Nabi. Jadhav's was the last wicket to fall, when he failed to force a ball from Gulbadin Naib over cover.

There were half-century stands for the second, third and fifth wickets. But the Indian batsmen made heavy weather of the Afghan attack, as its spinners shared five victims between them. Mahendra Dhoni's was an uncommonly pedestrian performance. Indeed, the relative newcomers to the global platform threatened an upset.

At 106 for three in the 29th over of their chase, Afghanistan needed to accomplish only a run a ball to clinch victory. This is when Jasprit Bumrah struck twice in the same over—to rock back the rookies.

The rugged Mohammad Nabi, though, was not finished yet. He had returned a tidy spell of two for 33 in his 10 overs with his off-spin in a tight performance by the four Afghan slow bowlers in tandem. Now he struck four fours and a six to blitz 52 off 55 balls, and Najibullah Zadran and Rashid Khan lent him merry support to prolong the suspense.

Finally, Mohammed Shami, who was selected only because Bhuvneshwar Kumar was unfit, intervened. Nabi lofted him off the back foot to long-on, but not long enough. Then, with the next two deliveries the Bengal pacer polished off the tail to complete a hat-trick—the second by an Indian after Chetan Sharma's feat in 1987. India won by 11 runs.

Toss: India
Man of the Match: Jasprit Bumrah
India 224/8 in 50 overs (Virat Kohli 67, Kedar Jadhav 52, Mohammad Nabi 2/33, Gulbadin Naib 2/51). **Afghanistan** 213 all out in 49.5 overs (Mohammad Nabi 52, Mohammed Shami 4/40, Yuzvendra Chahal 2/36, Jasprit Bumrah 2/39, Hardik Pandya 2/51).

27 June: Old Trafford, Manchester

It was back to the north-east, though this time on a fairly sunny and, by English standards, warm day. In 1983, India ominously lost the toss and were invited to bat in the face of a battery of fearsome West Indian fast bowlers. On this occasion Virat Kohli was fortunate with the coin and unhesitatingly took first strike, given the favourable batting conditions and a less threatening Caribbean attack.

It had rained in the run-up to the match, but the pitch was unaffected; indeed, it was on the firmer side. It thereby assisted the pace of Kemar Roach, who bowled incisively and fully merited his haul. Jason Holder, too, contributed with accuracy coupled with extra bounce. Six foot seven, he releases the ball from around 10 feet above the ground.

The in-form Rohit Sharma was adjudged caught behind off an inside edge by the TV umpire based on a murmur elicited by ultra edge. But on closer inspection the ball appeared to miss the bat; and Roach benefited. A second wicket stand of 69 between KL Rahul and Kohli—who recorded his fourth half-century—steadied the ship. After Kohli exited, pulling a slow bouncer from Holder to midwicket, a sixth wicket association of 70 runs involving Mahendra Dhoni—who scored an unbeaten 50, his first in the competition—and a brisk Hardik Pandya boosted the Indians to a defendable total, as long as they bowled to their potential.

In the event, the West Indians never quite got going. They were skittled out cheaply, with Mohammed Shami bagging four wickets in successive games. His and Jasprit Bumrah's economy rates restrained the Caribbean batsmen to such an extent that they were forced to resort to suicidal shots. The third wicket partnership of 55 between opener Sunil Ambris and Nicholas Pooran was the only stand of any substance.

With this defeat, the West Indies were no longer in the running for a place in the last four.

Toss: India

Man of the Match: Virat Kohli

India 268/7 in 50 overs (Virat Kohli 72, Mahendra Dhoni 56*, KL Rahul 48, Hardik Pandya 46, Kemar Roach 3/36, Jason Holder 2/33, Sheldon Cottrell 2/50). **West Indies** 143 all out in 34.2 overs (Sunil Ambris 31, Nicholas Pooran 28, Mohammed Shami 4/16, Jasprit Bumrah 2/9, Yuzvendra Chahal 2/39).

30 June: Edgbaston, Birmingham

India persevered with their choice of two wrist spinners on pitches not exactly providing them the bounce they needed. It was a flawed strategy in the first half of an English summer, when fast bowlers and to a certain extent finger spinners tend to flourish.

That the Indians had maintained a clean slate in the tournament was not justification for the move either. The success of Mohammed Shami, who ensnared another five wickets in this match to boost his tally in three appearances to 14, underlined the need to opt for three specialist quicks or at least one finger spinner. His victims included the centurion Jonny Bairstow, Joe Root and captain Eoin Morgan.

Before the tourney the Indian coach Ravi Shastri had spoken of a horses for courses team selection policy. In practice, the Indians pursued an opposite blueprint. Shami was not integral to the original plan and only came into the reckoning owing to Bhuvneshwar Kumar's fitness.

In contrast, England in this game replaced off-spinner Moeen Ali with paceman Liam Plunkett on a ground known to favour fast bowlers. In the two previous fixtures in the tournament at this venue, quicker bowlers had reaped rewards. India, however, continued to defy conventional wisdom.

Indeed, wrist spinners Yuzvendra Chahal and Kuldeep Yadav proved to be the most expensive in the Indian attack, costing 8.80 and 7.20 an over respectively, and consequently the weak links which cost India the match.

The Indians were locking horns with the hosts, but the setting could well have been back home for them, such was the overwhelming support for Virat Kohli's men from a sea of blue-shirted, tricolour-waving spectators.

England's opening partnership of 160 runs between Jason Roy and Bairstow set the tone for the match. The latter, albeit a bit streaky to begin with, proceeded to a run-a-ball century while his partner posted a 50, a lucky half-century as the Indians failed to appeal for a nick to Mahendra Dhoni down the leg side when the batsman was 21. Subsequently, Ben Stokes, batting at five, helped himself to 79 off 54 balls, studded with three sixes, before he scooped to fine leg off Jasprit Bumrah.

India were set a task of scoring 6.74 an over—by far the most challenging they had confronted in the championship. Given India's talent on paper, the target was not unachievable, but there was inevitably scoreboard pressure. With five wickets in hand, 104 runs off the last 10 overs—which is what was required—is often attained in Twenty20. But the English speedsters allowed few liberties to Dhoni and Kedar Jadhav.

Rohit Sharma registered his third hundred in six innings, having survived a dropped catch at slip by Root when he was on 4. Eventually he was caught behind off Chris Woakes. Rishabh Pant, Hardik Pandya and Dhoni scored over a run a ball, but they failed to convert their efforts to 50 or beyond, which is what was demanded. Kohli's fifth half-century in a row was comparatively more circumspect, though he stitched 138 runs for the second wicket with Sharma. The Indian skipper's innings terminated when he steered Plunkett to point.

India fell short against seamers who maintained a tighter leash than their Indian counterparts. The tall Plunkett with his extra bounce justified his inclusion in the eleven. Woakes operated with equal tidiness. England won by 31 runs.

Toss: England
Man of the Match: Jonny Bairstow

England 337/7 in 50 overs (Jonny Bairstow 111, Ben Stokes 79, Jason Roy 66, Mohammed Shami 5/69). **India** 306/5 (Rohit Sharma 102, Virat Kohli 66, Liam Plunkett 3/55, Chris Woakes 2/58).

2 July: Edgbaston, Birmingham

A 180-run opening partnership between KL Rahul and Rohit Sharma provided India with a launch pad for another 300-plus total. KL Rahul got his second half-century of the competition, while the vice-captain recorded back-to-back hundreds—his fourth of the tournament and at better than a run a ball. Sharma was the first to depart, mishitting to cover off the unfancied Soumya Sarkar. KL Rahul attempted to cut a ball from pacer Rubel Hossain not short enough for the stroke and was caught behind. The rest of the batting rather disappointed, and India could not capitalise on the start.

That was largely because Mutafizur Rahman, with his whippy left-arm deliveries blended with slower balls, exerted a stranglehold on the Indian lower middle order. He finished with a five-for.

Bangladesh's was a doughty reply. Shakib Al Hasan, batting at number three, reiterated his consistency in the tournament with another half-century, but he was deceived by a slower ball from Hardik Pandya which was swallowed at extra cover. Mohammad Saifuddin, entering the fray at the fall of the sixth wicket, followed in his footsteps with a lively 38-ball unbeaten 51. Jasprit Bumrah polished off the tail with two incoming yorkers.

For the first time in the championship, India opted for three specialist faster bowlers, reducing spinners to a solitary practitioner in Yuzvendra Singh. On a seamer-friendly pitch at this English Midlands venue, the move was justified, with Bumrah leading the way with a four-for. The chasers fell short by 28 runs and were eliminated from the knockout stage. On the other hand, India's win sealed their place in the semifinals.

Toss: India

Man of the Match: Rohit Sharma

India 314/9 in 50 overs (Rohit Sharma 104, KL Rahul 77, Mustafizur Rahman 5/59). **Bangladesh** 286 all out in 48 overs (Shakib Al Hasan 66, Mohammad Saifuddin 51*, Jasprit Bumrah 4/55).

6 July: Headingley, Leeds

Sri Lanka were in a crisis early as Jasprit Bumrah removed both openers by the eighth over. Two more wickets went down cheaply and the islanders were reduced to 55 for four in the twelfth over. Angelo Mathews and Lahiru Thirimanne then stemmed the rot with a sprightly 124-run partnership for the fifth wicket. Mathews registered a well-deserved century, before he drove to extra cover to present a third scalp to Bumrah. Thirimanne perished in the same fielding position off left-arm wrist spinner Kuldeep Yadav after posting a 50.

Bumrah finished with an economy rate of 3.70, which reflected his accuracy and penetration. The other Indian bowlers were less troublesome and more expensive. Bhuvneshwar Kumar was especially off-colour.

The task of accumulating 265 runs for victory was not challenging for India, but was not to be taken lightly either. The Indians, however, treated the target with contempt.

Rohit Sharma raced to his third hundred in three consecutive outings and fifth altogether (the most in a World Cup ever) in the tourney at more than a run a ball. KL Rahul collaborated with him to mount a 189-run first wicket stand. Sharma departed at this point, playing early to a slower ball from Kasun Rajitha to be caught at mid-off. Following this, the Karnataka batsman proceeded to etch his maiden World Cup ton before snicking to the wicket-keeper off Lasith Malinga.

India won by seven wickets with six and a half overs to spare. In so doing they reached the top of the league table.

Toss: Sri Lanka
Man of the Match: Rohit Sharma
Sri Lanka 264/7 in 50 overs (Angelo Matthews 113, Lahiru Thirimanne 53, Jasprit Bumrah 3/37). **India** 265/3 in 43.3 overs (KL Rahul 111, Rohit Sharma 103).

Semifinal, 9–10 July: Old Trafford, Manchester

It transpired to be a rain affected tie, which required resorting to the provision of a reserve day to arrive at a result. While the two teams fenced for a place in the final, the weather was at its changeable worst and mostly overcast during India's chase.

In retrospect, the toss rendered New Zealand a slight advantage. They made the best of it with two half-century partnerships for the third and fourth wickets. Both featured Kane Williamson, the Kiwis' helmsman and most accomplished batsman, who catalogued a 50. The experienced Ross Taylor, too, got a half-century before being run out by a bullseye throw from Ravindra Jadeja, arguably the finest fieldsman of his generation. Williamson was caught at point cutting at Yuzvendra Chahal. But considering the cloud cover, the Kiwis had posted a valuable total.

In swinging conditions, India's best exploiter of such an environment, Bhuvneshwar Kumar, was his side's highest wicket-taker. His victims, though, were lower order batters. Kumar and Jasprit Bumrah were perhaps a trifle unfortunate in not obtaining edges, whereas the Black Caps' left-arm Trent Boult and Matt Henry, more controlled in their movement, consigned India to five for three. The Indians' most consistent scorers in the competition—Rohit Sharma, KL Rahul and captain Virat Kohli—were the ones back in the pavilion, the first two caught behind off Henry and the skipper leg before wicket to Boult, as he swung one back.

Dinesh Karthik, who was persevered with instead of the promising and underutilised Jadhav, didn't open his account for 21 balls. Soon after, he edged a drive to be superbly caught at point by James Neesham. Karthik became man-of-the-match Henry's third wicket. India were now 24 for four.

Hardik Pandya joined the left-handed Rishabh Pant to mount a resistance. But Pant, after playing with promise, lost patience to hole out at deep midwicket. Then Pandya mistimed a slog to provide a skier. Both young Turks succumbed to underestimating the innocuous-looking left-arm spin of Mitchell Santner.

It's a matter of conjecture whether the calm and collected, not to mention vastly experienced, Mahendra Dhoni should have been promoted in the batting order to tackle the crisis, especially after the white ball had lost its shine. In the event, he and the enterprising Jadeja came together when India were at 92 for six and fought gallantly, at one point raising hopes of India breasting the tape.

They put together 116 runs for the seventh wicket, and at 203 for six, India needed 37 runs off 18 balls. Jadeja had ratcheted up his run rate to 130. But this is where pacer Boult beat the Saurashtra all-rounder with a slower delivery.

Dhoni played with comparative patience, probably a little too much of it. Eventually, in search of a second run, he fell short to a direct throw from Martin Guptill. It was curtains for India.

New Zealand, reputed for surpassing themselves in ICC events, won by 18 runs. It was their second entry into a World Cup final, that too in successive tournaments.

Toss: New Zealand
Man of the Match: Matt Henry
New Zealand 239/8 in 50 overs (Ross Taylor 74, Kane Williamson 67, Bhuvneshwar Kumar 3/43). **India** 221 all out in 49.3 overs (Ravindra Jadeja 77, Mahendra Dhoni 50, Rishabh Pant 32, Hardik Pandya 32, Matt Henry 3/37, Mitchell Santner 2/34, Trent Boult 2/42).

Semifinal, 11 July: Edgbaston, Birmingham

Only once before had the arch and ancient rivals met in a final in the World Cup, and England lost that duel at the Eden Gardens in Kolkata in 1987. In the round robin phase in the 2019 tournament too, Australia had prevailed.

This time, in mostly sunny weather, Australia elected to bat. But at 14 for three, they had reason to regret their decision. But when left-handed Alex Carey joined former captain Steve Smith, the pair produced a 103-run partnership. Carey clipped the leg-spinner Adil Rashid, who kept the Aussies guessing, into the hands of midwicket to quit the scene. Smith continued to hold the innings together before wicket-keeper Jos Buttler ran him out at the non-striker's end when he attempted to steal a leg bye. Glenn Maxwell raised Aussie hopes only to disappoint, deceived by a well-disguised slower ball from Jofra Archer. Mitchell Starc did his reputation no harm with a responsible knock.

The ball generally nipped around, and Chris Woakes cashed in. Archer's pace was at times unsettling; indeed, Carey was left bleeding and needed stitches after being hit on the chin by a nastily rearing delivery. Nonetheless, the Australians did not do justice to the pitch.

While it was easier to bat when it came to England's turn, they dismissively disproved the demons. Jason Roy was in his element, cracking a strike rate of 130. Joe Root's and skipper Eoin Morgan's strike rates were above 100. The hosts coasted home by eight wickets with 17.5 overs to spare.

None of the Australian quicks succeeded in extracting the life the English seamers had squeezed from the pitch. Starc and Nathan Lyon were profligate; while Smith, who is rarely called upon to trundle the leg-spin he used to initially in his international career, conceded 21 runs in his solitary over, as Roy smacked him for three consecutive sixes.

A triumph over the Aussies, even if not in the Ashes, is a matter of celebration for Englanders. So it was.

Toss: Australia
Man of the Match: Chris Woakes
Australia: 223 all out in 49 overs (Steve Smith 85, Alex Carey 46, Chris Woakes 3/20, Adil Rashid 3/54, Jofra Archer 2/32) **England:** 226/2 in 32.1 overs (Jason Roy 85, Joe Root 49*, Eoin Morgan 45*, Pat Cummins 1/34).

Final, 14 July: Lord's, London

Rain in the morning delayed start of play by a quarter of an hour. Thus, when proceedings got underway, conditions were not quite conducive to limited overs style aggressive batting, as was proven by only 33 runs coming in the first 10 overs of power play.

Thereafter, Liam Plunkett captured the prized wicket of Kane Williamson—caught behind slightly chasing a delivery. This was followed by Henry Nicholls's exit—bowled by the same tall pacer—but not before he had completed the only 50 of New Zealand's innings. Ross Taylor was a trifle unlucky to be adjudged lbw. Wicket-keeper Tom Latham arrested the fall with an unstylish but timely contribution before playing early to a full pitch from Chris Woakes.

The Kiwis were seven wickets down in the 49th over with the score at 232. That emphasised the conditions had been a challenge for them. However, they had runs on the board, and England still had to get them.

At 86 for four, it was certainly not proving to be plain-sailing for the Englishmen. But this is where Jos Buttler punched gloves with Ben Stokes in modern-day fashion and the two were unseparated until Buttler departed with the total on 196, holing out at deep cover to a slower ball from Lockie Ferguson. This was the 45th over and New Zealand were back in the match, but only just.

That changed as Woakes soon skied a hook off Ferguson to be held by Latham; Plunkett couldn't get a slow leg-cutter over long-off; and Archer was cleaned up by the same medium-pacer. The pendulum had slightly swung back New Zealand's way.

In the 50th and final over of the innings, England needed 15 runs to win. Stokes was on strike with two tailenders for company. The first two balls produced dots. The left-hander swung the next one to midwicket for six.

Then came a freak incident. Stokes pulled once more to midwicket and sped back to complete a second run. However, Martin Guptill's throw to the wicket-keeper accidentally hit Stokes's bat and got deflected to the boundary. The spirit of cricket expects a batsman not to run further in such a situation. The batsmen didn't, but the umpires signalled a six—two runs plus four from overthrows.

Simon Taufel, the distinguished retired Australian umpire, was quoted by the *Sydney Morning Herald* and *The Age* of Melbourne as saying, 'It's a clear mistake ... it's an error of judgement. They [England] should have been awarded five runs, not six.'

Law 19.8 as laid down by the guardians of the game the Marylebone Cricket Club says: 'If the boundary results from an overthrow or from the wilful act of a fielder, the runs scored shall be any runs for penalties awarded to either side, and the allowance for the boundary, and the runs completed by the batsmen, together with the run in progress if they had already crossed at the instant of the throw or act.' In other words, since Stokes and Adil Rashid had not turned for the second run at the instance of Guptill's throw, it was arguably one plus four runs or five altogether.

To be fair, that was only evident in hindsight and with the benefit of TV replays. The umpires could not be expected to have kept an eye on the exact timing of Guptill's throw. It may be argued the field officials could have referred the matter to the third umpire. But again, this is easier said on reflection.

Stokes drove the fifth ball – a yorker from Boult – to long-off and attempted a second run. But Rashid could not make his ground back to the no-striker's end. Then off the last delivery, with still two runs required for victory, Stokes turned a full toss to long-on. But once more a run out at the bowler's end precipitated by a pincer-like throw from Jimmy Neesham caught Mark Wood short, resulting in the first tie in a World Cup final as well as an historic and unprecedented super over.

England batted first and Stokes and Buttler were nominated to handle the face-off; Boult was given the responsibility to bowl. The homeside mustered 15 runs for no wicket, thereby setting New Zealand a target of 16 from six balls to win outright.

Jofra Archer was assigned the onerous task of bowling the critical over for England—a huge vote of confidence in the 24-year-old's abilities. The Kiwis chose Neesham and Guptill to confront him.

A hefty six from Neesham followed an extra run from a wide. Then a misfield resulted in a couple. In effect seven runs were now required off four balls. A couple from each of the next two deliveries narrowed the requisite to three off two.

Guptill faced the final ball with two runs needed to capture the crown. Archer fired in a yorker; the batsman shovelled it to deep midwicket to scamper through for a single but failed to cover his ground. Wicket-keeper Buttler lunged to complete a run out after an accurate shy from Jason Roy.

So the drama persisted; the two sides continued to be level even after the super overs. Only a contingency provision in the rules resolved the issue.

Toss: New Zealand

Man of the Match: Ben Stokes

New Zealand 241/8 in 50 overs (Henry Nicholls 55, Tom Latham 47, Chris Woakes 3/37, Liam Plunkett 3/42). **England** 241 all out in 50 overs (Ben Stokes 84*, Jos Buttler 59, James Neesham 3/43, Lockie Ferguson 3/50).

Super Over: England 15 for no loss, New Zealand 15/1.

England won the match on the boundary countback rule.

Conclusion

The 2019 Cricket World Cup evolved as the most watched edition ever. Live coverage of it reached a cumulative global audience of 1.6 billion in 200 territories—a 38 per cent increase over the 2015 instalment. This dispelled the cynical view in some circles that the 50-over game had reached its expiry date: 41 per cent of the audience were women.

The final attracted a unique audience of 15.4 million viewers on British channels. The most watched match of the tournament, unsurprisingly, was the India versus Pakistan fixture—273 million globally.

The outgoing Manu Sawhney, ICC's chief executive, was exultant. 'These astounding numbers demonstrate the power of live cricket to connect and engage more deeply with diverse audiences around the world,' he stated.

The 10 teams who figured in the finale in England, had a prize pot of $10 million dangled before them. Of this $4 million was take home for the winners, $2 million for the runners-up and $800,000 for the losing semifinalists.

Since the advent of Twenty20, pundits have been predicting the death of one-day cricket. However, with the next 50-over World Cup extravaganza in 2023 allocated to cricket crazy India, the demise of one-day cricket is unlikely to occur any time soon.

About the Author

ASHIS RAY is among the world's longest-serving cricket broadcasters and is the senior-most among those commentating today. He was the only Asian ball-by-ball commentator on BBC's coverage of the 1983 World Cup including the final that India won. He has also commentated on ABC, SKY, SONY, CBC, AIR and Doordarshan and written for every major British and Indian daily.